"In a poetic, powerful, passionate, and challenging book, Diane Langberg, with her many years of counseling experience, takes us on a disturbing (and healing) journey into the hearts of the survivors of many different types of terrible trauma all over the world—into our own bent and broken hearts, and then into the heart of an amazing, loving God who was humiliated, crucified, and abandoned so that we (and the whole creation) might be healed and delivered from the power of evil. This is a superb master-class in counseling and pastoral care with a gifted, experienced, and wise therapist."

Richard Winter, MD, Therapist and Professor of Practical Theology and Counseling, Covenant Theological Seminary

"Through this book, Dr. Langberg names one of the most insidious threats to spiritual health in our generation: trauma and the wounded heart. While disturbing, her unrelenting campaign identifies the next 'mission field' of the church, those who are suffering silently. This book is for all who hunger to help a loved one, congregant, or client apply the truth of God's Word as a healing ointment to the hidden anguish that trauma leaves in its wake."

Roy Peterson, President, American Bible Society

"This book reflects the glory and love of God throughout forty years of counseling experience. Diane is a masterful teacher and counselor for victims of abuse and violence. Reflecting Christ, she inspires new and experienced counselors and encourages them to bring the love of God to suffering hearts. This book is a masterpiece."

Luciene Schalm, President of REVER (Restoring Lives, Equipping Restorers) Ministry, Brazil; missionary of Comunidade Cristã Siloé

"We live in a broken world and evil is real. Where the true light of the gospel of Christ goes, the darkness of evil in this world retreats. William Wilberforce reflected the character of Christ into the eighteenth century British Empire and faithfully led the fight against slavery for forty years until it was outlawed. Diane Langberg has for forty years looked into the eyes of those wounded by evil and been a powerful voice for healing, justice, and truth. This book is a place of insight, wisdom, encouragement, and challenge for the body of Christ to love our precious Lord and to reflect his heart and love to the brokenhearted."

Greg Pritchard, PhD, Director, European Leadership Forum; President, Forum of Christian Leaders

"Diane Langberg has seen the effects of trauma all over the globe from Rwandan survivors of genocide, to inner city kids plagued with PTSD, to suburban moms trapped in violent marriages, to middle schoolers who cut themselves just to feel something, to big steeple pastors in American churches. Suffering is real and it really hurts body and soul. In *Suffering and the Heart of God*, Diane Langberg never diminishes the pain of suffering, but neither does she despair. By looking to the suffering of the cross of Christ, Diane Langberg leads us to hope and healing."

Frank A. James, PhD, DPhil, President, Biblical Theological Seminary

"This book is a powerful invitation into the fellowship of the suffering, a reparative work of the vulnerable, afflicted, and abused. Dr. Langberg is gentle and caring to the victims, confrontational to the abusers, and challenging to the church, which often fails to be a refuge. As a therapist and trainer, this is the best manual I've seen on what a therapist's heart should look like. A good portion of the book is dedicated to teaching how not to be consumed by the evil in this world, pointing to Christ who can offer restoration to all."

Stefana-Ioana Racorean, Family psychotherapist and trainer, Dianoia Institute of Family Therapy and Systemic Practice, The Association of Christian Psychologists in Romania

"As someone who has prosecuted, investigated, and confronted child sexual abuse for over twenty years, I have encountered dark suffering up close. As a Christian, I have spent many hours agonizing how to reconcile such suffering with a God who calls himself "love." *Suffering and the Heart of God* is an amazing book that does a masterful job in helping to see suffering through the heart of a loving God who knows and understands suffering and the pain it creates. This book brings hope to the sufferer who wonders where God is in the midst of it all. It's a must-read!"

Boz Tchividjian, JD, Executive Director, GRACE (Godly Response to Abuse in the Christian Environment)

"I challenge you to name a more influential Christian psychologist today than Dr. Langberg. This is not hyperbole! While an impressive communicator, brilliant thinker, and an astute therapist, the real reason for her influence is her willingness to be a student first—of broken people, of herself, and of God. Too often influential leaders spend much time touting themselves. This book will show you something different, in that you will see more of God and his heart for suffering people than you will of Dr. Langberg—just as she would want it."

Philip G. Monroe, PsyD, Professor of Counseling & Psychology, Biblical Seminary Graduate School of Counseling and Global Trauma Recovery Institute

"God never wastes a wound. He is in the midst of our darkest moment revealing himself—full of love, truth, hope, and healing. This book is an absolute treasure—a gift of grace to us all."

Tim Clinton, President, American Association of Christian Counselors

"Diane Langberg brings to these moving essays decades of experience working with trauma survivors in the United States and abroad. This is no arms-length reflection on the nature of human suffering. Throughout, she repeatedly points her readers to Jesus Christ, the Suffering Servant, who is the only hope for victim and perpetrator alike—and for the counselor who desires to be used by God to make a difference amidst terrible brokenness and sin."

Michael R. Emlet, MDiv, MD, Faculty and Counselor, the Christian Counseling and Educational Foundation (CCEF); author of *CrossTalk: Where Life and Scripture Meet*

"*Do not read this book* unless you are genuinely open to being led by the Holy Spirit to become more involved in ministering 'to the least of these' in Christ's name. Dr. Langberg has written a powerful and thorough summary of the complex reality of trauma in our world today. She has described Christ's Gethsemane weeping and his Calvary caring for those who are wounded and needy, and she calls us to weep and to watch and to care with him. She challenges us—Will we weep and watch and care, or will we sleep?"

Dr. Samuel Logan, Associate International Director, The World Reformed Fellowship, www.wrfnet.org

"As a Rwandan who lived through genocide, experienced my own trauma, and witnessed trauma for my people and my clients, I know firsthand the truth of what Diane teaches in this book. Until you understand the psychology of evil, sin, and suffering, many things will remain hidden and unanswered, but Christ can transform lives affected by emotional trauma into instruments to restore life and turn victim into victor. Thank you, Diane, for addressing this difficult and often hidden topic."

Baraka Paulette Uwingeneye, President, Rwandan Association of Christian Counselors; Director of Aftercare, International Justice Mission, Rwanda

"Diane drops insightful one-liners like others drop names. I remember the first time I heard her describe trauma as the 'mission field of the twenty-first century.' Suddenly, everything we were grappling with in the field made sense. A thousand lightbulbs went off. Synapses clicked. That *one sentence* opened up a new direction in my personal life and vocation. Read at your own risk because there's no going back to the way life was before."

John Walter, President, African Leadership; cofounder of The Trauma Healing Institute

"When I get the chance to listen to or read Diane Langberg's work, I take it. Of the five greatest talks I've heard in my sixty-eight years, she gave two of them. Her writing inspires. She is as tough-minded as people come, never underestimating the horrors of life. But walking with her through those horrors inspires me with hope. Because Diane walks with Jesus, and where Jesus is, *there* is hope. *Suffering and the Heart of God: How Trauma Destroys and Christ Restores* will turn your heart more fully to God in the midst of the evils and mundane cares of the world that you face. Please read it."

Everett L. Worthington, Jr., Author of *Moving Forward: Six Steps to Forgiving Yourself and Breaking Free from the Past*

"Stepping into the trenches with those whose lives have been blown apart by the heinous business of human trafficking means you're battling *alongside* them on many fronts: past, present, and future. The terrain is dark and hostile, and the Enemy seems to have won. But, as Langberg artfully reminds us, we are but chaplains in this war. The battle is the Lord's and the victory is certain. Be of good courage and press on!"

Jeanne L. Allert, MEd, Founder and Executive Director, The Samaritan Women

Suffering
and the Heart
of God

Suffering and the Heart of God:

How Trauma Destroys and Christ Restores

DIANE LANGBERG

New
Growth
Press

WWW.NEWGROWTHPRESS.COM

New Growth Press, Greensboro, NC 27404
Copyright © 2015 by Diane Langberg

All Scripture quotations, unless otherwise indicated, are taken from the *New American Standard Bible*, © Copyright 1960, 1962, 1963, 1968, 1971, 1972, 1973, 1975, 1977, 1995 by The Lockman Foundation. Used by permission.

Scripture quotations marked (NIV) are taken from THE HOLY BIBLE, NEW INTERNATIONAL VERSION®, NIV® Copyright © 1973, 1978, 1984, 2011 by Biblica, Inc.® Used by permission. All rights reserved worldwide.

Scripture quotations marked (NLT) are taken from the Holy Bible, New Living Translation, copyright © 1996, 2004, 2007 by Tyndale House Foundation. Used by permission of Tyndale House Publishers, Inc., Carol Stream, Illinois 60188. All rights reserved.

Scripture quotations marked (ESV) are taken from The Holy Bible, English Standard Version ® (ESV®), copyright © 2000, 2001 by Crossway Bibles, a division of Good News Publishers. Used by permission. All rights reserved.

Scripture quotations marked (KJV) are from the King James Version of the Bible.

Cover Design: Faceout Books, faceoutstudio.com
Interior Design and Typesetting: Lisa Parnell, lparnell.com

ISBN 978-1-942572-02-2 (Print)
ISBN 978-1-942572-03-9 (eBook)

Library of Congress Cataloging-in-Publication Data
Langberg, Diane.
  Suffering and the heart of God : how trauma destroys
and Christ restores / Diane Langberg.
    pages cm
  ISBN 978-1-942572-02-2 (print) — ISBN 9781942572039 (ebook)
1. Suffering—Religious aspects—Christianity. 2. Traumatism. 3. Caring—
Religious aspects—Christianity. 4. Helping behavior—Religious aspects—
Christianity. I. Title.
  BT732.7.L36 2015
  248.8'6—dc23
                                                                    2015015583
Printed in United States of America

23 22 21 20   7 8 9 10 11

Contents

Introduction

This book is borne out of forty years of listening to suffering and traumatized people. It has been a school; a discipline in many ways and I have learned much. Clients have come to me for help—with histories of abuse, violence, trafficking, and torture. They have been deeply shaped by those events and most come longing to be shaped differently. It has been my work to listen, to understand, to read, and to study diligently so that I do indeed help and not harm the already wounded.

However, I have come to see that in addition to coming to me for help they have been sent by God to help shape me. The years of absorbing evil, of deepening compassion, and boldness in truth have refined my life and my soul. The Redeemer has been in the room pursuing and changing shattered lives. That Redeemer has also been in the room continually working his likeness more deeply in me.

It is my hope that the words of this book, many of them originally talks given to God's caregivers around the world, will strengthen you in the caregiving you do. I would want you to gain knowledge of some of the great evils done to others and how those evils deeply alter lives so that a few true words will not simply make things right. I hope you will, as I have, grow in humility, losing the certainty that you know the answer and the way or conversely, that no study or expertise is necessary when caring for broken lives. We need the humility to enter in and sit with those who struggle—as our incarnated Lord did—and the wisdom to know when we are out of our depth and need to call in others with greater knowledge and experience so as not to trample fragile humans already trampled by others. To this end, the book is divided into sections—the first two designed for anyone who wants to learn to enter into the pain of others and the last two for clinicians who provide more specialized care. Further resources can be found on my website (http://www.dianelangberg.com) and at the website for the Global Trauma Recovery Institute (http://global-traumarecovery.org).

Yet even as the book increases knowledge and calls forth humility, it is my deepest hope that the suffering of others will open your eyes to the Suffering Servant who came in the flesh to explain the Father to lost and trampled humans and who, as you care for others, longs to teach you more about who he is and how he desires to transform your heart and life so that you bear the fragrance of Christ wherever you go. He bore every bit of ruin you will ever face in a life; even yours. Seek him in those ruined places—others' and your own. And as you seek him seeking you, you will find the Lamb who bore all the evil you will ever encounter. Look for his face in the ruined lives that sit before you and he will transform you into his likeness—so that those ruined creatures you counsel will look into your ruined face and see the Lamb of God.

SUFFERING, THE WORLD, AND THE HEART OF GOD

CHAPTER I

Trauma as a Place of Service

It is a numbing world. The digital world and media tsunami overwhelm us and we can often barely take in sound bites. For now, however, I would ask you to marshal the forces of your mind and heart and come with me for a glimpse of the world our God so loves, the world whose anguish he bears. He has asked us to look with him—to step away from the numbing and listen to *his* heart and *his* thoughts. So come, listen and see with me a small piece of the heart of our God for this fearful, fallen world.

While I was in Ghana a couple of years ago for a conference on violence against women and children, we visited Cape Coast Castle. Hundreds of thousands of Africans were forced through its dungeons and through the door of no return onto slave ships. There were five dungeon chambers for males, and descending into the darkness to one of those dungeons felt claustrophobic. Two hundred men shackled and chained together lived in that dungeon for about three months before being shipped across the Atlantic.

We stood in one of the male dungeons listening in the darkness to the whole horrific story when our guide said this: "Do you know what is above this dungeon?" Our heads shook. The chapel. Directly above two hundred shackled men—some of them dead, others screaming, all of them sitting in filth—sat God worshipers. They sang, they read the Scripture, they prayed, and I suppose took up an offering for those less fortunate. The slaves could hear the service, and the worshipers could sometimes hear the slaves (though there were those making them behave so as not to disturb church). It took my breath away. The evil, the suffering, the humiliations, the injustice were overwhelming, and the visual parable was stunning. The people in the chapel were numb to the horrific trauma and suffering beneath them.

We have dungeons in our world today too: Tent cities in Haiti and Ivory Coast; genocides in Rwanda, Bosnia, and Darfur; wars around the world; and relentless, systemic violence in our own inner cities. Do you know that all of these events produce traumatized human beings? One in four soldiers is a child, and 200 million children live on the streets of this world. Amnesty International says one in three females are beaten or coerced into sex or otherwise abused in their lifetime. One in three. Think about that statistic next time you walk through an airport or a city street, or sit in the pews in your own church. Child sexual abuse, child marriage, and female genital mutilation cause physical and psychological harm to countless females. Girls have acid thrown in their faces for attending school; they are stoned to death for being raped. Eastern Congo is the rape capital of the world. A recent UN human rights panel says that hundreds of thousands have been raped during the conflict there and 13 percent of the victims are children under the age of ten. Sex trafficking, the slavery of today, is a brutal and large-scale destructive force of girls and women today. And it is not just over there; it is here in our own streets and cities, in *your* city. The dungeons are here, sometimes sitting next to us.

All of these things from tent cities to abuse, things we find difficult to comprehend or hold in our minds, are endured by human beings one at a time. They result in traumatized human beings. Trauma means living with the recurrent, tormenting memories of atrocities witnessed or borne. Memories that infect victims' sleep with horrific nightmares, destroy their relationships or their capacity to work or study, torment their emotions, shatter their faith, and mutilate hope. Trauma is extraordinary, you see, not because it rarely happens but because it swallows up and destroys normal human ways of living. The dungeons of this world are filled with traumatized people.

As it was in Cape Coast Castle, the usual response to atrocity is to try to remove it from the mind. Those who have been traumatized want to flee the memory of its occurrence, and we who hear find that we want to flee also. We find it too terrible to remember and too incomprehensible to put into words. That is why we use the phrase *unspeakable atrocities*. The great tension is the futile attempt to forget the unspeakable, though it continues to live on and scream in the mind. That push-pull between the need to forget and the need to speak is the central dialectic of trauma, and that tension is not only experienced by individuals and families, but also by institutions and nations. It is experienced not only by the traumatized but also by those who bear witness to the trauma.

I know something of this tension because as a psychologist I have worked for forty years with sexual abuse, rape, and domestic violence as well as combat trauma, genocide, and trafficking. I have looked into traumatized eyes all around the world. I have seen this push-pull in my clients who are terrified to remember and speak, but who cannot forget. I have witnessed families, churches, and yes, nations deny the existence of evil, abuse, and trauma in their midst.

I also know this tension exists in those who bear witness, for it resides in me. You know, we see an atrocity on television or the internet, and soon after we look for ways to remove ourselves. Such stories threaten our comfort, our position, or our system. The stories are vile and messy and very disruptive. Traumatized people need attention and assistance, often for a long time. The trauma stories of our own families, institutions, and organizations get buried, and geographical distance and the push of a button enable us to do the same with entire nations. Ask Rwanda. We are in fact quite like the chapel-goers in the fort in Ghana.

So what are we to do? Choose complicity by turning away in silence? Flit from cause to cause trying to do something (which is sometimes about making ourselves feel better or feeding some voyeuristic need)? Render judgment and categorize the traumatized and suffering as *they*? You know, if *they* were more responsible and made better choices, then *they* would not be suffering.

Under the form of worship in that chapel in Ghana lay the darkness of slavery, oppression, and tyranny—all things that blight and destroy humans created in the image of God. But I think you know Christianity does *not* look like being folded up with evil and worshiping on top of dungeons. Following Christ *does not* look like complicity with a system that butters our bread and fills our coffers but is built on the backs of those created in the image of God. It does not look like praying and singing and giving money on top of screams, unspeakable suffering, filth, and death. Christianity is not calling others *them*—somehow unlike us, not human, deserving of their suffering. Our guide pointed up to the church above and said, "Heaven above; hell below." But I would argue that heaven was *not* above, for that is not what heaven does.

What does heaven do? Heaven leaves heaven—its place of comfort, songs, purity, plenty, and money to give. Heaven comes down. If the people of that chapel had truly worshiped God, they would have been in the dungeon, in the filth and the darkness and the suffering. They would have entered in *so that they might bring out*. Acts 17:6 says, "These men have turned the world upside down" (ESV). The church goes into the dungeon so that the dungeon becomes the church. God came down so as to lift up. God became like us so that we might become like him. He came to this dung-filled dungeon we call earth and sat with us, touched us, loved us, and called us to him.

He also enters the dungeons of our hearts and transforms them. He did not treat us as *them* but became one of us so that we might be his. God is power becoming little, coming down to embrace what is alien. There is no *them*; there is only us. We were the slaves in the dungeon, and he has *not* taken us out so we can stand on the heads of the oppressed and say we worship him for not leaving us there with them. He has called us as his body to follow our head, to go back into the plague-infested dung heap so other slaves might find freedom and go back with us to find yet more.

When our God interfaces with this world, he leaves the higher and descends. He leaves beauty and enters chaos; he leaves pure and goes into filthy. And he demonstrates that our God does not just speak words *but also acts—first* in the heart dungeons of human beings *and then* through the lives of those same people into the dungeons of this world. Jesus demonstrated in the flesh the character of God; his church is to do the same for the world. When God's people worship over and separate, untouched by dungeons, they are *not* worshiping the God of the Scriptures. There is *nothing* in the Scriptures to suggest that being complicit, neutral, or uncaring and deaf to the cries of humans is godly. Those Scriptures *do* say that the dungeons of Cape Coast Castle were below *because* they were *first present* in the hearts of the worshipers.

Sadly, the body of Christ has often failed to see trauma as a place of service. If we survey the extensive natural disasters in our time—earthquakes, hurricanes and tsunamis—and combine those victims with the human atrocities—the violent inner cities, wars, genocides, trafficking, rapes, and child abuse—we would have a staggering number. I think a look at suffering humanity would lead to the realization that trauma is perhaps the greatest mission field of the twenty-first century.

The people of God have sometimes hidden in chapels, worshiping, singing, giving money, and sticking our heads out to tell others what they were doing wrong. We have often blamed those who suffer for their trauma. We have failed to recognize that systems can be corrupt and power abused and that *like our Lord,* many people in this world suffer from totally undeserved injustice and trauma. We have not gone to the dungeons and have been blind to the fact that such refusal is merely an exposure of the dungeons of our hearts—hearts *not* like our God's, whose heart bore the anguish of this world and who entered the dungeons of this fallen world to make all things new.

Many of you see this and want to enter in, and I am glad. You are in places of power and influence, in alleys and brothels. You do not want to hide in the chapel and that is good. But listen, do not be seduced. The chapel is not a place; it is a Person; it is a Head with a body. And as in the physical realm, a body that does not follow its head is a sick body. Many of you see that. It is also true that the dungeon is not a place; it is the human heart. There is no corporate greed without humans; there is no rape and abuse without humans; there are no corrupt systems without people to protect and lie.

Our first call is not to places—be they chapels or dungeons—but to a Person. To love and obedience to Jesus Christ, no matter the cost; to hearts that tolerate no dungeon corner to exist hidden from his light. Many have thought that if you avoid the dungeons of this world, you stay clean. However, to do so is to fail to follow our Savior out onto the dung heaps of this world. Many of you are going—go. But remember this: the dungeon is first in us. That is what has created the dungeons out there. Do not fool yourselves into thinking you follow your Savior where others have failed to do so, all the while hiding dungeons in your own souls, whether it is in pride or pornography.

Given the numbers of suffering and traumatized, let me reiterate that *the trauma of this world is one of the primary mission fields of the twenty-first century.* It is one of the supreme opportunities before the church today. Our Head left glory and came down to this traumatized world. He became flesh like us; he literally got in our skin. He did not numb or flee the atrocities of this world or of our hearts. Will we, his body, also leave our spaces, our chapels and enter the trauma of terrified and shattered humanity in the name of Jesus? We are complicit with the perpetrators if we refuse to see and enter in. We are also complicit if we go ignoring the refuse in our own hearts. If the church does not enter in, then I would ask, is she really living as the body of an incarnated God? How I pray we will follow our Head, full of the light and life of Jesus Christ in the corners of our own hearts *so that* we might truly bring him to the trauma dungeons of this world.

CHAPTER 2

Justice vs. Complicity

In 1994, in a small and beautiful country in the Great Lakes Region of Africa, genocide occurred. About one million people were slaughtered in one hundred days—by friends, neighbors, classmates, and fellow church members—with machetes and hoes and nail-studded clubs. The world watched on television and did nothing. Over twenty years later Rwanda is still reeling and damaged.

I have worked with evil and its resulting trauma in hundreds of lives throughout my career. I have been to places like Burma and Ground Zero while the earth was still hot. The brutality, the frenzy, the scope, *and* the intimacy of the Rwandan genocide is unlike anything I have ever encountered. I have made several trips to this land of a thousand hills. There are one million orphans in the country. There are thousands of widows, many who were raped and now have AIDS, as well as raising AIDS-infected children born of those rapes.

The country was considered 90 percent Christian at the time of the genocide, and the church was complicit in the slaughter. Many people fled into the churches for sanctuary and were massacred within the church walls. Several churches around the country have been left untouched as memorials of what happened. That means you can go into these churches, where sunlight comes through broken stained glass and the Bible sits on the altar, and see the bones of thousands, lying just as they died—twenty-five hundred in one, four thousand in another, ten thousand in a third, and so on. Hell not only came to Rwanda; it came to the church. One woman said to me, "The churches were the ground of the genocide." How can such a thing be? How does the sanctuary of God become the house of death? How do people who call themselves Christians slaughter neighbors?

In visiting and doing training in Rwanda, I have been hit hard by what happened in the churches there. I continue to struggle with what I saw and heard. The evil was not done by the bad guys. It was neighbors, classmates, fellow church members, and friends. Rwandans were fed a diet of hatred for others—derogatory terms, ridicule, thinking of others as less than—lots of "tongue-murder" as Matthew Henry describes it.[1] Some of us know what it is like to think about others in this way—those who have hurt us, those we hold a grudge against or carry bitterness toward; those of another race or nationality; those of another political party; those of another economic class; or those of another faith or even another denomination.

Human beings do not go from dinner with friends to genocide in a day or a week. We get there little by little; blind, numb, and not noticing until the horrific seems normal and acceptable. We start with what John refers to in his epistle as hate, literally meaning to spit on another in your heart. It is a small, hidden thing. It is however the seed of demeaning and killing and injustice. First, like the church members at Cape Coast Castle, we think of others as *they*. *They* are not responsible. *They* do not drive correctly. *They* believe in the wrong god. *They* have a twisted sexuality. Then a name is attached to *they*. Stalin spoke of "enemies of the state," Hitler of "dirty Jews," and the Hutus of Rwanda called the Tutsis "cockroaches." If *they* have hurt you, disagreed with you, or do not believe what you do, then you slap on a label like cockroach. Well, we know what you do with cockroaches, right? It is not hard for humans to learn to think that mind-boggling evil and gross injustice is acceptable. It is a little-by-little seduction until we find ourselves thinking of another human being, created in the image of our God, as a nasty, threatening creature that ought to be stamped out.

Recognizing Egocentricity and Complicity

So what does the Rwandan genocide have to do with us? I have spent close to four decades sitting with the litter of injustice. I have heard stories of oppression, bondage, cruelty, terror, imprisonment, violence, deceit, malice, and rage. I have seen such stories on terrified faces, in dead eyes, and in trembling bodies. As in Rwanda, a good portion of what I have seen and heard—though certainly not all—has been wrought by the so-called church of Jesus Christ. So I come to this topic not as a victim of grave injustice, not as a theologian or philosopher with ideas about injustice, and actually not even so much as a psychologist. I come today as one who has borne witness, and from that place I would like to tell you something of what I know, what I have seen and heard, and what I long to see for his name's sake.

Elie Wiesel, survivor of the Nazi Holocaust, said this: "I swore never to be silent whenever and wherever human beings endure suffering and humiliation. We must always take sides. Neutrality [and I would add silence] always helps the oppressor, never the victim. Silence encourages the tormentor, never the tormented."[2] And so I want us to look at injustice and its polar opposite, justice, which we are told is a requirement of our God for his people. It is not a lofty idea; it is not a suggestion; it is not a liberal cause; and it is not simply for those who are not busy. It is a requirement of the God who is himself Justice.

Through the prophet Micah our God says this: "Hear now what the LORD is saying . . . 'the LORD has a case against His people. . . . What have I done to you, And how have I wearied you? . . . Indeed, I brought you up from the land of Egypt . . . the house of slavery [I brought you out from injustice]'" (Micah 6:1–4).

Some listening and seemingly tortured soul responds to God's query in verses 6–7: "With what shall I come to the LORD and bow myself before the God on high? Shall I come to Him with burnt offerings, with yearling calves? Does the LORD take delight in thousands of rams, in ten thousand rivers of oil? Shall I present my firstborn for my rebellious acts, the fruit of my body for the sin of my soul?" [A strange thought for approaching the God who said you shall not kill.]

Then the response follows: You want to know what God requires—which obviously means that he does require something—"He has told you, O man, what is good" (v. 8). God has not left us without revelation regarding what he requires. That word *require* includes a seeking, searching out. You know what God is seeking, what he is searching for. We do not have to guess or try various options. He has spoken to the people he himself freed from oppression and injustice. The answer: do justice, love mercy, and walk in humility with me. "How shall I come before God and bow myself down?" Is that not a question of worship? How shall I rightly worship God? Do justice. I, the God you worship, am searching for justice. In essence I am the Redeemer God who brought you out of the land of oppression, bondage, and injustice. If you would worship me, then you must look like me. Do justice.

"But we all, with unveiled face, beholding as in a mirror the glory of the Lord, are being transformed into the same image" (2 Corinthians 3:18). If we worship a God who is just, who hates injustice, and cannot participate in it for one second and remain himself, then we as his people will also love and do justice. We will be known for it. That means those of us who know God will render justice to those who are vulnerable. Our justice will serve as a memorial in the flesh of God's deliverance of his people. What would that look like? I can only answer by taking you to some of the places I have been and asking you to bear witness with me as we ask God to show us where we are not like him, and therefore fail to truly worship him.

Before asking you to bear witness with me, I would first like you to consider two things—I am sure there are more—that are major hindrances to our pursuit of justice. The first of these is our deeply entrenched egocentricity. During the years of my work I have been profoundly struck by the egocentricity of my own heart. I find I am not naturally moved by the evil, sin, and suffering of this world to do justice until it infringes on my world, my comfort, and my relationships. The evil, sin, and suffering that do not touch my world I work hard to keep at a distance. It is disturbing, messy, and inconvenient. God has used the work I do as a corrective measure in many ways.

Over the decades I have worked with many people—people the normal course of events would have never brought into my life. I have been inside things like abuse, suicide, terror, torment, trauma, trafficking, deception, abuse of power, and wordless grief. Such things were not mine; they belonged to other people. They were brought to me, however, and I was invited in. Going into such things has disturbed my thinking, my feelings, and my sleep. I have had to change my mind about things I was sure were true and ask questions I thought had been already answered.

In the last twenty years I have been involved in an inner-city counseling ministry that has brought me face-to-face with more disturbing things. Do you know that 50 percent of all babies born to women under thirty are born to unwed mothers? Think how many adolescents are growing up without fathers. Add to that corrupt systems, children treated like a number—or worse, like animals—homeless mothers or pregnant women, crack babies starved to death, violent police, hideous racism, filth and poverty and despair travelling down from one generation to another—all thirty minutes from my comfortable home and church.

Where are we? Why have I ignored my fellow human beings in the city? Why have I never even given a thought to those in the city who know and love the same Christ I do but cannot feed their families or afford rent? The Word of God says that what I do to the least I have done to my Lord. How is it that I even consider these human beings as *least*? Who am I to say another is *least*? Is that not making others *they*? But oh, I like to think of that Scripture when I do something for another that the world would consider "little." But does that Scripture also mean my failures or lack of loving and doing justice are done to Christ as well?

Outside my backyard, there is also the world. When I began travelling internationally, I would return home from hearing about the systemic sexual abuse in Brazil, the hideous oppression in Burma, the endemic rape in Congo, or the genocide in Rwanda and wait to "get over it"—to recover. I have learned through the years that God does not mean for me to get over it. I have met and worked with precious believers worldwide who have no training, no resources, no Bibles, and no books. These Christians love their people. They are committed to them. They long to help them. Meanwhile we are producing more books than we need in this country and building bigger churches. Do you suppose that is what justice looks like? I fear that we are often sleeping in the garden rather than watching with our Savior because the suffering is not ours. It does not touch our lives. It does not affect our world.

God is slowly dismantling my egocentricity and bringing me little by little into identification with his point of view. F. W. H. Meyers in his poem "Saint Paul" expresses it clearly: "Desperate tides of the whole great world's anguish forced thro' the channels of a single heart."[3] *That* is God's point of view; *that* is an expression of his heart. The whole world's anguish, including each of ours, has flowed through that great heart. My love of comfort and preference for protection from the tragedies and sordid nature of things in this world means I have a heart unlike his. He who dwelt in heaven, in the high and holy place, who donned human flesh and walked among the filth and torment of this world to the extent that the spit of others ran down his face as he suffered their injustices, has called us to identify with *his* point of view. He is seeking, searching to see justice. Does his church satisfy this cry of his heart?

You know another manifestation of this egocentricity is our thinking that everyone is like us. It is the inverse of thinking of others as *they*, the other side of the same coin. When I am working with young counselors, this egocentric thinking has to be confronted again and again. They tend to assume "sad" means what they mean when they say they are sad. They assume that saying "I stopped an addiction a long time ago" means years ago when it often means three days ago. They can easily assume the pain is less than reported, the depression lighter than stated, and the options available to the client more numerous than what they have heard. These assumptions are based on their own life experiences, their own levels of struggle, their own access to energy and resources, and their own levels of success.

We do this when we confront injustice, and this is where we see the same basic assumptions we had for people as *they*. If people worked harder, were more responsible, were not lazy, or simply thought differently, they would not be victims of injustice. We end up holding children morally responsible for sexual abuse, victims are blamed for rape, and battered wives own their husband's violence. Our egocentricity says to us, "You have experienced these things because you have _____ "—not been responsible; not loved your spouse well; not made moral choices, etc. We do the same for poverty and lack of jobs. Implicit is the idea that if they did what we did, made similar choices to ours, or behaved well, then injustice would not be present in their lives. If someone is downtrodden or oppressed, it is probably their fault. It is as if we think that all injustice is due to individual choices. Rather than lifting up the downtrodden, we walk on their heads in judgment and barely concealed disdain. All the while our God is seeking, searching for justice and has called us to do the same through the prophet Isaiah. "Learn to do good; seek justice, reprove the ruthless" (Isaiah 1:17). The ruthless? That must mean there are unjust people out there who trample on others no matter what they do.

I had this vividly taught to me by a pastor in Brazil many years ago. He had just moved with his family to pastor a church in a small town. He came to me at the end of a training session and told me the following: "Diane, all the men in my village are alcoholics—no exception. All the men in my village beat their wives—no exception. All the men in my village have sex with their daughters—no exception. Diane, can you please tell me how do I help my village?" Now understand when he said "all the men" he included all the police, the judges, and the pastors of that village. He alone was not doing what he described. Every system in that village was corrupted; injustice was the norm. No one growing up there ever saw anything different, and there was no one to turn to for justice. The developing world is full of towns, cities, or nations like this. Our own inner cities are full of systems like this. You can do right and still have everything turn out wrong. I am not certain where we got the idea that was not so, given that the one we follow and call God did do everything right and ended up treated with gross injustice.

So often, rather than suffer involvement with messy injustices and corrupt systems (sometimes even a system of which I am part), I choose the quiet way, the easy way, and sin against Justice himself. I turn a deaf ear to the voice of God saying, "I require; I am searching for justice." I would rather sin against Justice himself than allow the suffering of others and the injustices they live with daily to alter my schedule, my comfort level, and my tidy life.

The result of my egocentricity is that I find myself untouched by the great suffering and injustices in this world, down the street, and in the pews of my church or its neighborhood. I judge the oppressed as lacking, implying of course that somehow their grave experiences of injustice are in fact just, because if they had made the right choices, they would be justly treated. After all, isn't it true that if you work hard and do right justice will always follow? In thinking this way and acting on this belief I disagree with the God I claim to worship—the one who always did right and was met with murderous injustice.

Secondly, due to my desire to avoid suffering of any kind, I prefer the sin that allows me to keep things as they are in order to avoid distress and discomfort and pain. I do not want to see the injustices of the world, my world. I do not want to know about the corruptions that occur in places of power, the cover-ups, the victims silenced, and the poor, the widowed, the orphaned, and the alien ignored. I do not want to face the claim others have on my life simply because I am a follower of a just God.

Several years ago I stood before a plaque in the genocide memorial in Kigali, Rwanda. Following the definition of genocide is the list of those things that are punishable as genocide. Number five is complicity. The word literally has to do with folding together. It means to be an accomplice, a partner in wrongdoing. To be silent about the injustices in this world is to be folded together with those who carry out violence and evil and corruption. As the church of Jesus Christ we are to be witnesses to what is true. And yes, that means speaking boldly about the God who came in the flesh to redeem broken humanity. But it also means speaking the truth *about injustice* and calling evil by its right name. A truth-teller disturbs, alerts, wakens, and warns against indifference to injustice and complacency about the needs of human beings. The world knew what was happening in Germany in the 1930s and remained silent. The world knew about the Warsaw ghetto and Auschwitz and remained silent. The world knew about the genocide in Rwanda and remained silent. We know now that Haitians are not okay; the Rwandans are not okay; the Congolese are not okay. We know our cities are sick. The poor are beaten down, receiving totally inadequate education and dying in the streets. We know girls in our cities and towns are being trafficked. Some of us also know of abuse in our families and our churches and have done and said nothing so as to protect the structure, the institution, rather than the victim. When it comes to injustice, silence is not a virtue; it is a vice two times compounded because it contains both indifference to the victims and complicity with the destroyers. In such instances we have failed to do justice. The call to do justice is the call to be like God. In failing to do justice, we do not look like Christ in this world. In not looking like Christ, we have failed to worship him.

Hearing Testimonies of Injustice

Now I would ask you to come with me and bear witness to a few of the injustices I have seen or confronted in various forms. Hear from some individuals what injustice was like for them. Let us consider some of the world's great anguish that has forced a channel through our great God's heart. This is a tiny portion of anguish and injustice borne by our God.

The voice of Elie Wiesel in *The Night Trilogy*, his account of his time in the Nazi death camps:

> Never shall I forget that night, the first night in camp, which has turned my life into one long night, seven times cursed and seven times sealed. Never shall I forget that smoke. Never shall I forget the little faces of the children, whose bodies I saw turned into wreaths of smoke beneath a silent blue sky. Never shall I forget those flames which consumed my Faith forever. Never shall I forget that nocturnal silence which deprived me, for all eternity, of the desire to live. Never shall I forget those moments which murdered my God and my soul and turned my dreams to dust. Never shall I forget these things, even if I am condemned to live as long as God Himself. Never.[4]

He was fifteen years old and had just entered Birkenau, the reception center for Auschwitz. The world knew. And over that

world is a God who says: do justice. Do you know there are genocide survivors from Germany, Cambodia, Bosnia, and Rwanda in
our cities?

The voice of a woman in the 1800s:

> It was in a Bible class . . . that I defended some religious opin-
> ions which conflicted with the creed of the church in that
> place, which brought upon me the charge of insanity. . . . I
> was kidnapped when my husband forced his way into my
> room through the window with an axe. . . . Two doctors felt
> my pulse and without asking a single question declared me
> insane. This was the only medical examination I had and the
> only trial of any kind I was allowed. . . . I was forced from
> my home and had to leave my six children and precious babe
> of eighteen months. . . . When once in the Asylum I was be-
> yond the reach of all human aid. . . . I lay closely imprisoned
> three years, being never allowed to set my foot on the ground
> after the first four months. . . . I returned to my husband and
> little ones, only to be again treated as a lunatic. My husband
> cut me off from my friends, intercepted my mail, made me a
> prisoner in my own home and began to plan how to have me
> incarcerated for life.[5]

The act was carried out by so-called men of faith, but in fact
the husband wanted a different wife and this injustice provided
the way. Women continue to be silenced and abused by prominent
men in power in the very churches where we worship. Is it safe for
them to speak?

Gerry, a troubled woman in her early twenties, experienced a
chaotic childhood and family history that is so familiar among the
multi-crisis poor that we could reconstruct her past without knowing the details. As a foster child she was abused intermittently and
raped more than once. She lived in eight different homes and at-
tended six schools, most of them full of violence and no resources.

She never finished high school. As a member of a large, disorganized family she was often ignored and sometimes pulled back in to serve as caretaker for others. Over the years she has lived in shelters, been addicted to drugs, grappled with drug programs, and maintained on-and-off relationships with many men. She has seen her children placed with other families and has tried to comply with the conditions for their return. She has told her story in multiple agencies, none of which have ultimately been helpful. The caseworkers are overworked and the news report just came out that the higher-ups had been embezzling money meant for clients. She has had to trade sex for food and twice traded the same for early release from the local jail where she landed due to trading sex for food.

Gerry is poor, abused, uncertain, confused, depressed, and irresponsible. She does not want the life she has but cannot find a way out. Actually she finds it hard to even envision anything else. Her life looks like her mother's before her.

Our cities are full of women like Gerry. Our God is searching for justice.

Gilbert Gauthe was the first Catholic priest in the nation to face a criminal indictment on multiple charges of child molestation. The indictment charged that he had molested 36 children in all. When Ray Mouton, the lawyer asked to defend him, dug around, he learned that the Louisiana diocese knew about seven other pedophile priests and had done nothing. The story is long and complicated, but in the end the priest went free with no required supervision. He never was sent to the psychiatric facility as promised when he pleaded guilty. He was given long furloughs to his mother, given a private prison office, and took teenage prisoners as assistants. He took them into his "office," shaved their body hair, and had sex with them. He served seven years of a twenty-year sentence and, aided by an old family friend, was set free in 1995.

I repeatedly get calls from churches and Christian organizations around the country about sexual abuse in their midst. They want help but hope no one has to know—children abused by dynamic youth leaders the church wants to protect or pastors abusing four to six women in a congregation. "But, Diane, he is so charismatic and the church has grown." *Do justice.*

She was twelve and lonely. Her parents were members of the church and quite active. She was required to attend youth group and the new twenty-six-year-old pastor paid special attention to her. He included her in things and she often ran errands with him to keep him company. He bought her some nice things and took her for ice cream or lunch. He said she was pretty. Then he started texting and sending emails. It was a little weird, but she felt important. One day he asked her to meet him for an errand he had to run and then drove the car to an out-of-the-way place and raped her. He told her if she ever told, no one would believe her because the families of the church all loved him.

Obviously there are forms of coercion that can be effected without physical force against those who are vulnerable. He had raped her about thirty times before she found the nerve to tell her parents. They did not believe her at first and then wondered what she had done to cause it. They went to the head pastor. He told her she was seductive and ruining a young man of God. She was forced to sign a confession and ask forgiveness. The pastor said it would ruin the church if people found out and certainly ruin a promising minister's future.

She left home at seventeen and the folks there have often talked about what a troubled girl she is and how she is making terrible choices. They do not understand why someone from such a wonderful home and church could turn out that way. They heard rumors but of course they could not possibly be true. "He is, after all, such a fine young pastor." *I, the Lord, love justice.*

"Cry loudly . . . raise your voice . . . declare to My people their transgression . . . on the day of your fast you find your desire, and drive hard all your workers. . . . Is this not the fast which I choose? To loosen the bonds of wickedness, to undo the bands of the yoke, and to let the oppressed go free? Is it not to divide your bread with the hungry and bring the home-less poor into the house? . . .

"If you remove the yoke from your midst, the pointing of the finger and speaking wickedness, and if you give yourself to the hungry and satisfy the desire of the afflicted, then your light will rise in darkness. . . . You will be like . . . a spring of water whose waters do not fail." (Isaiah 58:1–11)

Who is like the LORD our God, who is enthroned on high? . . . He raises the poor from the dust and lifts the needy from the ash heap. (Psalm 113:5–7)

For I, the LORD, love justice. (Isaiah 61:8)

My brethren, do not hold your faith in our glorious Lord Jesus Christ with an attitude of personal favoritism. (James 2:1)

Religion that is pure and undefiled before God, the Father, is this: to visit orphans and widows in their affliction, and to keep oneself unstained from the world. (James 1:27 ESV)

And in the old Scottish Psalter, psalm 82: "In the gods' assembly, God doth stand; he judges gods among. How long, accepting per-sons vile will ye give judgment wrong? Defend the poor and father-less; to poor oppressed do right. The poor and needy ones set free; rid them from ill men's might."[6]

Serving the God of Justice

The word of our God down through the centuries tells us that he himself is justice. That same word also calls us to bear his image in the world. We do that first by loving and worshiping him, and second by living that worship out—looking like him in this world. Our first and grandest mission in life is to love God. But this God we adore happens to be in love with humanity. That means that true worship is seen or played out in our relationships to our fellow human beings.

If we love God, if we reverence his holy name, then his love and justice and humility will be seen in us. Like the Word of God—both written and flesh—the church is an instrument in the world for the revelation of God. Whatever God's heart is toward the cities of this world—toward victims, toward the poor, the orphaned or alien, the alone, the vulnerable, the abused, the victim of deception or corruption—that should also be the attitude of his church. It is also true that whatever his heart toward the arrogant, the deceivers, and the powerful that use power to hurt others—that too should be the attitude of the church.

My father was a colonel in the United States Air Force. He graduated from a military school, went on to flight school, and then headed for Europe and World War II. He returned home with medals he never displayed. When I was thirteen, the man who flew for Strategic Air Command and was a superb athlete was retired due to a debilitating illness no one could diagnose. He spent the next thirty-two years becoming increasingly disabled and lived out the last years of his life in a nursing home.

As my father's disease progressed, his body went from coordinated athlete to unable to tie his own shoes or get out of a chair. Eventually he was unable to get his feet to walk down a hallway. I learned many lessons from my father's life. Here are two primary ones: First, a body that does not follow its head is a sick body. My father was a bright man who knew many things. He certainly knew how to tie his shoes and how to walk. However, he could not get his body to do what his head knew how to do. His body would not follow his head. The church of Jesus Christ has a head. Our Head has called us to follow him. Where we do not, we are sick.

Second, unchecked, untreated disease—whether due to denial or lack of treatment options—will eventually infest, strangle, and destroy the entire system. It will become less and less able to function as it was meant to. Initially my father's body continued to follow his head; the deviations were small and could even be hidden. Over time, it gradually and more obviously failed to do so. At the end it turned that coordinated, 6-foot-4-inch body into a wreck of its former self. His head no longer directed his body, and eventually, his body died.

We follow a just God. He has said he loves justice. He stood on this planet and declared himself anointed to bring good news to the afflicted; to bind up the brokenhearted; to proclaim liberty to captives and freedom to prisoners. God, whose doctrine is certainly impeccable and infallible, apparently saw the need for it to be fleshed out, lived and seen in a body. He still does. He has us here to follow his head, and where we do not look like him we have unchecked, untreated disease. And we can remove ourselves from the faces that remind us of our failures—we can live apart, never enter in, turn off the news, make quick judgments to relieve ourselves of responding—but eventually the small deviations we have deceived ourselves into finding acceptable will lead to greater disease and the voice of God disobeyed will lead to the voice of God, our head, unheard. That is a very dangerous place for a soul to live.

In closing, let's revisit the dungeons of Cape Coast Castle and chapel sitting above it. I have wondered since then: What if that one body of those who said they were believers had gone down into the dungeons and set the captives free? What if they had taken them out into the light, fed them, clothed them, educated them, and set them free? They would have had to stand up against their superiors, the pattern and print of that age, their cultural norms both secular and Christian, and the greatest empire on earth at that time. They would have caused a stir of rage and indignation on at least three continents. But when our God interfaces with this world, he leaves the higher and descends. He leaves the beauty and enters chaos; he leaves the pure and goes into filthy. He goes against the mainstream, certainly culturally and economically, but even more he demonstrates that God is one who does not just speak but actually does things in this world—first in the hearts of human beings, and then through the lives and bodies of those same human beings. Jesus gave us a manifestation in the flesh of the character of God; his church is to do the same for the world.

Those churches that worship over and separate and are untouched by dungeons are not worshiping the God of the Scriptures. There is nothing in the Scriptures to suggest that being hateful, unjust, neutral, or uncaring and deaf to the cries of humans is godly. The dungeons of Cape Coast Castle were not just below; they were also rampant in the hearts of the worshipers.

The dungeons are not just out there—though they exist all over the world and in our neighborhoods. They are in here, in our hearts. John says to us: "Whoever has the world's goods [money, influence, reputation, expertise, power], and sees his brother in need and *closes his heart against him,* how does the love of God abide in him?" (1 John 3:17, italics added). Earlier we said that when John talks about hate in the heart, it literally means "to spit on someone in your heart." God is concerned about the dungeons of our hearts—our favoritism, our discrimination, our prejudice, our harsh judgments, our choices to be blind and deaf, and our self-protections—as much as he is concerned with the dungeons we are neglecting "out there" in our cities, communities, churches, and families. We are not fit to do the justice of God in this world unless he has first brought light and life into the dungeons of our souls. How else will we bring the life of God to the oppressed? Programs, education, clean water, medicine, food, jobs, and counseling all matter greatly to desperate human beings. We are called by God to do those things, but we are called to do them with hearts that have gone from being dungeons and are transformed into the sanctuary of the God who loves human beings—including us.

And so my fellow believers, I pray we will recognize ourselves first and foremost as the "they." We are the enemies of the kingdom; we are the dirty alien worthy of elimination; we are of the impure race; we are the "other," the less-than, and we have worshiped the wrong god. We are the unwashed and imprisoned; we are the fatherless. As we see these things, we will walk humbly with the Almighty God we say we worship. And as we see him we will see him take a towel, love the alien, lift up the fallen, touch the unclean, and welcome into his kingdom those utterly unlike himself. He came to serve; not to enslave men to serve him, lift him, or ensure his pleasure. He is the antithesis of Cape Coast Castle. When we see him as in a mirror, beholding the glory of the one who became like us, we will be transformed into the same image.

I, the Lord, love justice.

What does the Lord require of you? Do justice, love mercy, and walk humbly with your God.

CHAPTER 3

The Psychology of Evil and Sin

It is striking how little the Christian counseling world speaks of evil. It is certainly not discussed in the realm of psychology, with few exceptions such as O. Hobart Mower, M. Scott Peck, Karl Menninger, and Erich Fromm. In Christian circles we speak more of individual sin but not so much about evil and even less about systems perpetrating evil on vulnerable people. However, underlying all trauma, violence, and abuse lies evil, and the result of evil is always some kind of suffering. In considering these topics some guidelines are in order. If we do not, we will end our journey damaged rather than enlightened, for we are dealing with things that are of the nature of explosives.

One thing my study has engendered in me is a deeper sense of humility. We are approaching that which is largely a mystery to us. We will be traversing the heart and mind of God himself and in essence attempt to comprehend and hold an ocean with a thimble capacity. That humility must be with each other as well as creatures before God. Our knowledge and experience is varied. We need to hear and learn from each other. I look forward to that.

Secondly, we are also, at least in some measure, trying to see what is unseen. We are called to do that. Paul says, "Look not at the things which are seen, but at the things which are not seen" (2 Corinthians 4:18). We will try to do so with the aids God has given us—his written Word, the Word made flesh, the presence of his Spirit, and the thoughts of saints who have preceded us, in writing if not in time. We will still be sorely limited. Nevertheless, we want to try to pierce the appearance of things and get at what is, never forgetting that we see through a glass darkly. That means we will misread and misjudge.

Finally, we who are dealing with these things are ourselves infected by them. We are not healthy doctors working with sickness. We are sick doctors who are trying to grasp the nature and impact of a life-threatening disease that has invaded our own souls, minds, and hearts. Whatever this disease does to our so-called patients, it has done or can do to us. Not only that, any contact with the disease in the lives of others can make us sicker. We do not approach our subject objectively, clear-minded, and untainted. We approach our subject mired in, clouded by, and stained by the very thing that we are attempting to study. Let the student take note.

Those of us who counsel work with sin and evil everyday. We see firsthand the destructiveness wrought in others' lives by their own sin and the evil and sin of others. The turbulence in our world and in the lives of those who seek our help affords us a platform on which to speak truth about these matters. I pray we will have the courage to do so, the wisdom to do it well, and the grace to remember that we ourselves are included in anything we say. Oswald Chambers said the following: "Be careful to maintain strenuously God's point of view."[1] I will attempt to do that as we move through this chapter, fully acknowledging that I can only do so as a finite and sinful creature, albeit one blessed by his Word and his Spirit.

Why Is This Topic Important to Us?

You and I are Christians. We have already stated that many Christians in the fields of psychology and counseling rarely speak about evil and sin. We talk about pathology, dysfunction, abuse, and aberrant behavior. Now all of these are realities and we need to talk about them. These words are descriptive regarding the things we see. Descriptions can be helpful and even powerful in working with people. I do not want to suggest that we should throw such words out. However, the vocabulary of psychology and counseling refers to those things that are seen—symptoms, behaviors, words, and the thoughts behind them. You and I also know that there is a reality that is unseen. It is powerful and impacting, and it demands our attention. The topic of evil and sin is critical and foundational for Christians who would work with those maladies described by the vocabularies of psychology and counseling. Why is that? Let me answer by giving you some points that are basic to our discussion.

First, we are told in the beginning that our Creator God made mankind in his own image. Whatever that phrase means (and that could fill a book itself), we know that it means something good, beautiful, and having inherent dignity. And though we also know that these God-imagers are now fallen, the Scriptures still refer to us as being made in the image of God. Some of what was there is still present. Have you ever been to a museum and seen shards of porcelain gathered during an archaeological dig? The shard may be small and jagged but you can clearly see that the whole was exquisite. You and I are a bit like that shard. The damage is hideous, but a remnant of our former glory still can be glimpsed. The very fact that we were created to reflect the glory of God in the flesh makes the study of evil and sin crucial because it is what destroyed us. That which has the capacity to destroy what God has created deserves our serious attention.

Second, though psychologists and others have offered descriptions of the disease and even palliatives for its lesser forms, they can and have offered no soul cure. Descriptions of personality disorders such as narcissistic, borderline, and sociopath can be helpful in our understanding of what we are working with (or against), but it is commonly accepted that such disorders are highly resistant to change and the descriptions with which we work are merely one way of talking about what we see. The etiology is not really understood. And even more than that, anyone who has been in clinical practice for some time knows that our diagnostic tools are far from exhaustive. One can encounter many arrangements of pathology that do not fit into typical clinical categories. For example, we also know that a category such as sociopath is only descriptive of observed symptoms. It is merely descriptive of the seen. Nothing about the unseen is put forth in the vast majority of psychological literature. If the pathology you are working with is rooted in the unseen, do you think your methods will be curative if you only treat what you can see or describe? It would be the equivalent of treating the symptoms of arsenic poisoning without removing the arsenic.

My friends, where have we been? It is a question that has often arisen during my study. We who know this Creator God, the One who has spoken to us and indwells us, where have we been? I would like to give you two answers to that question because I believe they are important observations of the Christian counseling community. We have been divided. Speaking of evil, division is a great tool of the Evil One. We seem to set up what I call "forced choices" and argue among ourselves. Is healing in the counseling office or the local church? Are we dealing with pathology or sin? Do you follow psychology or theology? Let me tell you something: the choice itself is a fallacy. Cannot the work of God occur in both the counseling office and the local church? And ought they not to work together? Are we not dealing with both pathology and sin? The fallenness of this world is surely so pervasive that it wears many faces. Pathology and sin can occur separately and/or together in the physical realm. Why not in the realm of our thinking, feeling, and willing?

You cannot wrap wire around a sapling tree, bend it over, and tie it to a peg in the ground and then expect it to grow tall and straight. No more can you pin a three-year-old girl under a grown man's body for sex for fifteen years and expect her to grow tall and straight. Both tree and girl will be twisted. Will all trees tied in that manner grow the same way? No. It depends on many other factors, such as light and rainfall. Will all girls tied in the manner described grow the same way? No. It depends on many factors such as exposure to truth and support from others, and unlike trees, in the case of girls, their own sinful propensities will shape them as well. You cannot twist and tie up things, training them in the way they were never meant to go, and not have pathology as a result. At the same time, just because someone has been twisted and tied into a pathological shape is no reason to assume that is the sole source of what we see. Surely in such an environment their own sinfulness is even more likely to contribute to the shape of their lives.

Our divisions weaken us, and we treat each other as enemy rather than brother and sister. Not only are we arguing among ourselves, we also have often divided so that we only talk to those who sound just like us. We talk Christian with Christian. We need to do that, though I fear we often only talk with those particular Christians who agree with us, who are like us, and who use the same vocabulary. Do we really think that our perspective is so full and complete that talk with those who see things differently is unnecessary? I have watched Christian organizations and churches die a slow death, corroding from the inside out because they have failed to cross-pollinate with other believers. Statements remain unquestioned, wrestling ceases, and arrogance results. The subject of evil and sin is a difficult subject for many reasons, not the least of which is that we are all infested with it. We need to talk with each other. We need to be challenged, questioned, and prayed for.

We also need to dialogue with and listen to the non-Christian world. I have learned a great deal by reading the writings of those who do not believe as I do. Sometimes I learn because I do not agree with what they say. Other times I learn because their observations and descriptions are quite profound. John Calvin said,

Whenever we come upon these matters in secular writers, let that admirable light of truth shining in them teach us that the mind of man, though fallen and perverted from its wholeness, is nevertheless clothed and ornamented with God's excellent gifts. If we regard the Spirit of God as the sole fountain of truth, we shall neither reject the truth itself, nor despise it wherever it shall appear, unless we wish to dishonor the Spirit of God. . . . These men whom Scripture call "natural men" were, indeed, sharp and penetrating in their investigation of inferior things. Let us, accordingly, learn by their example how many gifts the Lord left to human nature even after it was despoiled of its true good."[2]

The second thing we have done is unthinkingly echo the secular psychological or counseling community. Let me give you an example. We were told for years that problems in human beings were largely the result of what was called "low self-esteem." This was the answer for violence, bad behavior in the classroom, and trouble in marriages. If we could just raise someone's low self-esteem, they would be fine. The Christian world dutifully followed along and swallowed these statements. If you look through popular Christian books you will find many laced through with or founded on this teaching. There is a problem with it: it is not true.

As more and more research has been done, the evidence has not supported the belief that low self-esteem causes violence. In fact, violent acts follow from high self-esteem. Perpetrators of violence are typically people who think very highly of themselves. Violence ensues when people feel that their favorable view of themselves is threatened or disputed by others. This has been shown to be true across a broad spectrum of violence, from playground bullying to national tyranny, from domestic abuse to genocide, from warfare to murder and rape. Roy Baumeister has a great deal to say about this in his book *Evil: Inside Human Violence and Cruelty.* Now if the Enemy of God, Satan himself, who is in his essence evil, landed there by way of pride, how is it that the Christian community did not see the flaw in popular reasoning? Were we sleeping? Do we not know the Word of God? Why would we merely echo those who say they neither know nor do they believe in the very One who created them?

Now we need to be careful here. I am not suggesting we return to those twisted versions of self-evaluation that the church has often given. Scripture does not call us so much to high or low self-esteem as it does to an accurate or true picture of the self. In speaking truth, we call good that which is good, but we will also call evil that which is evil. To value a self that is riddled with sin is to be deluded. To fail to value a soul for whom Christ died is an affront to God.

The souls of human beings are very precious in the sight of God. As pastors and counselors, we work with these souls and are charged by God himself to do so with care and watchfulness, for some day we must give account. The battle is fierce, the Enemy wily, and the casualties many. We need to learn all we can, we need to weigh what we learn according to the Word of God, and we certainly need each other.

Evil and Sin

Let us look more specifically at evil and sin. The Word of God says this: "Be of sober spirit, be on the alert. Your adversary, the devil, prowls around like a roaring lion, seeking someone to devour" (1 Peter 5:8). You and I, and those with whom we work, have an adversary whose business is to destroy the soul. We have front row seats to the wounds, overthrows, cruelties, and captivities of this enemy. Though we may see more of his work than many, if we are honest, the mystery of darkness remains great. We cannot plumb its depths or fully bring the hidden things to light. We cannot know the mind of our God who yet allows this enemy to pursue us. However, we need to be wise regarding his strength and power if we are to be rightly vigilant. What do we need to know about this enemy?

1. He is the author and father of sin. He was an angel who excelled in strength and beauty. He had the great privilege of serving before the face of God and in that glorious place attempted to supplant the only One worthy of worship. He took many angels with him and proceeded to take the human race as well.

2. He is the father of lies. He is the Deceiver. Nothing he says can be trusted. He who has seen the face of God and knows his character would have us believe God is neither good nor worthy of our worship. He would have us follow him in his attempt to supplant the Almighty. He will say anything, use anything, and twist anything to achieve his end. He will use the words of God himself. Note that it is a great and powerful weapon because that is also what he used with Christ.

3. His power emanates from an implacable malice, his cruelty is insatiable, and he is relentless to pursue. Nothing is beneath him. Not only will he stoop to any evil imaginable, he will use any good to aid his cause. Do not forget the Scriptures describe him as an angel of light. Light is what we associate with God. He comes looking like God as much as he is able in order to deceive us and delude us into thinking we are following God when in fact we are walking after the Evil One himself.

Do we believe these things? Not do we simply know these things—do we *believe* them? Do we hold these truths close as we work with people? Are we aware of the presence of this enemy in the lives of our counselees and in our own life? If we believe these things what should be the result?

1. We should approach life in this world, and in particular our work as counselors, with fear and trembling. How do you think the people around Washington DC felt about going outside when the sniper was on the rampage? Afraid?

Vigilant? Like hiding somewhere? One much greater than the DC snipers or the 9/11 terrorists is here. And we are fools if we think our techniques and interventions and book knowledge and wits are a match for this devouring one. Such things are the equivalent of hiding in fire trucks near the World Trade Centers to avoid the disaster. Our only safety is in our Refuge, our Rock, and our Stronghold. To live in this world and do this work without clamoring for greater understanding of what it truly means to hide in Christ is the height of stupidity. If the work of counseling has not driven us to our knees in search of our Refuge, then we are either asleep or fools. The Christian counseling community, because of its keen awareness of evil and sin and its profound impact on lives, should be known as a praying community.

2. We will be humble and repentant. If one who has seen the face of God had the capacity to rebel against him how much more should we fear for ourselves? We who are frail and who walk by faith not by sight, we who have never seen his face nor watched him create the worlds, we whose limitations and finiteness far exceed that of our finite enemy should grasp to some degree our own capacity for rebellion and deception. We will daily, moment by moment, acknowledge our need of the Word, the Spirit, and the Body to keep us from falling like our enemy did. We will run to him like a passenger on the *Titanic* ran to the lifeboat.

3. If we understand the truths we have laid out, we will know that we can never solve the riddles of the Deceiver. I am saddened when I hear of those in the counseling profession who spend their lives talking about the demonic, describing what they learn, naming them, figuring out what the Enemy is doing. What makes us think we can figure out one who is in his essence a lie? Have you ever

worked with a hard-core addict? The perpetual question is: what haven't you told me? Addicts have practiced lying to themselves and others for so long they cannot simply stop. It is a practice woven into their very being. If a human being who is addicted to a drug or sex or food is so full of lies that you do not believe what they say, then why do we think that the *father* of lies can be believed when he says things to us about what he is doing? The deception we have swallowed is to think that we can discern what he is doing. I cannot even tell how a good magician does his card tricks when they happen before my eyes! To attempt to discern the detailed workings of the Enemy in someone's life is to enter a maze that goes on forever. What did Jesus say to his disciples when the work of the Enemy was resistant to their efforts? "This kind does not go out except by prayer and fasting" (Matthew 17:21). Those activities are directed toward God. And the more we see of the Enemy in a person's life, the more we need to seek after God.

A discussion of evil and psychology cannot help but raise questions about demonization. People often ask me, "What do you think about it? Does it exist? Have you ever encountered it?"

First, yes, I believe it exists. Our Lord encountered it in the Scriptures. He demonstrated his authority again and again by casting out demons. He encountered those with more than one spirit in them, and he showed great compassion for those so afflicted. Some suggest that such things do not occur anymore. I see no scriptural grounds for such a conclusion.

Second, it is an area where many have shipwrecked. They have gone in and never come out. They speak far more of the Enemy than the Savior. They focus on understanding the father of lies, neither a possible nor laudable goal. They also have lost sight of the workings of sin in all of us and so leave many in their sin by attributing things to the demonic rather than to the human in front of them. There is then no call to repentance. Now whose deceptive work do you think that is?

Third, yes, I have seen it. I have worked at times with those who have been actively involved in witchcraft and Satanism. However, I believe it is far more rare than some of the popular Christian literature would have us believe, at least in this country. I recently spoke at conferences in Brazil on abuse and know from the missionaries and national pastors there that black magic, Espiritismo, and Satanism have borne ugly and real fruit in the lives of many. When I have concluded that the demonic is actively present in a life, it has been infrequent and only after much prayer, both private and corporate. If you ever encounter it, treat it like quicksand and get on your face before God. It has an enormous capacity to derail you and deceive you, while leading you to think you are doing God's work.

Sin

I want us to consider sin. Let us begin by noting that the connection between evil and sin is seamless. We do not always treat it that way. We often speak of evil as out there, unusual, extreme, and foreign. We associate evil with Satan, terrorists, and sadism, not usually with ourselves. We must maintain strenuously God's point of view. God says evil is not lodged in "them" over there. He says evil is lodged in us. He says we have met the Enemy and they are us. Not just him (though Satan is our enemy and God's) and not just them (though they may sometimes act as enemies). We ourselves are at enmity with God. We serve clients who are at enmity with God. There are no exceptions. A terrible life of unjust suffering does not erase this truth. Severe handicaps do not change this fact. No human being, no matter how wounded by others, grossly handicapped, or anything else, is exempt from being at enmity with God.

Secondly, evil is not just something we *do*; it is something we *are*. Sin is not merely wrongdoing; it is wrong being. It is how we think, what we desire, how we are motivated. Scripture says that every intent of the thoughts of the heart was only evil continually (Genesis 6:5). That does not leave any room for having a good day, does it? Jesus said, "If you, being evil . . ." Jesus quotes Isaiah saying that people's hearts are far away from him. Can that be anything other than evil? He says in Mark 7, that which comes *out* of us is what defiles us. He lists a great many evils and then says that all this evil proceeds from within.

Let me give you some characteristics of sin. These come from a book by Jeremiah Burroughs titled *The Evil of Evils*. He says that evil, or sin, is opposite to God. It opposes his nature; it works against him; it wrongs him. Evil is so opposite to who God is that if one drop resided in him he would cease to be God. Evil resists God; it walks contrary to him; it despises him. He is life; evil is of the nature of death. Sin wrongs God more than anything else. It strikes at the very being of God.

Second, sin or evil is opposite to man's good. It has defaced the image of God in us. It defiles us, hardens us, isolates us, deceives us, deadens us, and deforms us. Sin is opposite to the image of God, the life of God in me. Sin is the object of God's wrath and hatred. It defiles all that we meddle with and us as well.

Third, sin is poison. It contaminates; it spreads; it seems to change shape and easily delude us so that we pick up that which is evil and call it good. It is contagious. Pastors and counselors are experts in the worst of all infectious diseases. It is not just that we might catch it from another but that it already resides in us and can quickly be inflamed and envelop us even as we try to help another.

So sin exists, outside us certainly, but inside us as well. It is in our families, our churches, our culture, the media, and our schools. It is in us infecting all of those institutions as well. It is subtle and deceitful and it is often that which looks good to us. It is contagious. It is the thing that God calls the worst thing in the world.

I have been struck by the fact that the Christian community does not talk about sin very much, or if it does it often seems to do so in a naïve and superficial way. Cornelius Plantinga, in his book *Not the Way It's Supposed to Be,* says he is trying to "retrieve an old awareness that has slipped and changed in recent decades. The awareness of sin used to be our shadow. Christians hated sin, feared it, fled from it, grieved over it . . . but the shadow has dimmed."[3]

I have thought long and hard about a way to try to cut through both the denial and naiveté and so, at the risk of offending you, I want to present you with an image to help us grasp what we are talking about. I would like us to think about sin as the sewage, the excrement of human souls. Now the concept of sewage is inherently repulsive. We all immediately back up. It is not a subject considered appropriate to discuss in polite company. And frankly, anyone who does not seem repelled but rather drawn in is someone we would consider very, very sick.

Now remember this is sewage that is not just an external problem. We are constantly creating it ourselves. We are contaminating our worlds, our homes, and ourselves with it. No amount of cleaning gets rid of it. It is a perpetual problem until we die. Not only that, because we work with people, we are those who have the divine vocation of latrine duty. We have been called by God to deal with the sewage in others' lives—not just their own but also sometimes years of the sewage of others that is on them and in them in a multitude of hidden ways. And we come into that work with our own as well.

There is another complication. My West Virginia great-grandmother had a saying that went like this: "You get used to hanging if you hang long enough." Now obviously, if you get used to hanging you are dead. So it is with latrine duty. We get used to our own sewage and that of others. We use the equivalent of Clorox and air fresheners and scrub brushes, forgetting that the source is internal and more will simply take its place. We get used to the smell, our eyes become dull, and we no longer see clearly. We explain it away. If those other people had not come around, we would not have this problem. The real problem is that we are not using the right brush. The air freshener needs freshening.

Now listen to me carefully. In a literal sewage problem you would need brushes and Clorox and air fresheners. Many years ago I had a young man walk into my office off the street and defecate all over my waiting room. We used Clorox, scrub brushes, and air freshener. These are not bad, wrong, or useless things. They are helpful and even necessary. But they do not stop the production of sewage! We do not have a forced choice situation here. Both components are necessary. We need to find the source of the sewage and deal with it. We also need to do cleanup and help those who come to us do the same.

That leads us to a major problem. Who among us can stop the flow of sewage from human souls? Our own or another's? I cannot even figure out half the time where mine will show up next. I am layered, complex, hidden, and deceived. Worse, I do not often enough have the sense to recognize the stuff, especially in my own life. My critical remark was "helpful insight," my arrogance is labeled "wisdom," my impatience is called "weariness," and my demandingness is merely a "need." Even worse—a thought which seems astounding in the context of this analogy—we *like* some of our sewage. It comforts us, we are used to it, it is what our family did, it is what our church or denomination does, it is what our culture adheres to, it is justified because others put it in our lives and we cannot help it. We forget that it is sewage.

Now understand, if we truly see sin from God's standpoint, we will be as repelled by it as we would be by overflowing sewage. We would run, or we would react to sin as a burned child reacts to the fire. Do we see how dull we are? How deceived our minds and hearts? How clouded our eyes? How lulled into sleep our spiritual senses? We are talking about something that distorts our character, originally designed to carry the image of God. It pollutes our thoughts, emotions, speech, and actions. It twists up the things that are good so that we use them for evil. It runs as a thread through the atrocities found throughout the world such as disease, abuse, starvation, genocide, and death.

What is to be our response to these things as Christians in the helping professions? You and I come into contact with evil and sin every day of our lives, internal and external, seen and unseen. It is the nature of life in this world. You cannot escape it by finding a "Christian" fortress to hide in, for your very presence will mean it is no longer a refuge. Or as G. K. Chesterton put it when asked what was wrong with the world, "I am." As those who work with people for the specific purpose of ministering to their broken places, we encounter evil and sin in an intense manner. We cannot help but be profoundly impacted, and if what I have said about the nature of evil and sin is true then we will be ignorant of many of the ways that is occurring.

Conclusions

I have a few conclusions from what we have considered.

1. While we must study and learn, grasp, and wrestle with an understanding of evil and sin, we must never forget that we cannot fully know. The Scriptures say we cannot fully plumb the depths of our own finite and deceitful hearts. We will certainly never completely understand the Enemy and his ways, the heart of the human being in front of us, ourselves, or our God, who while being eternally good, loving, wise, just, and merciful has permitted such things to be. Humility rather than adamancy will be our badge.
2. If we grasp the wily nature of the Enemy of our souls, we will constantly seek new ways to flee into Christ, to wear

his armor, to stand in his strength, and to learn how to pray. We become like that which has a hold on us, like that which grips us. If we constantly pursue the Enemy, seeking out his ways, lost in the maze of trying to understand one who is perennially false, we will look more like him than the One whose precious name we bear.

3. We will hate sin wherever we find it, in others, in institutions secular and sacred, in our clients, and in ourselves. We will fear it, dread it, agonize over it, and flee it. We will be those who would rather lose anything than gain by sinning. We will be courageous in dealing with the sins of others. We will hate sin more than we love acceptance or approval or belonging.

4. We will not be naïve about the nature of sin wherever we find it. We will not think it is merely bad deeds or bad words. We will comprehend to some degree that when a person has been gravely sinned against, someone has poured sewage all over and into the life before us. If you are going to work compassionately with someone like that, you must first understand how they have been contaminated and help clean them off before you begin to consider ways they are producing sewage of their own. When Jesus responded to the woman found in an adulterous relationship, his first response was to the sewage of her accusers and then he mentioned her own. It is harsh and ignorant to sit with someone who is poverty-stricken, living in a neighborhood of violence, in a home filled with abuse of all kinds, to think that merely dealing with their particular sins is all that is needed.

5. We will also be keenly aware that human nature will use any excuse it can find to avoid dealing with its own sin. We must be careful not to allow our compassion and understanding of the sewage of others that may be burying another's life to lead us into failing to consider the individual

sins of the one so sinned against. Understanding of the impact of others on a life is necessary for effective help to occur. Understanding one's own production of sewage and the ensuing damage is also vital. Oswald Chambers said that the world and those who inhabit it need a surgical operation and that if we can help others by our sympathy and understanding alone we are traitors to Jesus Christ. Every response not embedded in the cross of Christ will lead astray.

6. One of the things God has often done for me is use my awareness of sin and evil in individuals or institutions to give me a picture of who I am before him and outside of Christ. As I have sat with self-centered, grabbing, demanding individuals who tax me to the limit and sought him to teach me how to respond with both grace and firmness, he has shown me the evidence for such things in my own heart or life and then reminded of who he has been to me. Apart from such lessons, we would easily become proud and Pharisaical. Listen to the words of Father Brown as written by G. K. Chesterton when he was asked how he was able to figure out who a criminal was in a difficult case which the police were unable to solve:

> They get outside a man and study him as if he were a gigantic insect. . . . When the scientist talks about a type, he never means himself but always means his neighbor. . . . I don't try to get outside the man. I try to get inside the murderer. . . . No man is really any good till he knows how bad he is, or might be, till he's realized how little right he has to all his snobbery and sneering and talking about "criminals" as if they were apes in a forest 10,000 miles away; till he's got rid of all the dirty self-deception of talking about low types and deficient skulls;

till he's squeezed out of his soul the last drop of the oil of the Pharisees; till his only hope is somehow or other to have captured one criminal, and kept him safe and sound under his own hat.[4]

7. Finally, we will never for a moment forget that the most precious truth of all time and eternity is that there is a Redeemer. There is One who did for us what Father Brown talks about in the above quote. There is One who became sewage for us that we might be clean and pure and holy. He was not just littered with our sewage; Scripture says he became the thing itself. He did not come to earth to study us; he became like us, and he got inside us. We will look more at this in a later chapter. Suffice it to say for now, that he, who was nothing like us, became what we are so that we, who were nothing like him, might become as he is. He who was all beauty and glory became garbage for us so that we, who were at enmity with him and proliferating sewage all over his world and his creatures, might share in and reflect that beauty and glory in this world and in our work.

Sin becomes the most frightening thing in the world when we understand these things. The souls and lives of those we live and work with become very precious, for we begin to understand the great lengths our Savior went to in order to redeem them. The work of ministry and of counseling is a sacred work in light of these truths, for it is an arena where we see the work of the Redeemer manifested. And we, who sent him to the cross, are privileged to do that work with him. Who can fathom the mysteries of God?

CHAPTER 4

The Psychology of Suffering

There is a window in my office across from the chair I sit in day
after day. Outside that window I have placed a bird feeder. I
originally put it there in order to remind me of beauty so that
as I listened to stories of evil, sin, and suffering I could see the
red cardinal who comes and feeds alongside the beautiful gold-
finches. One day as I was listening to a horrific story of trauma
and abuse from a woman I had come to love dearly, I looked up
and saw a flock of sparrows at my feeder. The following Scripture
came to mind: "Are not two sparrows sold for a penny? And yet
not one of them will fall to the ground apart from your Father.
So do not fear; you are more valuable than many sparrows"
(Matthew 10:29, 31). If two very inexpensive, dispensable creatures cannot suffer apart from our Father, how much more so for
the woman I was listening to.

However, these verses contain a familiar dilemma. The Father
who watches over them knows the sparrows. They cannot fall
without his knowledge. And yet, they still fall. Falling hurts. If
we had written these verses, we would have concluded with "So
do not fear; you are more valuable than many sparrows and your
Father will catch you." That is not what is says, is it?

The dilemma of suffering is inherent in the Scriptures.
Suffering cannot occur apart from the Father. Suffering occurs
with the knowledge and oversight of the Father, who obviously

cares and considers us valuable. The precious woman in front of me was describing a horrific story of repeated abuse and neglect. She definitely qualified as a fallen sparrow. She is of far more value than a fallen sparrow. Her fall did not occur apart from the Father who loved her then and continues to do so while she struggles heroically in my office to face the truth and grow. How are we to explain such a seeming contradiction?

I am not unacquainted with the tension this question brings. As I mentioned before, I am the daughter of an Air Force colonel who had to retire at age forty-two because of a then-undetermined illness. He was increasingly disabled for thirty-two years until his death at seventy-four. I had a front-row seat growing up to the kind of suffering that is progressive and slow, attacking someone little by little. It was a suffering that chewed away at the man I called Daddy until he was but a shadow of the colonel in blue.

I have been a psychologist for over forty years. I have worked in the area of trauma and abuse all of that time. Those of you involved in such work know that you cannot sit with such suffering and not suffer too. Certainly it is not suffering of the same magnitude as those I sit with, not by any means. But it does involve suffering nonetheless. Anyone in a helping profession knows that the weeks prior to the holidays are wild. Whatever hurts, hurts worse. One year seemed particularly bad to me. I sat with suicide, Ground Zero, cancer, a divided and dying church, clergy sexual abuse, and all of these amidst the usual caseload of abuse survivors and other trauma. I did not sleep well and struggled with nightmares as the suffering of others worked its way into my heart and mind and then into my nighttime hours. The abuse was not mine, the cancer was not mine, the suicide was not in my family, but the suffering of the people I saw ended up in my life as well. Suffering is like that. That is why so many people back up from it and do not want to hear about it.

We will not solve the dilemma and questions that surround the topic of suffering. It is, however, something we all struggle with, both personally and professionally. I hope our discussion will better equip us in that ongoing struggle.

Evil and Suffering

One of the things I have struggled with in preparing this chapter is the unnatural division, necessary because of time, between evil and sin on the one hand, and suffering on the other. They go hand in hand really. We cannot separate them. Sometimes because they have often been wrongly joined together, we in the counseling field work hard to separate them. We have seen the suffering inflicted by so-called helpers when they have assumed that suffering meant wrongdoing in the life of the sufferer. In our sadness and perhaps anger over that, we have often erred on the other side and so we only deal with evil and sin as they occur in the lives of those who have hurt our clients, not in our clients themselves. Again, we must go back to our statement in the last chapter: "Maintain strenuously God's point of view." We need to heed Paul's admonition to look not merely at the seen but at the unseen. It is so easy for us to see an error, particularly when it causes suffering in the lives of those we want to help, and simply react against it. If we fail to pull the lens back and see the whole from the perspective of Scripture, we will merely produce another error.

We all know that in the beginning we are told that "God saw all that He had made, and behold, it was very good" (Genesis 1:31). God's creation was saturated with goodness and beauty and life. His creation reflected his glory. There was no evil or suffering in what he had made. But very shortly, a mere two chapters over, we find evil, enmity, pain, domination, shame, seduction, deception, and death. Sin has come in and made the basis of things wild and not rational. It has created chaos and darkness, ugliness and death. All of creation has been altered; nothing is as God intended it. It is very crucial, however, that we say that in the midst of this hideous contorting and twisting of creation, God himself has not changed. "For I, the LORD, do not change" (Malachi 3:6). The one who said "It is good" is exactly the same One who said, "I will greatly multiply your pain, and thorns and thistles will grow for you" (Genesis 3:16, 18, author paraphrase).

These two facts—that all of creation is altered and God himself is not—are facts that you and I have difficulty absorbing and, in fact, frequently reverse. As creatures we tend to reason from creation to the character of God, rather than from the character of God to creation. There are reasons for that. One is that you and I are supposed to be able to look at what is and see his invisible character. Romans 1:20 says: "For since the creation of the world His invisible attributes, His eternal power and divine nature, have been clearly seen, being understood through what has been made." Who God is, is apparent in what he created. We have all experienced the truth of this, standing under heaven's expanse, watching the waves roll in, examining a tiny mountain wildflower lodged in a rock crevice, or seeing a baby born. He is there and his power, his creativity, his beauty, his might, and his care for all that exists are apparent.

Then all of a sudden it makes no sense. Lightning falls from that heaven and a family's home is burned to the ground along with the three children inside. The waves roll in during a hurricane and towns are wiped out and many people die. A volcano erupts and the wildflowers are decimated along with many human beings. The baby is born but he is severely handicapped and will never take a breath on his own. Who is God in *these* places? Can we look at his world now and see his invisible attributes? Is he then uncaring, cruel, oblivious, or punishing? How are we to know when the world accurately reflects him and when it tells us lies about who he is? It is a complex and confusing problem, and we, as human beings, have made many mistakes in our attempts to answer the question. I am sure we will continue to do so.

What are some of the ways we have attempted to solve the dilemma? We do it in a way not unlike a child who is being abused.

The child-mind attempts to understand what is happening and concludes that the abuse must be someone's fault. In that child-mind are two possible choices. The abuse is either her fault or it is the abuser's fault. Now when the abuser is her father, the idea of it being his fault is terrifying, for how can she then feel safe in the home? She is little and he is big. He has power; she does not. People listen to him; no one listens to her. So she decides it is her fault. It gives her a small sense of control. If the abuse is my fault because I am bad, then if I can figure out how to be good, I will be able to stop the abuse. There is some shred of consolation in that hideous conclusion and so it is held onto tenaciously. Anyone who has worked with survivors knows how difficult it is to unwrap the fingers of a mind that clings to such a belief.

Now obviously the abuse is the father's fault. Though in working with such issues we also know it is far more complex than that. The odds are high that the father, who was once a powerless little boy, was himself a victim, equally shaped and molded by the evil perpetrated against him. Perhaps he coped by assuming he needed to do whatever was necessary to make himself feel better and so a couple of decades later his choice has led to the belief that he has the right to hurt his own child because no one will take care of him. And on it goes. Sin and suffering intertwined together and perpetuated through the generations.

Do we not think similarly when it comes to evil, suffering, and God? In our struggle with *why*, we assume somebody has to be at fault. Is it me or is it God? To think that it is God is a bit terrifying since he has all the power and is in charge. So many of us say that the sufferer is at fault. This was the choice of Job's so-called friends. If you are suffering, then it is obvious you have done something wrong. When you figure out what that is and stop doing it, then your suffering will be over. The greater your suffering, the greater the evil you have done. It is a nice, neat package of direct correlations. Many of us in the counseling field have picked up the pieces in lives where Job's friends have abounded. The damage has been even greater when those "friends" have been people in authority such as pastors or Christian counselors.

"I was told my wife was unfaithful because I travel for my job."

"I was told that my husband beats me because I am not a good wife."

"Our daughter is on drugs because we were not good parents."

"I have chronic illness because of some sin in my life." Or the version I got from a Christian woman when I was a teen was that my father was sick because I was a bad daughter.

The clear implication of such statements is that the speaker is not suffering from such things because they are good, righteous, and therefore deserving of a pain-free life.

Does our sin contribute to our suffering? Sometimes it does, but certainly not always. Scripture says we can suffer for righteousness' sake. It also makes clear that suffering can occur simply because there are wicked people in the world. The Psalms are full of such instances. David talks about "those who would destroy me are powerful, being wrongfully my enemies" (Psalm 69:4).

Some Christians resolve the dilemma by blaming it all on Satan. It can get a bit ridiculous. I burned my toast this morning because of the toaster demon? Is the Enemy of God involved in this world? Absolutely. He is called the prince of the power of the air (Ephesians 2:2). We are told "our struggle is not against flesh and blood, but against the rulers, against the powers, against the world forces of this darkness, against the spiritual forces of wickedness in the heavenly places" (Ephesians 6:12). We are told in 1 John 5:19, "We know that we are from God, and that the whole world lies in the power [the embrace] of the evil one" (ESV). So is he here? Yes. Is he involved with the evil and suffering of this world? Certainly. Is he powerful? Yes. Does that explain it? No. Ultimately we still come back to God with "WHY?"

Elie Wiesel, who has taught me a great deal about trauma and suffering, states the problem eloquently for us. Wiesel was sent to

Auschwitz with his family. He was the sole survivor. He entered the camps as a fifteen-year-old Jewish boy steeped in the belief that God was omnipotent and loving. The terrible evil and suffering he witnessed in that place swallowed his faith. He says that we are not to think that saying God exists solves the problem at all. In fact, he says it simply states the problem. His mind, he says, can manage God and not Auschwitz, or it can manage Auschwitz and not God. How is a mind to grasp God *and* Auschwitz? Each seems to cancel out the other. They appear to him to be irreconcilable realities.

I cannot answer the why for you. I have never been able to do so for my clients. I do not believe though that suffering and God are two irreconcilable realities. I will get to the reason for that conclusion later. For now, the point is that we need to be aware that we are dealing with complex, sacred matters beyond our comprehension. While we may know some things about this issue, we cannot know all things. Comprehending these matters is a bit like trying to grasp the ocean from a thimbleful of water. Now if we had a thimble of ocean water, we would know some truths about the ocean. We would know it was wet. We could taste its saltiness. We might find sand in it, and if we put it under a microscope, we might see creatures. But we would never understand the depths. It would be impossible. So it is with God. We know from his world and his Word many things about him. But that very Word says, "Oh the depth of the riches both of the wisdom and knowledge of God! How unsearchable are His judgments and unfathomable His ways!" (Romans 11:33). We are to seek and we will find. We are to search and we will know. But oh the depths! They are infinite and therefore unfathomable.

What then can we conclude from the above?

1. As in our previous discussion, it is clear that we must approach this subject with humility. We are the creatures. Our understanding is limited. Not only is that humility

necessary before God, it is also necessary when we sit with the suffering of another. We cannot pass judgment. We cannot say why. Even when consequences seem a direct result of an individual's choices (such as lung cancer for a lifetime smoker), the question still remains—*Why* did this smoker get cancer when others did not. Bad choices do not always result in equally bad outcomes.

2. Sin has tainted every aspect of our world, our lives, and our very beings. The basis of life in our fallen world is tragic. It is irrational. That means what we see will not make sense to us. Don't expect it to. Good people experience bad things. Bad people have good lives. And since before God we are all bad people, why are we not surprised that any of us have good in our lives at all? Things are not just or fair in this world. Sin is at large, and all the created world is captive to it.

3. The Enemy of our God is involved in suffering in many ways. He asked permission to wreak havoc in Job's life, and it was granted. Jesus said Satan had bound the woman who was bent double for eighteen years. If, as John says, the world lies in his embrace, then surely he is involved with our suffering.

4. Whether we understand it or not, have faith to believe it or not, the Scriptures say that the character of our God is unchanged since before time. Who he was before the dawn of time is who he was at creation, is who he was at the cross, is who he was at Auschwitz or Ground Zero, is who he is in my life today.

Suffering

For each human being the question of suffering represents a continuous challenge. The more present suffering is to us or those we love, the greater our struggle. It is when our struggle ceases to be academic or abstract and becomes highly personal that we wrestle most intensely. I wrestled early on as a result of my father's illness. I have continued to do so through the sorrows and deaths of friends and through the suffering of the clients I have seen for forty years. Let me tell you some things I have learned about suffering.

The first thing I learned early on in my life was that suffering *is*. I learned that health is never certain, that maintaining it is often not under our control, and that disease, suffering, and pain can rise up out of nowhere and completely alter a life. I saw that health is not worthy of our worship, for it is a tentative, changeable and often fragile god.

My father had a marvelous mind, an amazing sense of humor, and was an excellent athlete. He flew a lead plane over Normandy during World War II and came home with medals I never knew him to display. When I was twelve, he was told we were being sent to Iran so he could head up the flight training school for that country's military. We never went. At the age of forty-two he was instead retired with an as yet undiagnosed disease.

My world changed radically. My father lost his job, his security, his status, his income, his future, and the use of his body as he had known it. I left friends, home, and the only lifestyle I knew to move to a new place, with a sick daddy and an uncertain future. If life and its value depended on health or the lack of suffering, then ours would have been over.

You don't need my story to know that suffering *is*, do you? Watch the news, read the newspaper, listen to your clients or parishioners. Look at your own life. Read the Word of God. Peter says, do not be surprised (1 Peter 4:12). Jesus says, in this world you shall have trouble (John 16:33).

I also learned that suffering seems unreasonable, irrational, and unjust. How many times have you encountered suffering in a life and thought it was fair? Perhaps if we encounter suffering in someone we consider evil, then we deem it fair. That is rare and I have never known someone who was suffering to think that what they were dealing with was just. Suffering rarely makes a great deal of sense. Oh, we work hard to make sense out of it. We write books and have conferences trying to make it seem rational. Frankly, I often think that the ability to easily explain suffering is the clearest indicator of never having suffered. It is a mystery in many ways, and those who have suffered demonstrate humility and respect for that fact.

Jesus indicated that it could not all be balanced out. He and the disciples passed a man blind from birth, begging by the road. "Who sinned?" they asked. "Did this man bring this on himself or did his parents do something? Tell us this is fair because of something someone did." Now given my earlier statements about forced choices, you will know that I am delighted with Christ's answer. The disciples said, "Is it A or B?" Jesus said, "C." You can rarely balance it out. There is no balance in the gang rape of an eleven-year-old. There is no justice in the brutal molesting of a child. There is no fairness in the suffering of an AIDS baby. There is no justice in the rape of a missionary nurse who works selflessly on an isolated station in the service of others. You cannot make suffering fair.

I also learned that suffering is not good. That seems obvious, doesn't it? Death is not good; abuse is not good; violence is not good; cruelty is not good. These things are wrong and were not intended to be. However, I am sure you have encountered those who try to say suffering is good. We sit across from indescribable suffering and glibly pronounce, "All things work together for good to those who love God." Now do not get me wrong. I believe that verse with all my heart. But it is *not* a glib verse and it does *not* say that suffering is good. It does not say, "Do not worry about what you are enduring because it will all turn out nice in the end." What it does say is that the God we worship is capable of redeeming the deepest agony, the most hideous suffering, the pain beyond words, into something that gives life and brings glory to him. But make no mistake, the transfiguring of agony cost Jesus Christ inestimably.

Death does not transform into life easily. Redemption costs, and whenever we encounter it, we can be certain we have stepped into the realm of the supernatural.

Another lesson I learned through my father's continued and deteriorating illness was that though suffering is inevitable, we are not to respond passively. We are not to sit back and let evil, sin, suffering, or the Evil One have its way. We are called to do battle.

My parents responded with strength and courage. They pursued answers. It took a year just to get a diagnosis. One week we were told it was terminal, the next week it was not. My father pursued jobs. Very few people were interested in a forty-something retired colonel who could do air refueling and had an undiagnosed disease. My father, who had been vice commander of an air base, swept out a truck stop for awhile to fight against the economic ravages of the disease. My father tried many drugs and aids to attempt to stay the relentless progression of his condition.

For me, one of the most profound ways I learned to actively fight against his disease was that I learned how to wait. It is a lesson that has reverberated down through forty years of clinical work. We lived with an increasingly handicapped man who was still trying to tie his own shoes and bait his fishhook. Rather than railroading over him and destroying his dignity, we learned to wait. We could not stay the physical progression of the disease, but we could inhibit its destruction of his dignity and honor. That lesson has borne fruit in my office often as I wait for a terrified woman who has been battered for years by her husband to find words or while I wait for the parent of a child just taken by a drunk driver gasp for air and struggle to speak. It plays out when I work with those who were sexually abused as children and whose ambivalence about trusting me is a roller coaster ride that lasts for a long, long time.

Over time I learned that suffering is universal. It happens to all of us. It is inescapable. Even those who appear to go through life relatively unscathed must deal with death, their own and the deaths of those they love. All of us must walk through the valley of the shadow of death. If we look at the crucifixion, we see three crosses. They show us the universal heritage of suffering. Suffering is the heritage of the bad as seen in the unrepentant thief. It is the inheritance of the penitent as seen in the repentant thief. It was also the heritage of the perfect Son of God. None escaped. Neither will we.

It is amazing to see that when people find out you know something about suffering, they come out of the woodwork to tell you about theirs. Perhaps they sense they are safe in the presence of one who has suffered. They think they may be understood. People began talking to my parents about their lives and their own suffering. They told stories of what went on behind closed doors. I found it so myself. Kids in school came to me about alcoholic parents, beatings, promiscuity, and cruelty.

Another lesson I learned as a result of my father's illness is that when it comes to suffering, human beings tend to fall into one of two camps. One camp is made up of those of us who would flee from suffering, disease, defects, pain, and death. It makes us very uncomfortable. We do not like how it looks, how it sounds, how it smells, and how it makes us feel. We do not know what to say. We cringe at the thought of touching a diseased body or sitting with someone who is wracked with sobs. We are ever trying to avoid pain and suffering, not just that of others but our own as well.

Those who sit with the suffering occupy the second camp. We sit with people as they die. We hold those who cannot stop crying. We care for others, wait on others, and take care of others. We easily get lost in the suffering. We end up drowning in the sickness and suffering of others, easily resentful of those who are not doing as we are.

As the years went by and my father's illness progressed, I watched my mother struggle with this balance. She was committed to caring for my father. His disease completely altered her life.

THE PSYCHOLOGY OF SUFFERING

She gave up many things for his sake. One by one I watched her pursuits fall by the wayside. The last years of his life were spent in a nursing home, and daily she would rise, organize her day, and go to spend the afternoon, dinnertime, and early evening with him. It was a costly sacrifice.

She often had to be reminded by her children to take breaks or go on vacation. It was easy for her to lose sight of the fact that there was something in life besides sick people in a nursing home. She believed God had called her to love and care for my father with faithfulness, but she periodically needed to be reminded that she herself was not sick and her life needed to reflect that truth as well. At the same time, she often struggled with feelings of uselessness given the small size of her world. She had traveled the world as the "colonel's lady." She was outgoing and involved in many lives. Wherever we lived, she taught women's Bible studies. The phone rang. Life was full. A hospital bed with a crippled man in it who shared a room with a tube-fed boy who would never eat, speak, or walk was a drastic change.

During that struggle of many years mom and I experienced a growing awareness that there was a larger picture. Yes, there is terrible suffering in this world and we are not to run from it. We are to look it full in the face, confront it with courage, sit with those who are suffering and minister to them. However, suffering is not to rule our lives. It is not our master. We were created to bring glory to God. That purpose has not changed since the beginning of the world. Suffering has not altered our purpose. We are to fight against pain and suffering, but that is not our ultimate goal. God help us if it is, for we will often lose.

Finally, I learned from my father that God uses brokenness. My father's use and value did not cease as his body ceased to work. His impact on many lives continues to be felt. It is certainly apparent in my work, for his life and his suffering has shaped mine in profound ways. I can see the impact on my sons, whose formative years were full of experiences with my father. Our culture teaches us that usefulness is in proportion to beauty, health, brains, and ability. It is a terrible lie.

I have a dear friend who has lupus. She struggles often with the smallness of her world and how her suffering impacts and limits her. It is easy to feel useless in such circumstances. Yet she is a wonderful intercessor and wages war in the heavenlies—only eternity will tell what fruit her life has borne. Her life is not small at all because it encompasses far more than what is seen.

Our Response to Suffering

In 2001 I had the privilege of speaking at two conferences in Brazil on sexual abuse. It was a marvelous experience and I am not sure I will ever be the same. Its impact on me was not unlike that of spending a night in the pit at Ground Zero. Both experiences have altered me by giving me pictures of life in this world from the perspective of the unseen. Let me tell you just a few things about Brazil because it is relevant to our discussion of suffering.

The poverty was overwhelming. Brazil was in an economic crisis. Millions of people lived in makeshift "homes" such as cardboard boxes—without jobs, unemployment checks, education, and social services. The church was alive and growing, but it had no resources. The second conference took place in northeast Brazil. The problem of sexual abuse was rampant throughout Brazil, especially in this area. Incest was considered "part of the culture." There was a saying in that area according to a pastor's wife I spoke to: "Other men may have my daughter, but I get her first." The sex slave traffic was exploding, second only to Thailand in the world. Young girls and teens were on the streets prostituting themselves. They came to get "away" from the abuse at home.

The church desperately needs help. Christian counseling is pretty much unknown. Those with degrees in counseling or psychology learn nothing but Freud. There are few books. Many times in that beautiful country, among people I came to love, I felt like I was again standing in the pit of Ground Zero looking at the rubble of what was the world. The suffering was incomprehensible. The rescue workers were few and weary. The work was slow and hard. The darkness, the stench of death, and the grief were very powerful. It is into these places that the church of Jesus Christ is called to go, for it is into such places that he went when he was here in the flesh.

Jesus Christ has called us to follow him into the fellowship of his sufferings. He asks us to do so in varying capacities, but all of us are asked. Some of us are asked to go there in our personal lives. Some of us are asked to go by way of the suffering of others. And some of us are asked to traverse both paths, as did our Lord. None of us are exempt from this call if we follow Christ because that is the way he went. As he weeps in the Garden of Gethsemane, Christ calls us to watch with him. Will we watch or will we sleep?

We do not want to watch. Watching means coming into close quarters with the great enemy in the souls of God's people. Watching means facing horrific and terrifying evil washing over the lives of others. Watching means a desperate struggle with the Prince of Darkness, and with everything his rage can stir up in the shape of obstacles, vexations, oppositions, and hatreds, whether by circumstances or the hands of men. Watching is a serious task. Watching means facing the deceitfulness of our own hearts, our lust for comfort, and the approval of men. We prefer to flee into the anesthesia of sleep. Will we sleep or will we watch?

I believe that the people of God have been extended an invitation by God to enter into atrocity, evil, and suffering in his name. Such a call, which R. C. Sproul calls the divine vocation of suffering, is really nothing other than a call to follow in the footsteps of our Lord, who entered into the terrible atrocity of this world and our hearts for our sakes. He came in a body of flesh to walk among us and our sin and suffering. He, who now stands at the right hand of the Father interceding for us, still has a body of flesh on this earth. We are that body, called out of love and obedience to the Father, to walk among others in their sin and suffering.

In recent years I have begun to understand that the call of God on my life is a bit unusual. It is a clear call to enter into the fellowship of his sufferings. It is a call to weep with those who weep. We must not forget that we serve a God who weeps, for he never calls us to something we do not first find in him.

As God opens my blind eyes bit by bit, I am staggered at the radical difference between that which is seen and that which is unseen. I am as a creature so utterly tied to this earth. It shapes my thinking, my feeling, my values, my occupations, and my choices. God has called me to have fellowship with what I cannot see. Not only that, what I cannot see is in direct opposition to my own ways. He says die. I want to live. He says humble yourself. I want to be lifted up. He says follow me while not seeing, not fully knowing. I want to know and I want to see. He says enter the fellowship of my suffering. I prefer the fellowship of joy. He says I am to count suffering a joy. Suffering appalls me. I hate it; I fear it. The experience is something like this. All of my life I have been told that humans need oxygen to survive. Since that is true, when you go under water, you are to hold your breath. If you breathe, you will die. God says come into the water with me and breathe so that you can live. My heart quails. My mind screams. He waits.

Fellowship means communion; intimate familiarity. What a strange idea to seek familiarity with suffering. It is however, not just any suffering. I have been asked into familiarity with *his* suffering. I, like Peter, James, and John, have been asked to enter Gethsemane and watch with him. They fell asleep. How easy it is for me to sleep. Not just physically, but emotionally, intellectually and spiritually, in the face of his sufferings. They overwhelm. They frighten me. They staggered the Son of God so it is no surprise that they stagger me. But I desire to watch with him. I desire to learn how to look upon this world as he does. To watch with Christ is to pierce the appearance and get at what truly is.

The Scripture calls us to weep with those who weep. The first one I must weep with is the Son of God. I must listen to and understand *his* weeping if I am to benefit any other weeping souls. He is called the Suffering Servant. He is a Man of Sorrows and intimately acquainted with grief. Men hid their faces from him. They did not want to watch with him. To watch with him is to see the horrors of this world. Pierced, crushed, scourged, afflicted, and oppressed. Can I bear intimate familiarity with such things? Will I prefer resting and sleeping as the disciples did? Will I prefer care for myself—the anesthetic of sleep and withdrawal from the horrors?

You and I live in a time when Christian counseling is a strong force. It has not always been so. Christian counseling has been criticized. We have been told we ought not to exist. We have been told we are not truly Christian. We have been told we are robbers who steal the church's work and secularize it. We have a choice before us. It is a very serious choice.

We can throw criticism back. We can hunker down and disconnect from the body of Christ. We can overreact and end up fighting one error with another. I suspect we can find occasions where all of these choices have been pursued. Or we can go another way. We can choose to watch with Christ and enter into the fellowship of his sufferings and then speak into the world and the church from that place. What does that mean?

1. It means first and foremost that we know our roots must go deep into Christ, who he is and his work in this world, or we will not suck in grace, and all we do will be wood, hay, and stubble. We will tend with steadfastness and discipline to our own walk with Christ, knowing we will not resemble him unless we truly know him.
2. If we know him and our roots go deep into his character, then we will know, even in the face of terrible suffering, that the unseen, the invisible things of God, are not

clearly perceptible in what has actually happened in the seen world except as they are manifested in the cross of Christ where God demonstrates for us his character and his heart.

3. If we know him and our roots go deep into his character, then we know he is holy and we will hate sin wherever we find it—in ourselves, in the church, and in our clients. We will speak with a humble boldness because we will know that the greatest suffering is not from disease, loss, trauma, abuse, or death. Rather, the greatest suffering is to be lost in one's sin, forever at enmity with God. Every other kind of suffering is temporal—for a moment—and will be exchanged for the glory of living with Christ face-to-face.

4. We will open our mouths for the afflicted and for the rights of the unfortunate. We will open our mouths for the oppressed and the needy. Our Lord cared for those who suffered. He spoke on their behalf to the people and systems that were crushing them. We will do so because we know that glibness in the face of suffering is not a reflection of the heart of God. Those who know him understand the terrible burden of suffering, its erosion of humanity, its complexity as it weaves its way through a life, and the awful toll it takes on those who love and care for the sufferer. Though suffering can be for the glory of God, it nevertheless leaves destruction in its path.

In the life of Joni Eareckson Tada, we have seen much of the glory of God. She is still bound to a wheelchair, must have everything done for her, and lives in constant pain. In this world, the glory of God does not eradicate the pain and destruction. In this world, the glory of God is seen *in* the pain and destruction. The cost to the sufferer to display the glory of God is tremendous. It is so easy to hastily point a sufferer to the promise of glory. Our God entered into our suffering; he became like us;

he bore witness to the suffering of humanity. He brought glory as he screamed, as he bled and contorted and died. We often assume that if sufferers are bringing God's glory into it they will not scream or bleed, but sit quietly, hands folded and smile peacefully. Glory is never found in such pretense.

As we enter into suffering—our own or another's—seeking him in the dark places of our lives, the glory comes. It is not from the end of suffering or its effects, but from little by little being transformed into his image as we suffer. We begin to wear his patience, his grace, his love, and his kindness into suffering even while joining in his scream.

5. We will understand that while God has called us to look not at the seen but at the unseen, he has also called us to work in the seen world. The techniques, interventions, and methods we have are to be used to alleviate suffering for his glory. In Matthew 25, we are told that when the Son of Man comes in his glory, and all the angels with him, that he will sit on his throne and separate the people spread out before him. Those he will call his own will be recognized by their acts of giving water to the thirsty, food to the hungry, clothes to the naked, and visits to the prisoner. These are very mundane acts of human compassion given to those who are suffering. The King says those who minister in such ways have ministered *to him*. As we do the ordinary human things we know to do, in some mysterious way we are caring for our Lord in his sufferings. Think about it. I just spoke to a friend who spent time with someone she loves who has been crippled by strokes. She cared for her by sitting with her while she cried and wiping the tears off her face. She does not like to cry alone because she cannot wipe her own tears. I think of my mother buttoning my father's shirts, brushing his teeth, and tying his

shoes. Think of a therapist sitting with someone wracked by grief and simply listening or a counselor gently nudging a survivor to face the truth of her life so she can find freedom. Each is doing ordinary human things for others, but in caring for the body of Christ we care also for its head, our Savior. In that context, entering into the fellowship of his sufferings becomes the greatest privilege ever given—who would not want the opportunity to be present to Christ in his sufferings and tend to him? You and I have been called to serve as his body on earth. We are called to be his character once again made flesh. In that call is also the privilege of caring for him as he continues to suffer in this fearful, fallen world in the lives of his people.

CHAPTER 5

The Fellowship of His Sufferings

Researchers once asked random people how long they thought it took the average person to grieve the loss of a loved one. The general conclusion was two weeks. That answer must surely have been given by those who have never stood at the graveside of a loved parent, spouse, or child. Such a response certainly was given without grasping the immense suffering entered into both individually and corporately due to the earthquakes in China or Haiti, the AIDS crisis in Africa, or the genocides in Bosnia and Rwanda. Such events have turned the world upside down for those who were there and will continue to do so for a long time.

One of the questions such losses raise for me is, how should Christians respond to suffering? Before we can speak about response we must begin by naming truly what has occurred. These events were traumas. And a trauma is unspeakable because it is by its horrific nature so staggering that words are utterly inadequate to communicate what happened, not just externally, but internally as well. The natural human response to that which is unspeakable is to attempt to drive it from the conscious mind. What happened, what was seen is too terrible to speak out loud. The result is an attempt to put the trauma away, to forget, to go on as if it had not happened.

The paradox is that in order to heal from such atrocities one must learn to speak the unspeakable. What seems too terrible to hold for long moments in the mind must be remembered and re-flected upon. That which is unspeakable must be spoken. The in-describable must be described. As you work with people who have lived through trauma, you will find this tension expressed over and over: the need to forget or bury and the need to speak. You will observe this dynamic in individuals and in groups. It is the push-pull between "getting on with our normal lives" and talk-ing, processing, reliving, the events of the trauma. It exists not just for those who endured the trauma but also for those who listen to them. Atrocities are unbearable by definition. Hearing them re-peated over and over is overwhelming as well. Just as the trauma victim struggles to face what is not to be endured, so the listener struggles to stay connected and present.

In spite of this tension, I have come to understand that God's call to his people is to face life as it truly is in this fallen world. Many have experienced the depths of human depravity. We as Christians must not dodge their ghastly revelations. We are called to face life as it truly is in this dark world of ours. Any voice we give to the truths of redemption must take into account the reality of such events as Rwanda or sex trafficking rather than be founded on denying that these events occurred. We who call ourselves Christians blaspheme the name of Christ if we pretend that the evils of genocide, the rape of little children, or the events of a massive earthquake are less than they truly are. Any redemption that fails to take such evil into account is no redemption at all.

As those who minister to people in the churches and commu-nities and on the campuses of this country, you have by virtue of your calling, been invited to enter into atrocity in the name of Jesus Christ. Such an invitation is really nothing other than a call to follow in the footsteps of our Lord, who entered into the terrible atrocity of this fallen world and endured the unspeakable. He who did so for our sakes has called us to do the same for those who are suffering. He came in a body of flesh to walk among us in our darkness, our fear, and our atrocities. He who now stands at the right hand of the Father interceding still has a body here on earth. We are that body of flesh, still called out of love and obedience to the Father, to walk among others in their darkness, their fears and atrocities in a way that explains the Father to others.

Remember that day in 2011 when the World Trade Centers were destroyed in New York? On televisions around the globe the world watched them fall. Consider those rescue workers who came to that scene of destruction as an example of a Christian response to trauma and suffering. They were people who came to a scene of ruin and entered into what they found. Day after day they worked in the place of death, sifting through the rubble to look for people. Their task was backbreaking, grim, and dangerous. They faced the trauma again and again. They never got away from it. Their eyes were opened, and they have seen too much horror to pretend. The work they did will mark them for the rest of their lives. It will haunt their sleep and it has changed the way they think about themselves, their lives, their faith, and their future. Some have died as a result of breathing in the toxic air. What they did stands in sharp contrast to the values of this world. There is no quick success in the ruins, no material gain, no easy gratification—values that we who follow Christ have often pursued.

As the people of God we have been called in many ways to serve as the rescue workers of this world. We are invited into the fellowship of the sufferings of Christ. That means we are called into the place of darkness and death because that is where he went. He opened his public ministry with these beautiful words from Isaiah 61:1–3 (ESV):

> The Spirit of the LORD God is upon me, because the Lord has anointed me to bring good news to the poor; he has sent me to bind up the brokenhearted, to proclaim liberty to the captives and the opening of the prison to those who are bound; . . . to comfort all who mourn; . . . to grant those who mourn in Zion . . . the garment of praise instead of a faint spirit.

Those verses bring us comfort, but we often fail to see that if we are to follow him we must walk into poverty, brokenness, prisons, darkness, mourning, and despair. These are not places we desire to go. These are places of death. In essence, you and I, like the rescue workers, have been called to live and work among the tombs. Think about that for a minute. Suppose I came to you with a career idea and asked how you would like to spend your days in the catacombs of Rome, talking to the people there and helping them. It is an irrational sounding proposition, is it not? But isn't it what the workers at the World Trade Center did day after day? And isn't it what God has called us to? He has called us to live and serve him in this dark place of death, this world, moving among those who are dead in their trespasses and sins, calling them to life and light.

What is it like to live and work among the dead day after day? Ask the rescue workers. Death is a place of darkness; there is no light there. It is a silent place; there are no words. It is a rigid place; there is no movement or growth. There is an awful stench. To enter into the darkness of trauma in the life of another is not unlike this description. Fear, which is the core of trauma, leads people to hide in darkness. Fear silences them because words are inadequate. Trauma brings with it a sense of powerlessness. You have experienced that helplessness, that sense of being overwhelmed by events you couldn't control. When people have been traumatized, they repeat things over and over, trying to grasp what cannot be understood and trying to carry what is unbearable. They carry the smell of trauma with them into their relationships, their work, their thinking, and their choices. They will not be completely better next week or even next year. Those who have endured previous traumas may be utterly crippled by a new one. Those who have lived through one trauma and seem better at some point can be catapulted back into what happened by the experience or even hearing of another trauma. If we want to help others, we need to learn how to sit with, listen to, and care for those who have been traumatized. That call, I believe, is merely a specific manifestation of the call of God to his people who are living in a world that has been traumatized by sin and suffering.

Christ Adjusts Your Value System

Long before the World Trade Centers collapsed, you and I, as the people of God, were called into partnership with his sufferings. It is not the kind of invitation most of us like to receive. He is the Man of Sorrows and familiar with suffering. You and I would rather be familiar with success. He was despised and rejected. We prefer acceptance and applause. He took up our griefs and carried our sorrows. We desire to take up awards and carry accolades. He was crushed for our sins, oppressed, judged, and cut off from the land of the living. And you and I, as the servants of God, are called to complete in our lives what is lacking in regard to Christ's sufferings, for the sake of his body. It is not unlike the rescue workers, who are filling up what is lacking in this terrible suffering for the sake of this world our God "so loves."

How can you and I persevere, living and working among the tombs, in the places of death? And how can we fulfill this call and not be so twisted and impacted by the death all around us that the aroma of the life of Christ is not destroyed? Paul, who speaks of the fellowship of Christ's sufferings in Philippians 3:7–10, tells us:

> Whatever were gains to me I now consider loss, for the sake of Christ. What is more, I consider everything a loss because of the surpassing worth of knowing Christ Jesus my Lord, for whose sake I have lost all things. I consider them garbage, that I may gain Christ and be found in him. . . . I want to know Christ—yes, to know the power of his resurrection and [the fellowship of sharing] in his suffering, becoming like him in his death. . . . (NIV)

Whatever was to my profit I now consider loss. What has been to our profit in the church? Many have profited by such things as fame, success, numbers, reputation, and growth. So often we have absorbed the values of the culture, and we bear the print and pattern of the age we live in. We who follow a scarred Savior have valued wholeness, prettiness, productivity, speed, and efficiency. We value big. He became little. We value recognition. He was despised. We value beauty. He was marred. Paul says that whatever was a success, whatever made him look good, whatever made him special, those things he considered garbage that he might gain Christ. He begins with knowing Christ.

You and I will live and work among the tombs according to our personal relationship with Christ. The degree to which we know and truly follow this scarred Savior will determine the degree to which we will be able to live and work among the tombs in a way that resembles him. The call to share in the fellowship of his sufferings is preceded by the call to worship, the call to truly know him as he is. You and I cannot face things as they actually are in this dark world without getting twisted, unless we do so from the place of worship.

That is so for two reasons. First, unless we see him who is high and lifted up, exalted on the throne and worthy of all honor, power, and glory, the reality of things as they are will efface our faith, throw us into cynicism, and put us into a panic. You cannot face the rubble of the World Trade Centers, the rape of a child, the mass murder of a people, or the destruction of an earthquake without devastation to your own soul—that is without worship of the Lamb who sits on the throne.

Second, unless we begin from the place of worship, we will not have power to descend. Worship always leads to repentance. We cannot walk among the traumatized and the suffering with humility, patience, compassion, and comfort in a way that honors the Man of Sorrows until we have truly seen ourselves before him. Isaiah did not hear the voice of the Lord saying "Whom shall I send?" until his sin was atoned for. Without that we will respond with pride and superiority, impatient that people are not better yet, intolerant of their repetitions and prolonged fear. Worship must come first because though the earth shake and the mountains fall into the sea, God is on his throne and is our eternal refuge. Worship must come first or we will exalt ourselves and think that the drab drudgery of the rubble is not meant for us. If you would walk well among those who are suffering, then begin on your knees worshiping the God who must permeate your being if you are to bring life to dead places.

Paul says first we must know him, or keep tryst with him as we come into contact with things as they are. He points then to knowing the power of his resurrection. Knowing him precedes knowing of the power of his resurrection, for without an ongoing life with Christ, power of any kind will be used for our own purposes and is therefore dangerous. If you think about yourself living and working among the tombs, the power of his resurrection is a necessity. Go back to my image of working with the people in the catacombs of Rome. Go back to the image of the rescue workers. You talk, you cry, you intervene, and what happens? The dead stay dead. You read; you try something creative and new and the dead stay dead. They are buried and wrapped in grave clothes. The traumatized are buried under layers of fear, self-protection, previous traumas, depression, layers of their own sin, and the litter of others' sins against them.

We cannot persevere for long in such circumstances. I cannot envision getting up every morning and driving to the catacombs to talk with the people who reside there. The stench, the darkness, and the deadness will drive us away, or we will cope by convincing ourselves that there really are signs of life in order to keep going. Neither is sufficient, is it? I mean, if you are going to work among the dead, what you really need and want is a resurrection. Paul says that we can know the power of his resurrection.

What does that mean? I believe that one principle of Scripture is that in order for any truth to bear fruit as God intended, it must be worked out in me prior to my delivering it to others. If I am to bring the power of the resurrection to bear in the lives of suffering people, I must first allow the Spirit of God to bring that power to bear in the dark and dead places of my own life. How can I bring liberty to captives if I myself am enslaved to sin? How can I bring freedom from fear, if I myself walk in relationships full of fear? Service to God always begins with worship and a bowing to the work of redemption in my life. If you would bring the power of the resurrection to bear in the lives of the traumatized, you must begin on your knees, repentant and seeking the work of God in your own life. Paul speaks in Ephesians of the greatness of God's power for us who believe as being the same power that raised Christ from the dead. You cannot lead a traumatized individual into the power of his resurrection unless that same power has been exerted over the bondages and fears of your own life.

When you and I think about bringing the power of his resurrection into the lives of others, I expect we tend to think of ways to "make it better." We want to help people get away from suffering. We want to make it as if it did not happen.

However, when we look at the resurrected Christ, what do we see? Scars. Thomas put his hands *in* Jesus's wounds. If you and I were in charge, I suspect the resurrected Christ would be free of all wounds. Scars are not pretty. Scars are something people try to hide. Christ's will endure for all eternity. The victory of Jesus Christ, his kingdom and his glory, come by way of the scars, by weakness, by suffering. Do you hear the hope in that for victims of trauma? Nothing you can do will make it as if that tragedy did not happen. Those who have been traumatized by abuse, violence, war, or earthquakes will *never* be the same. Lives are permanently altered. The message of the scars in the resurrected Christ is not that the resurrection takes the suffering away, but rather that the resurrection catches it up into God's glory.

When we get to eternity, the most beautiful thing there will be the scars of Jesus Christ. Apart from those scars, you and I would never see him except as judge. The terrible suffering of Christ is caught up in his glory. Our God will not merely rearrange the broken pieces of trauma. Our God is holding the suffering from the traumas of this world and catching it up into his glory. You can see some evidence of that in many responses to tragedy. He has taken self-sufficiency and transformed it into mutuality. He has taken evil and transformed it into compassion. He has turned devastation into tenderness. God catches up ugliness, death, and sorrow, and uses it for his glory. Have you not seen such evidence in your own lives? No evil, no suffering is outside the pale of his ability to catch it up in his glory. As you live and move among the tombs, the devastation, the tragedies, do so knowing him who has called himself the resurrection and the life, bringing to the places of death and despair the hope of scars made beautiful. Your work in this world is resurrection work.

Consider the work of Christ among the tombs where Lazarus was buried. When Jesus finally comes after a wait of three days, Mary and Martha both say to him that if he had been there, Lazarus would not have died. Jesus gives a phenomenal response. He does not say, "Yes, I could have done something," or "even now I will do something." He says, "I Am something. I am the resurrection and the life. I am the thing itself." As we follow Jesus to the tomb, we find what we usually find around tombs. The words used tell us Jesus is deeply agitated, indignant, and angry at the presence of sickness and death. He is so troubled he shakes under the force of it. And he weeps. Truly he knows our griefs and has carried our sorrows.

Jesus then does an interesting thing. He engages human beings in the resurrection process. Now, someone who can raise another from the dead is surely not troubled by a little stone being in the way. It was not necessary that people remove the stone, but he catches them up in his resurrection work. He calls Lazarus out and engages humans again. "Unbind him." Lazarus has to make his way blindly out of the cave toward a voice that calls him. He cannot see, is bound with clothes that restrict him, and he stinks.

Jesus calls people to assist. He does not need their help. He raises himself without assistance. He could just as easily have Lazarus come out free of grave clothes. Stones and sheets are not a big deal if you can raise the dead.

God has called you and me to participate in his resurrection work. We do ordinary things like move stones and remove grave clothes. He has called us to go with seemingly ordinary methods into the place of death and darkness. The result is transformation to the glory of God because the Resurrection and the Life goes with us and in us. Participation in God's work requires that we know how to do what he has called us to do well. If you try to handle the trauma of others in ignorance of its impact and without knowing how to respond, you will damage those who are already severely hurt. For us, doing that work well will mean understanding trauma and its effects on human lives. It will mean learning to respond to frightened humans who have been overwhelmed by atrocity. It will mean persevering because the nature of trauma is that its effects far outlasts the event that caused it. Hopefully this book will give you some of those tools. You need to do your part well. It matters.

Christ Is the Power

At the same time you need to recognize that those tools, however necessary, are not the power. This will lead you to do your work with humility. No matter how good you are at rolling stones, handling stench, and removing grave clothes, you cannot raise the dead. *He* is the resurrection and the life. The power is of him, and I am not to confuse my work with his. It is easy for us to get caught up in our ways, our models, and our interventions. Can't you just hear the talk in Bethany that night? "Did you see? *I* rolled the stone." My friends, rolling stones and removing grave clothes is one of the greatest privileges I know, for it means being called to work in partnership with my Savior. But such work must be stamped with the fruit of humility because it is *he* that is the thing itself. He is the resurrection and the life. The work is done by him because he is in us. It is done for him that he should be glorified. It is God condescending again and again, as he did in Bethlehem, to bring down into flesh and blood, the power of his resurrection.

Paul says knowing him is first and foremost. Knowing him is to be the value that eclipses all else. To know him is to be infused with his life, that through us he might bring life to dead places, catching up the terrible evil and trauma and suffering of this world into his glory.

Paul also lets us know that such a life brings us into partnership with his sufferings. Note that the verse calls it a fellowship with *his* sufferings. It is a truth I think we often miss. This truth is expressed in Matthew, chapter 25. Jesus says that one of the ways those who know him will be recognized is because they gave *him* food when he was hungry, water when he was thirsty, clothes when naked, etc. The righteous are surprised at such a description. "When did we see you in such conditions?" And Jesus says, "Whatever you did for the least, the smallest, the most unnoticed, you did for me, the Highest." Isaiah says he bore our griefs; he carried our sorrows. Do you understand that when you sit with someone who is suffering, grieving, sorrowing, that you are sitting face-to-face with a grief that Christ has borne? There is no tragedy—or sin for that matter—that you will encounter in another's life that your Lord has not borne. When you care for the suffering, you are caring for him. When you care for the survivor of sexual abuse, of domestic violence, of war, of a natural disaster, you are caring for him. He has said it is so.

Amy Carmichael expressed this idea eloquently.

At last the day came when the burden grew too heavy for me; and then it was as though the trees . . . were olive, and under one of those trees our Lord Jesus knelt, and he knelt alone.

And I knew that this was his burden, not mine. It was he who was asking me to share it with him, not I who was asking him to share it with me. After that there was only one thing to do: who that saw him kneeling there could turn away and forget? Who could have done anything but go into the garden and kneel down beside him under the olive trees?[1]

An invitation into the fellowship of his sufferings is an invitation to Gethsemane. If you will do this work of bending down to bear the burdens of others, you will find that many aspects of your world will be disrupted. Tragedy and suffering turn schedules upside down. Those who suffer are often repetitive as they try to assimilate tragedy. They are slow, for suffering minds move slowly. Nights are worse than days for darkness renews fear. Suffering is messy and sometimes loud as tears and groans and wailing become avenues of expression when words fail. Suffering also means listening to questions that cannot be answered—tortured, tormented questions—for voicing what is indescribable is part of healing. Such things as these do not fit into schedules driven by what is successful, efficient, reasonable, and proper. In essence, you will be entering relationships centered on suffering. What a concept! Fellowship means communion; intimate familiarity. What a strange idea to seek familiarity with suffering. We typically center relationships on productivity, success, gain, mutual interest, celebration, or love.

Those of us who are called to follow the Man of Sorrows into the fellowship of his sufferings willingly enter such relationships in order to reveal the Author of all things, not as one who stands aside as complacent, but as One crucified. And here, in this place, the place of the cross, is the joy of this strange brand of fellowship. An invitation into the fellowship of his sufferings is also an invitation to Calvary.

The Crucified is the One most traumatized. He has borne the World Trade Center. He has carried the Iraq war, the destruction in Syria, the Rwandan massacres, the AIDS crisis, the poverty of our inner cities, and the abused and trafficked children. He was wounded for the sins of those who perpetrated such horrors. He has carried the griefs and sorrows of the multitudes who have suffered the natural disasters of this world—the earthquakes, cyclones, and tsunamis. And he has borne our selfishness, our complacency, our love of success, and our pride. He has been in the darkness. He has known the loss of all things. He has been abandoned by his Father. He has been to hell. There is no part of any tragedy that he has not known and carried. He has done this so that none of us need face tragedy alone because he has been there before us and will go with us. And what he has done for us in Gethsemane and at Calvary he asks us to do as well. We are called to enter into relationships centered on suffering so that we might reveal in flesh and blood the nature of the Crucified One.

As you and I enter into the suffering of the Son of God in the lives of others, one of the things that will result is that we will see him resurrect the dead places within us. We go to help and find we are helped. I know this is so, for he has resurrected such places in me, places of death I did not even know I carried within me. And he continues to do so. God will use the suffering of others to drive you to himself for more of him. If you will enter into the suffering of people, you will be entering darkness. Such darkness would overwhelm and lead to despair were there not a treasure there. The treasure in the darkness is the Crucified Christ. He who can sympathize is there. He who knows anguish is there. He who has felt tormented, abandoned, unheard, and crushed waits there in the darkness. To enter into the fellowship of his sufferings is to find him.

My prayer for you is that you will know him deeply and well, infused with the power of his resurrection, and will willingly enter into the fellowship of his sufferings. When the darkness, the suffering, and the trauma overwhelm you, as they will, get down on your knees and cry out for more of him so that you may persevere until that day when the kingdoms of this world are become the kingdom of our Lord and Christ—that day when the resurrection will mean the redemption of all tragedies, of all things; that day when all suffering will be caught up into the glory of God.

CHAPTER 6

The Spiritual Impact of Abuse

Those in the counseling field are talking more and more about what is called "making meaning." It is a spiritual concept that has to do with what gives meaning and purpose to a person's life. Trauma has the capacity to shape meaning. For example, a boy who grows up in an urban setting in poverty, with a largely absent father who is an alcoholic and physically abusive when present, whose mother keeps getting evicted due to drug use so they are periodically homeless, and who has been raped by some men in the neighborhood has meaning and purpose shaped by trauma: Life is chaotic and disordered; no one can be trusted; get what you can when you can and watch your back unceasingly.

On the other hand, trauma can shatter meaning. A young girl grows up in an intact home, nurtured and cared for with many opportunities and goes off to the college of her choice. One evening on the way back from the library she is violently, brutally raped. The meaning and purpose she has for her life is now shattered. Nothing makes sense, trust is destroyed, and the meaning held to by the urban youth now makes more sense to her than her own.

When a situation is destructive to familiar, comfortable beliefs, a person's distress level is high. When someone's pre-trauma beliefs and meaning are resilient and have the capacity to include trauma, suffering, and injustice, the ability to weather the trauma without destruction of meaning and purpose is much higher.

Rigid, pessimistic, or incoherent meanings, particularly those that assume protection from all suffering, seem to prolong trauma symptoms and leave one vulnerable to chronic PTSD. Therefore, I think it is critical that we grasp some of what sexual abuse does to the meaning and purpose of a child and the adult they become, as well as what is involved in helping them find true meaning and purpose not based on pretending the trauma never happened or that it did not really hurt.

Sexual abuse has a spiritual impact. Let's consider more specifically what the spiritual impact of trauma might be and what responses are helpful. There are three things to keep in mind as we move into this area. The first is that much of a survivor's thinking is "frozen" in time. A woman who was chronically abused by her father for fifteen years thinks about herself, her life, and her relationships through the grid of the abuse. She may have encountered situations where people proved trustworthy, but she does not trust. She may have heard thousands of words about how God loves her, but she believes she is trash, somehow an exception to the rule. Trauma stops growth because it shuts everything down. It brings death. The input from many other experiences, relationally and spiritually, often does not seem to impact the thinking that originated within the context of the abuse.

Second, the abuse occurred to a child, not an adult. Children think concretely, not abstractly. Children learn about abstract concepts like trust, truth, and love from the concrete experiences they have with significant others in their lives. They learn what love is by how Mommy and Daddy treat them. They learn about trust by the trustworthiness (or lack) of Mommy and Daddy. In essence, they learn about intangible things, ideas, and values through the tangible. If those who teach them are repeatedly untrustworthy, cruel, hurtful, and lying, then to grasp the meaning and living out of concepts like trustworthy, safe, loving, and truthful seems like an exercise in the ridiculous. Children can be impacted in these ways not just by sexual abuse but by domestic violence, by physical abuse, by ongoing verbal and emotional abuse, by neglect, and by addictions and rage in the home.

Third, not only do children think concretely and therefore learn about the abstract by way of the concrete, I believe that as adults, we continue to be taught about the unseen through the seen. We are of the earth, earthy. God teaches us eternal truths through things in the natural world. We grasp a bit of eternity by looking at the sea. We get a glimmer of infinity by staring into space. We learn about the shortness of time by the quick disappearance of a vapor. Jesus taught us eternal truths the same way. He said He was the bread, the light, the living water, and the vine. We look at the seen and learn about the unseen. Consider the sacraments—water, bread, and wine. We are taught about the holiest of all through the diet of a peasant. This method is used all the way through understanding the character of God himself. God in the flesh, God with skin on. God explains himself to us through the temporal.

If we consider the combined impact of these factors, we see that many survivors exhibit this quality of thinking frozen in time in that they learned repeatedly through the concrete how to think about the abstract, and they learned repeatedly through the seen what to believe about the unseen. One area that this profoundly impacts is the spiritual. God is viewed through the lens of abuse. Who he is and what he thinks about the survivor is understood based on who daddy was, or mommy, or grandfather, or youth pastor, or whoever. They have learned about love, trust, hope, faith, through the experience of sexual abuse. They have also learned about the unseen through the visible. The ins and outs of ordinary life have taught them many lessons about who God is. That is why a therapist or pastor may have the experience of speaking the truths of Scripture to a survivor, truths desperately needed, and yet finding that they seem to have no impact. They don't go in. Many times I find that survivors can speak eloquently to me of the truths of Scripture, but on an experiential level their lives are lived out in the context of what the abuse taught them. Intellectually, truth is rooted in the Word of God. Experientially, or personally applied, the truth is rooted in the lessons of abuse.

Sometimes, of course, we find an exception. God is certainly still capable of the miraculous. They are few and far between however. There are also those who *seem* to experientially know the truths of Scripture and apply them to themselves, but on inspection are able to do so because they have yet to face the truth of the abuse they endured.

There was an article in the *Philadelphia Inquirer* about a young man from Bosnia whose life was touched profoundly by the war there. He wrote an essay about a friend who found his dead mother, and said the following: "Her body was white because the grenade that struck her apartment turned the wall into a fine white powder. . . . He kissed his mother before they covered her, and then he went into a small nearby room. *He needed to get away from her so he could think she was still alive.* He needed to believe in that because he needed time. Although he used that time in self-deceit, he needed that time to get carried down to the reality slowly."[1] Oftentimes I find that survivors can hold on to their belief in God because they are doing what this young man did—they are living in self-deceit. "It was not really abuse." "It wasn't that bad." "He didn't mean it." In other words, "I can believe God is really alive, or truly loves me, because I have in essence 'gone to a nearby room' away from the abuse."

For many survivors of sexual abuse, two irreconcilable realities exist: the reality of a God who says he is both loving and a refuge for the weak, and the reality of the ongoing sexual violation of a child. Each seems to cancel out the other, yet both exist. Again, the human mind can manage either alternative—the sexual abuse of a child and no God, or God and protection from sexual abuse. What is one to do with the rape of a child *and* the reality of God? Most survivors will come down on one side or the other. They have faced the rape and God is not to be trusted. Or they hang on tightly to God and the rape is a blip on the screen. The dilemma is not easily solved.

I want to make sure that we grasp the profound impact of ongoing abuse to a child's understanding of God. Let us consider some specific examples.

Sarah is five. Her parents drop her off at Sunday school every week. She has learned to sing, "Jesus loves me, this I know, for the Bible tells me so. Little ones to him belong. They are weak, but he is strong." Sarah's daddy rapes her several times a week. Sometimes she gets a break because he rapes her eight-year-old sister instead. The song says that Jesus loves her. It says that he is strong. So she asks Jesus to stop her daddy from hurting her and her sister. Nothing happens. Maybe Jesus isn't so strong after all. Or at least not as strong as Daddy. Nothing, not even Jesus, can stop Daddy. The people who wrote the Bible must not have known about her daddy.

Mary is seven. She lives in a house where she is taught about God. God seems to have a lot of rules. God says children have to do whatever their parents tell them to do. Mary tries very hard to do what her mommy and daddy say. When she doesn't obey, then Daddy hurts her and says this is how God told daddies to teach their little girls. Mommy sends her to Daddy when she is angry with Mary, and Daddy hurts her then too. She guesses that if you don't do what God says then he will hurt you too. She will try very hard to be good.

Stan is a young boy whose father abandoned them. Many nights his mother requires him to get in bed with her. She tells him that God gave him to her to take care of her since his dad left. She says God knew she couldn't live without him. Stan feels angry with God and wonders why he demands such confusing and repulsive behavior. He is full of shame because he also finds pleasure in it. God seems an enigma at best, or at worst, cruel.

A child is told to get down on her knees nightly by her bed and pray with her father. As he tucks her in he molests her, saying,

"Why are you such a whore that you make me do this after we have prayed?"

Michael went away to overnight camp at age seven. He was scared and homesick. His counselor paid him special attention. It made him feel important. But then it got strange and scary. The counselor would teach the Bible study at night and then take Michael for a walk and make him do things he didn't like.

What does incest teach about fathers? That they are untrustworthy. That they have a great deal of power. They are unpredictable. They inflict pain on those they are supposed to care for. They betray, they abandon, deceive, use, and rip you apart. They speak love and reassuring words and then suddenly abuse. Trust is out of the question.

What does abuse teach about God? That he is cruel, impotent, or uncaring. He does not hear, or if he hears, he does not answer. He thinks children are expendable. He does not keep his word. He is not who he says he is. That since he says he is powerful—distance is wise. Trust is out of the question.

What does the survivor learn about herself? That she is unworthy, trash. She is not loved and probably never will be and her prayers are useless. That she brings evil to people or makes them do evil things. No effort on her part brings change.

What does the survivor learn about things like trust and faith? Those are things you never do unless you are an idiot. Love? Love is a word you use when you want to make someone do something they do not want to do. Hope? Hope is a setup. Nothing ever changes anyway.

Emotions Accompanying Traumatic Memory

The trauma of sexual abuse brings out all sorts of emotion with which the Christian community is largely uncomfortable and is often condemning. It is important to see and understand this as we move on to consider how to respond to the spiritual impact of abuse. Abuse results in fear (God has not given us the spirit of fear), anxiety (be anxious for nothing), anger (let not the sun go down on your anger), and grief (let not your heart be troubled). We have precious verses that speak to such emotional states, but I fear we often hurl them like projectiles at the victim in an attempt to make feelings we are uncomfortable with or have been taught are wrong, go away as quickly as possible. If you are going to enter into the suffering of those who have been traumatized you have to learn how to sit with and listen to fear, anger, and great grief with compassion and understanding. You will also have to learn how to do it for far longer than you prefer.

Many who are traumatized will be afraid to face and feel the feelings related to the trauma. They fear losing control of themselves and enduring pain and suffering. These fears are understandable, for the feelings surrounding the trauma are powerful and such emotions can quickly recreate the trauma in which the survivor felt overwhelmed and helpless. It feels safer to let oneself down into the emotions of trauma in small bites and in the presence of someone who will listen, normalize, and not condemn. Dealing with and healing from such feelings will never occur in a straight line. Feelings will alternate with numbness and exhaustion. Those breaks are necessary and must not be rushed.

One of the things you can do for the trauma survivor who is wrestling with these overwhelming emotions is encourage them to do restorative things with safe people in their lives. Going for a walk and making a note of the beauty that is seen, listening to music, doing aerobic exercise (especially helpful when anger or agitation is a struggle) can help quiet the mind and rest the body. Doing them with someone who feels stable and safe is also restorative, giving the message that strong feelings have not isolated them as they did during the abuse.

Anger can be toward others, especially the perpetrators and silent bystanders or anyone seen as responsible for their loss. Anger can also be expressed in guilt and self-blame. The child mind is egocentric and so often the victim rages against herself for being abused. The older sibling who believed she should be able to protect her younger sister from sexual abuse and failed will struggle with guilt. Seeing the self as damaged goods and carrying great shame can bring on self-loathing.

Grief can take several forms. Grief can manifest because a childhood is lost, a way of life is gone, a hoped for home, a safe parent, health, or a hoped-for future have disappeared. People may have lost the faith they had in life or human nature. Another aspect to grief is the sense of powerlessness that pervades. Not only were survivors helpless to stop the trauma, they are helpless to restore what—and who—is gone. You cannot resurrect the dead. No mater how successful or wealthy someone becomes they cannot restore a lost limb or a lost person or an innocent childhood. Our sense of power in this world may be largely delusional, but nonetheless we grieve when we lose it.

One characteristic of dealing with survivors of trauma is the repetitious nature of that work. Survivors will say the same things over and over—"How could my father do that to me . . ." They will be repetitious in dealing with their emotions—"I am so angry that . . ." And they will repeat their losses again and again—"I cannot believe so-and-so is dead . . ." Expect it, and learn to sit with it. The magnitude of the trauma is so great that repetition is necessary. The mind cannot imagine what happened. It cannot hold such a thought. Bearing the intensity of emotions is impossible and so the feelings must be tried on again and again. These are attempts to bear what cannot be borne. They are struggles to integrate into life what does not fit because there are no categories. Be patient, and then be patient some more.

Developing the Heart of God

The essence of working with trauma survivors is about bearing witness to their story and suffering, entering in and demonstrating in the flesh the heart of our God toward them and the evil they experienced. If we have not personally come to know and understand the heart of our God in response to evil and suffering we will either avoid entering into the experience of evil in our client's lives or we will glibly apply the words of Scripture without an accurate representation of the God of Scripture. This work has exposed to me the egocentricity of my own heart. I find I am not so much touched by evil, sin, and suffering in this world and the hearts of human beings unless it infringes on my world, my comfort, and my relationships. The evil, sin, and suffering that do not touch my world I work hard to keep at a distance. It is disturbing, messy, and inconvenient.

Through the years God has used the work I do as a corrective measure, as I have worked with many kinds of people—people I would otherwise have had no contact with. I have been inside things like abuse, suicide, terror, torment, psychosis, trauma, obsessions, and wordless grief. Such things were not mine; they belonged to other people. They were brought to me, however, and I was invited in. Going into such things has disturbed my thinking, my feelings, and my sleep. I have had to change my mind about things I was sure were true and ask questions I thought had been finally answered.

I have also learned, to my dismay, that I consider suffering in my life to be far more odious than sin. In fact, I have on occasion, sinned in order to keep from suffering. Is that not what we are doing when we tell "only a little lie" in order to protect ourselves from criticism, correction, or disapproval? We forget that the heinousness of sin lies not so much in the nature of the sin committed, as in the greatness of the Person sinned against. Do we not fall into the habit of comparing one sin to another as a way of deciding how serious it is? We hear this with clients all the time. "Well, at least I just looked at pornography on the Internet and did not have an affair." When Bill Clinton, as the then-President of the United States, said in his now infamous line: "I did not have sex with that woman," part of what was implied was that whatever he did it was not so bad because he did not do something else that would have been worse. In 2 Corinthians 10:12 we are told, "Comparing themselves with themselves, they are unwise." Is not such comparison merely a form of self-deception that is, in itself, a narcotic for our souls?

According to the Word of God, sin is the greatest evil. If I am to maintain God's point of view, then my sin must be viewed from his position of untainted holiness, not from the perspective of another sinner whom I deem to be worse than myself. How often we say things like, "I cannot imagine doing *that*!" or "At least I did not do *that*!" John Donne wonders why his soul is not as sensible to sin as is his body to pain. "Why is there not always a pulse in my soul to beat at the approach of a mere temptation to sin?" Think about your physical response in preparation for something painful, even a simple needle in the arm. You become vigilant, you steel yourself, and you prepare your mind to endure. Oh, that we would do similarly at the approach of any sin. Remember we said that sin is the excrement of the human soul. Yet, I find I often protect what should in fact repulse me.

Slowly, God is increasing my sensitivity to and awareness of sin. Ernest Becker, who did not know Christ but often told the truth said the following: "I think that taking life seriously means that whatever you do must be done in the lived truth of the evil and terror of life, of the rumble of panic underneath everything, otherwise it's phony."[2] Such a growing awareness is frankly, rather uncomfortable. If the truth is told, many of the things God does in my life are uncomfortable. I am becoming more aware of the massive generation of sin by my own heart.

Unfortunately, I tend to also be more aware of the sins of others. That is problematic on two counts. One, it means I am then inclined to sin in my attitudes toward them with judgment, criticism, or arrogance. Two, it means I cannot, if I am to truly love, ignore such things. Discernment of wrong in the life of another is always a call to intercession and sometimes to involvement. It is truthfully easier not to see; it is easier to anesthetize myself with the narcotic of self-deception. However, the dealings of God the Father with his Son on the cross demonstrate for us the evil of sin. To ignore it or dilute it anywhere, including in our own lives, is to refuse his point of view. To accept his point of view is to often feel weighed down by the burden that comes. Charles Haddon Spurgeon said the following (and I think it is applicable to those of us in the counseling field): "Our work, when earnestly undertaken, lays us open to attacks in the direction of depression. Who can bear the weight of souls without sinking into the dust? To see the godly grown cold, pastors abusing their privileges, are not these sights enough to crush us to the earth?"[3] When the eyes of the heart face the truth of things as they actually are and face sin, our own and others', from God's point of view, we will cry, "God, be merciful to me, a sinner" and with David, "How long, O Lord, how long?"

Thirdly I have been reminded again how much sin is the antithesis of humility. I am aware that there has been a lot of twisted teaching in Christian circles about pride and humility. Humility has been seen as something equivalent to self-hatred and in fact, ends up being an obsessive focus on the self, which is certainly not what true humility looks like. We have seen many lives destroyed by the church's wrong teaching on humility. We have also had years of a focus on self-esteem, a term that has often been poorly defined and misused. I have been struck by Roy Baumeister's statement: "The most potent recipe for violence is a favorable view of oneself that is disputed or undermined by someone else—in short, threatened egotism."[4] He is saying that people are inclined to do violence or evil when another contradicts their inflated view of themselves.

In Isaiah 14 we read about Lucifer, star of the morning, the shining one. He has fallen, and that fall occurred when he said, "I will ascend above the heights of the clouds; I will make myself like the Most High" (Isaiah 14:14). I think it would be safe to say that

God threatened Lucifer's favorable view of himself, and surely we could say violence was the result! He then appears in the garden and says to the humans there, "Indeed, has God said, 'You shall not eat from any tree in the garden'?" When Eve corrects him and says no, only one particular tree he says the following, "You shall not surely die! For God knows that in the day you eat from it your eyes will be opened, and *you will be like God*, knowing good and evil" (Genesis 3:4–5, italics added). There is the phrase again, "like God." It is a subtle twist of the truth. We were created *in the image of* God. The goal Satan offered was close to the real goal. It had to be or it would not have been capable of deceiving. Dorothy Sayers describes it in her usual magnificent way:

> One of the most important things we have to do is to distinguish the Devil as (in the sight of God) he is, and the thing which may be called the diabolic set-up. The underlying actuality is miserable, hideous, and squalid; the set-up is the façade that the Devil shows to the world—and a very noble façade it often is, and the nobler, the more dangerous. The Devil is a spiritual lunatic, but like many lunatics, he is extremely plausible and cunning. His brain is, so to speak, in perfectly good working order except for that soft and corrupted spot in the center, where dwells the eternal illusion. His method of working is to present us with the magnificent set-up, hoping we will not use either our brains or our spiritual faculties to penetrate the illusion. He is playing for sympathy; therefore he is much better served by exploiting our virtues than by appealing to our lower passions; consequently, it is when the Devil looks most noble and reasonable that he is most dangerous.[5]

The problem came when Adam and Eve left their position as creatures dependent on the wisdom of the Father. They thought they were ascending and assumed a rather inflated view, which God threatened, and violence resulted. Whenever we wiggle out of our position as creature, dependent on our Father, and elevate ourselves, violence, sin, and evil will result. We still, like our for-bearers, want to know good and evil. We still do not like our position as creatures, dependent, finite, and frail. We are often insulted that God will not explain things to us. We are impatient with him because he has not told us enough.

He has said, "In the world you have tribulation" (John 16:33). He has said, "The whole world lies in the power of the evil one" (1 John 5:19). He has said, "For I, the LORD, do not change" (Malachi 3:6). And he has told us the goal—that we should be conformed to the image of Christ, be creatures that look like him. He has made the result plain, but he has kept the working out of that result mysterious.

How hard it is, in this time and place, with sin and suffering rampant in us and around us, to bow the knee and acknowledge ourselves as creatures and Jesus Christ as Lord. I believe we can trust him and bow in humility because I have seen something of the heart of God. The cross of Christ is the manifestation of the heart of God in time and space. The cross of Christ is where our two seemingly irreconcilable realities, sin and God, come together. The cross of Christ is where God and sin crash together—and the crash is on the heart of God himself.

He bore the slaveries of this world, the child prostitution, the inquisitions, the racial injustice, the Holocaust, Rwanda, Bosnia, Uganda, the Khmer Rouge, the Black Plague, AIDs, Ground Zero, the suffering in our bodies and sickness in our souls. My friends, he knows our griefs and carried our sorrows. He was wounded for our transgressions and by his stripes we are healed. He was wounded and crushed for our sins. It was God's good plan to crush him and fill him with grief. Yet when his life is made an offering for sin, he will have a multitude of children, many heirs. When he sees all that is accomplished by his anguish, he will be satisfied. Because of what he has experienced, he will make it possible for man to be counted righteous. He will be given the honors of one who is mighty and great because he exposed himself to death. He was counted among those who are sinners. He bore the sins of many and interceded for sinners (Isaiah 53).

As you wrestle with evil, sin, and suffering, let *this* be a sign unto you—you shall find the Redeemer robbed of his clothes and hanging on the cross. He compels us to notice him and to note what he allows his enemies to do to him.[6] Let us sit there and see. The cross speaks. Have we sat and listened?

He was made the subject of shame as absolutely as was the custom in that day. Grace abandoned him. In other words, he descended into hell. The Creator is destroyed. Life becomes dead. Glory turns to shame. Beauty is obliterated. Living water thirsts. All Power becomes powerless. The great Clothier of everything is stripped naked. All-Honor is despised. Holiness becomes excrement. Love is forsaken. Heaven enters hell. These truths mean many wonderful, eternal things. They also mean that our God understands trauma.

A young Japanese man, who teaches conducting at a university and came to Christ through listening to Bach's cantatas, recently taught us something beautiful based on Bach's Cantata for the 19th Sunday after Trinity. One of the arias reads like this: "I will the cross-staff gladly carry; it comes from God's loving hand. It leads me after my torments to God, into the promised land." The German word *Kreuzstab* means cross-staff. He said Bach is portraying the cross as both an instrument of crucifixion and the staff we lean on.

Certainly we think of it as the instrument of death. There our Savior died and sin died with him. That means sin can die in us so the life of God can be borne in us. We see the suffering and grief Christ bore for us. We see the sicknesses, all the sicknesses of this world, borne in that one body. He did that so that all of those things might die forever. But is it not also the staff on which we lean? Where else can we go when our own sin horrifies us and yet we cannot stop? Where else can we go when sickness, sorrow, and grief overwhelm us? Does not the cross sustain us in such times?

As I bow before God and allow him to produce his viewpoint in me, several things will result.

First, I will know without question that evil is not just "out there"; it is also "in here." I will never see the world as divided between "them" and "us." There is no "them" because we are all "them." God's point of view will lead me to hate sin wherever I find it, including in myself. When I understand that it is the excrement of human souls, I will respond as he did. I will go to any lengths to see it killed, both in me and in this world. I will rather endure suffering than sin against a holy God.

Second, those who are suffering will know that I will give time and compassion because I am called to identify with the sufferings of Christ. To evade them is to evade him. What I do to the least, I have done to him. I will understand that I will never encounter any human suffering that Christ has not borne. He has carried every kind of suffering you find. When I sit with those who suffer, I sit with him. I will understand that God would assuage the anguish of this world through his people. Wherever creation groans, the method of healing its deep wounds and assuaging its convulsive grief is by planting the children of God in its midst. Wherever men and women of God live *there* is some measure of healing the world's wounds and soothing its sorrow. The weeping of girls and women, boys and men in the dark and cruel places of this earth is heard and healed by the living presence of the Word of God in the lives of those *who incarnate what they say they believe.* We "comfort those who are in any affliction with the comfort with which we ourselves are comforted by God" (2 Corinthians 1:4).

Third, I will walk this world with humility. Humility will come because I know that with the sinfulness of my own soul I can never point a finger, raise my head in arrogance, or react with impatience to a struggling sinner. Humility will come because I know I am a finite and frail creature that is utterly dependent on my Creator for life and godliness. Humility will come because I follow in the footsteps of the Servant of servants.

Finally, I will be wise to discern truth from error. Wisdom will come because I know the cross of Christ must be central in all my thinking. Wisdom will come because I make a practice of forcing my mind to think through what it so readily and comfortably accepts. Wisdom will come because I know keenly my use of the narcotic of self-deception.

The Response

You and I become the representative of God to the survivor. Our work is to teach in the seen that which is true in the unseen. Our words, tone of voice, actions, body movements, responses to rage, fear, failure all become ways that the survivor learns about God. I believe the reputation of God himself is at stake in our lives. We are called to represent him well.

While we try to represent God, the survivor struggles with questions about God: Who is he? What does he think about my abuse, my rape, the loss of all things? What does he think about me? Am I loved? Am I forgivable? Does his patience run out? Why should I have hope?

In this case, words are initially meaningless. What are words when you grew up hearing "Daddy loves you," and then Daddy raped you? Or when Grandfather called you over to sit on his lap, and when you were afraid he said not to worry because this time it would be okay, but it never was. When the therapist says, "This is a safe place," the survivor responds "Right." "Oh, sure." Or she may have become so desperate that words are believed no matter what actions might suggest, making it easy for her to be abused again.

Our task is no less than living out before them the character of God himself. Early in my work with survivors I longed for a woman who had been chronically abused to truly know the love of God. I tried telling her about it but realized that she was only politely listening. I clearly remember getting down on my knees before God and begging him to help her see what she so desperately needed to see—that he loved her. What I heard back from God was "You want her to know how much I love her? Then you go love her in a way that demonstrates that. You want her to know that I am trustworthy and safe? Then you go be trustworthy and safe." Demonstrate in the flesh the character of God over time so that who you are reveals God to the survivor.

That, of course, is the incarnation, isn't it? Jesus, in the flesh, explaining God to us. Jesus, bringing the unseen down into flesh and blood actualities. The survivor needs us to incarnate God for two reasons. One, we all need that. Secondly, this need is intensified for the trauma victim because what has been repeatedly taught to a child in the seen is the antithesis of the truth of God. She has learned about fathers, power, trust, love, and refuge from one who emulated the father of lies.

If you want the survivor to understand that God is a refuge, then be one for her. If you want her to grasp the faithfulness of God, then be faithful to her. If you want her to understand the truthfulness of God, then never lie to her. If you want her to understand the infinite patience of God, then be patient with her. And where you are not a refuge, or are tired of being faithful, or are fudging in your answers or growing impatient with the necessary repetition, then get down on your knees and ask God to give you more of himself so that you might represent him well.

The second aspect of the response is to speak truth. When people have experienced interpersonal evil, especially as children, they carry deeply embedded lies within. Such lies need to be exposed, gently and slowly, so the light of the truth can take their place. There are usually particular aspects of certain memories that burned those lies into the brain and help keep them there. For example, a woman who was sadistically abused during childhood told of being forced to kill a loved pet or risk further pain. She was told repeatedly that she was evil and no one would ever love her. Her vivid memory of killing her pet and the blood on her hands provided tangible proof of her evil and burned that lie into her brain. It took a long, long time of carefully picking our way through that memory and all its pieces for her to even begin to grasp the subtlety and hideousness of the lies it had taught her.

This can happen in any kind of trauma. It is prevalent in combat vets—particularly when they experience moral injury, e.g., they participate in or bear witness to things that violate conscience; things they would never do under any other circumstance. It can also occur when they could not save a buddy—even when the expectation is completely unrealistic. It is powerful in a victim of domestic violence who frequently is told she is the cause of the violence with such statements supported by twisting Scripture.

In my experience the deep struggles of the soul cannot truly be considered until the trauma victim has experienced a relationship that bears the fragrance of Christ in hard places. We need the Word made flesh first. We also need some of the darkness illuminated so we understand the lies that have been wrapped around our souls from the evil done to us. Then the questions about God and who he is come and the ground is plowed for a much deeper understanding of the work of Christ on the cross. He knows the depth of the evil done; he has borne the great sorrows; he has been wounded so that we might be healed.

I send my clients on a search to uncover that the cross of Christ is God with us—in our sin, our suffering, our grief, and our sorrow. When trauma victims are struggling with spiritual questions, I often direct them to a particular passage or raise a specific question. Rather than simply teaching them I send them to study and learn. The work has far more power when they wrestle with it themselves. This is *not* something I do early on in therapy—it falls more toward the end of the second phase and into the third (see chapter 14 for a discussion of treatment phases). One of the reasons I wait is that many times people who have experienced child sexual abuse or relentless or overwhelming trauma come into counseling with some very confused spiritual ideas that will govern any work we try to do. Another of the major reasons for this is that I find they will grasp the profound truths of the cross far more readily and deeply if they have seen some representation of those truths in their relationship with me. They have been able to speak the unspeakable. They are known. They are loved. No matter what they tell, they remain safe. I can forgive. I have hope for them. Out of that experience in flesh and blood, they can then turn to the person and work of Christ and his identification with them. I have without exception found it a powerful way of teaching truth and of bringing healing.

A female survivor expressed her growth in a poem, which serves as a succinct summary of a long and grueling process. You can see how she begins with understanding Christ's identification with her suffering, and then moves to using her suffering to identify with his suffering. Finally she begins to identify with his victory and his glory.

The Victim
Abused
 abandoned
  battered
   broken
Emotions ridiculed
  body penetrated
   soul invaded
Stripped
  taunted
   cursed
    beaten
The Victim
  lay prostrate–
   on a cross.

Robed
  in light-years
   of grace and glory

Love
    incarnate
        now exalted
Blessed
    and lauded
        praised
            and honored
The Victor
    sits
        beside His Father.

            Cherished
                chosen
                    redeemed
                        radiant
            Gowned
                in perfect
                    bridal splendor
            Cleansed
                and glowing
                    guilt-free
                            blameless
The bride
    will stand
            beside her Bridegroom
    (Hebrews 4:15)

I want to close by giving you three elements that are necessary if we are to do this work and do it well. First, know about people. Know about trauma. Understand what trauma does to human beings. And yet, in knowing, never assume you know. No matter how many survivors you see, each is unique. If we do not understand such things, we will make wrong judgments. We will prematurely expect change. We will give wrong answers. We will fail to hear because we think we know. Listen acutely. Study avidly.

Second, know God. Know his Word. Be an avid student of that Word. We need to be so permeated by his Word that we learn to think his thoughts. George MacDonald said, "If you say, 'The opinions I hold and by which I represent Christianity, are those of the Bible,' I reply, 'that none can understand, still less represent, the opinions of another, but such as are of the same mind with Him.'"[7] May we never forget that to know his Word, according to him, means it is woven into our lives and we are obedient to it. Where we do not live according to his Word, we do not know God.

Finally, do not do this work without utter dependence on the Spirit of God. Where else will you find wisdom? How will you know when to speak and when to be silent? How will you discern the lies? How will you love when you are tired or be patient when you are weary? How can you know the mind of God apart from the Spirit of God? How can we possibly expect to live as a person who demonstrates the character of God apart from the Spirit of God? How can we think that the life-giving power of the work of Christ crucified will be released into other lives unless we have allowed that cross to do its work in our own lives? You cannot bring life to the place of death unless you walk dependent on the Spirit of God.

Trauma work is difficult. The task of serving as a representative of God in the seen so that the unseen can be grasped, understood, and believed in some measure, is far beyond our capability. It is a work, however, that can take you to your knees with a heart hungry for more of God so that you might in turn make his presence known.

MINISTRY IN THE CONTEXT OF CHRISTIAN COMMUNITY

CHAPTER 7

Ministry to the Suffering

Twenty centuries ago baby girls were considered a liability. Demographics in the first century in certain parts of the world were stunningly imbalanced male to female. Female infanticide was not uncommon. Infant girls, often considered the equivalent of deformed, were killed by exposure. In essence, it was permitted by law to leave them outside the city on the dung heap to die. That is about as clear a judgment of "worthless" on a human life as can be made.

There was, however, a growing group of people who seemed to think the judgment was an error. Rather than accept the culture's assessment regarding the value of females they went outside the city to the dung heaps to find and rescue the abandoned baby girls. The decision was both risky and sacrificial. It required standing against the mainstream and making a judgment that ran counter to the culture of that time. It meant the giving of life, time, and goods to someone else. It meant extending the circle of one's responsibility. It meant being devalued and disdained for stooping so low as to treat that which was deemed worthless as precious. It meant entering into a crisis and sacrificially serving the suffering.

Who were these people? They were the church, the body of Jesus Christ. They followed the Lamb who went outside the city gates to make the ultimate sacrifice and give his life a ransom for many who were deemed worthless. By his death, he judged them precious. His first-century body followed him outside the gates to the garbage heaps of those days to rescue baby girls. The call that was answered by our first-century brethren is the same call that now sits before us in the twenty-first-century church. It is the call of our God, as his body in this world, to follow our Head in his tender care for the suffering in our midst.

I began my counseling practice with Vietnam veterans and moved to working with survivors of rape, childhood sexual abuse, and domestic violence. I have also worked with pastors and Christian leaders for many years and as result have sat with missionaries captured, raped, tortured at gunpoint, etc. I have sat with workers and chaplains from Ground Zero, nationals in Burma who live under a hideously repressive military regime, and undercover investigators who rescue girls from brothels. I have travelled often to Rwanda and listened to survivors of a hideous genocide.

* * *

Suffering is prevalent in our world. Let's put some facts to that. Statistics are about real people. Some of you are part of the numbers I will give. When I give you the figures, I would encourage you to process them not just as numbers but by thinking about those with whom you work or are walking alongside.

Statistically, 31 percent of the women in this country will experience at least one episode of violence from a husband or a partner.[1] That translates to one in three in your women's ministry. More than three women are murdered daily by their husbands or boyfriends.[2] Pregnant women are more likely to be victims of homicide than to die of any other cause.[3] The statistics for rape are not that different. At least 20 percent or 25 percent of adult women, one in four or five, and 12 percent of adolescent girls have experienced sexual assault or rape during their lifetimes. According to the American Medical Association about seven hundred thousand women are sexually assaulted each year.[4] That is more than one woman per minute. Close to one hundred thousand males are raped every year in the US (CDC).[5] Two-thirds of rape victims had a prior relationship with the offender. Seventy percent of reported assaults occur to those seventeen years or younger.[6]

Childhood sexual abuse occurs in the lives of one in four women before the age of eighteen.[7] Child sexual abuse has been reported up to eighty thousand times a year, but it is believed that the number of unreported instances is far greater.[8] One in five teenagers reported being solicited for sex on the Internet.[9]

One in five males or 20 percent report being victims of child sexual abuse before age eighteen.[10] *The Philadelphia Inquirer* had an article regarding the abuse of boys in November 1998.[11] Sex abuse against boys was referred to as America's hidden epidemic. Boys who are sexually abused are far more likely to become drug addicts, suffer from mental illnesses, and become sexual preda-tors. Child sexual abuse can be a one-time occurrence or span many years. The average age at which it begins is six for girls and ten for boys. Sadly, the number of physically abused children is sta-tistically similar. One study suggested that 27 percent of women and 29 percent of men suffered physical abuse as children; others suggest one in three.

United States statistics suggest that there are approximately four hundred thousand runaways every year.[12] One out of three of those teens on the streets are lured into prostitution within forty-eight hours of leaving home.[13] About 150,000 teens then are lured into prostitution per year. Most of these are middle-class runaways from troubled homes who begin selling their bodies at about age twelve. They usually come from homes where there has been significant abuse.[14] Currently, as many as 2.8 million children live on the streets in this country.[15]

In the United States youth homicide rates are ten times higher than that of other leading industrial nations.[16] In 2004 an average of fifteen youth between the ages of fifteen and twenty-four were murdered daily. Persons less than twenty-five years of age account for 50 percent of those arrested for murder and 62 percent of those arrested for robbery. For children between sixth and tenth grade the statistics suggest that one in six are victims of bullying.[17]

There are six million car accidents annually in the US.[18] One hundred fifteen people die in car accidents every day, which is about one person every thirteen minutes. Probably everyone reading this has been touched by cancer in some way—in yourself, a family member, or a friend. There are seventy thousand people suffering from PTSD as a result of the destruction of the World Trade Center and thousands more struggling from the ongoing trauma of hurricanes Katrina and Sandy. We are hearing more and more of the large number of Iraq and Afghanistan veterans returning home with PTSD and the escalation of suicides and sexual assault in the military. When you consider the global picture, the numbers are staggering.

We are not okay on this groaning planet, and I believe wholeheartedly that the body of Jesus Christ is called to step into the mess and bring light and life. He has not called us to live cloistered lives away from the mess. And frankly, given the stats we cannot if one in four women and one in five men in our pews have been sexually abused, one in three experience domestic violence, one in five have been raped, our children are being bullied, our streets are not safe, and our families are losing loved ones to war, suicide, and disease. All of these things exist among the people of God just as they exist in the world at large.

I assume that you are reading this book because you care about and desire to minister to people who are suffering or in crisis. A crisis is literally "a separating." It is something in life that is so significant that it becomes a marker. You think of life before and life after a crisis. A rape, the first time someone hits you, the pronouncement of cancer, the loss of a child, the death of a spouse, financial ruin, and infidelity are all separating moments. It is a turning point; a crucial time in a person's life. It is also a frightening time. The road map with which you are familiar no longer points the way. What was known is gone, what felt safe now feels unsafe, and what seemed predictable is uncertain. A crisis is essentially an alarm moment in a life.

Oswald Chambers talks about having "staying power in the alarm moments of others' lives."[19] Think about when you accidentally set off an alarm and you hear a sample of what people in crisis are experiencing. There is a lot of emotional noise in their lives; there is chaos. They cannot think what to do. They are afraid. They feel like they are in danger; something is wrong. They want someone to help. They want the noise to stop. They want the fear to subside. They want to feel safe. They want to be able to think.

If people seek you out during their alarm moments, they will bring you their noise. They will walk into your life and bring anger, violence, sobbing, ranting, terror, panic, fear, and anxiety. You may even become the recipient of their anger, accusations, or fear. How hard it is to stay at such times. They will bring you their silence. Pain brings silence, for often suffering is so great that there are no words. The psalmist says, "I am shut up and I cannot go out" (Psalm 88:8). They will bring tears, sometimes wrenching sobs. We tend to respond by simply handing out tissues, often a subtle hint that the crying should be over by now. We prefer human beings with clean faces. We feel awkward with sobs that are loud. We are uneasy in the face of unadulterated terror or pain. When an alarm goes off, we want it stopped. The noise bothers us; it disrupts our world. When an alarm goes off, fleeing is a normal response. Alarms mean things are not okay. How can we have staying power in alarm moments like these?

Anytime a person in crisis walks into your world you are facing an alarm moment. It is a separating time for that person. It is actually a separating time for you as well. The fact is that anytime someone brings us their crisis they create one for us as well. The question is whether or not we will allow their crisis to turn us away from our own routine, our own comfort, and our own preferences to become a staying force in their life. Will we enter in and if so, how should we become a help and support, rather than a contributor to the noise and chaos?

It is crucial that we understand something of what we encounter if we are to minister to a person who is suffering. I fear we often think that helping people in crisis is simply about telling them good and true things so they will listen and get better. I am afraid it is rarely as simple as that.

One thing you will encounter as you move in to help is ambiguity. Interactions between humans on a good day are often fuzzy and confusing. Interactions while a life alarm is going off are frequently unclear. You think you understand an issue and then it shows up in someone's life and what you know does not seem to fit. Or someone brings you a problem and then you realize it is not the real problem at all. People want to feel better. They want answers. You can find yourself quickly feeling like you have no idea what to do or seeing what you thought was the right response end up producing a more complicated mess.

Those in crisis want change—or do they? They do, but we forget that change makes humans nervous. Change requires massive effort, and they are exhausted. Change is not something that usually occurs simply because someone told you the right answer. Not only that, when a person does decide to do the work of changing, he/she potentially frightens and angers others in their world. They push back and that creates more crises. That feels like going in the wrong direction!

Change is not just in the wings for the person who is suffering; it is there for you as well. Somebody in crisis walks into your life with an untold story. This person and their story *will* impact you. You cannot let yourself into another's life without being impacted. You cannot be present to abuse, violence, trafficking, deceit, addiction, brokenness, terminal illness, and darkness without being affected. You will find yourself thrown by the things humans do to one another. You will struggle with disbelief. You will want to say it could not be true.

Repetition is necessary for someone in crisis. You say something, and then you say it again. You live it out in the flesh and they still question its truth. You cannot confront the debilitating effects of chronic childhood abuse, domestic violence, oppression, or addiction without having to be repetitive. You speak truth, and watch it devoured by a sea of lies. Over and over you rework the ground of trust, only to have someone say, "But can I trust you here too?" And so you must restate, rework, relive, what you thought was so clear. Not, of course, unlike how we are with our God.

You will have to learn how to wait. You will wait for a thought to bubble to the surface of a confused mind. You will wait for truth to penetrate a dark mind. You will wait while an addict fails *again* and old ground has to be reworked. You will wait while the Spirit of God works internally in a life with no outward sign of growth. You will wait because God's timetable is not yours and he is teaching you about waiting as much as he is teaching the person for whom you are caring. He is teaching you how to think and love *while* the alarm is going off.

You must never forget that you are dealing with a combination of suffering and sin when you work with people in crisis. Suffering silences people and scars lives. Silence and scars are not proof of sin in a life. You have only to look at the life of Christ to know that. You do not push someone to tell you how the alarm got set off while it is still screaming in their ears. They cannot think clearly. Sometimes people suffer because of another's sin, not their own. David suffered because of Saul's. His suffering was undeserved. Remember that when you sit across from suffering. Do not add to the burden of the suffering one by going on a sin hunt. Sometimes we suffer because we live in a fallen world and no one's sin is involved. For example, a person may live with chronic illness and be faced with never-ending grief and loss, and pain and body chemicals that result in unremitting depression, yet none of his suffering is a result of anyone's sin.

You will, of course, also encounter deep and habituated sin, not necessarily in the person you are caring for but perhaps in others in their life. It is critical that we not be naïve about the impact of such sin on others' lives. A woman who grew up with chronic sexual abuse has been shaped and trained by evil. A person who has lived with control, rage, battering, or constant verbal abuse has been profoundly impacted in their thinking, their emotions, their spiritual life, and their relationships. A person who has had a drug, sexual, or alcohol addiction has practiced self-deception for years, and truth will only penetrate slowly and in small doses. People who have been beaten down by shame, rage or humiliation cannot suddenly stand up straight. People who have lived with habituated sin—their own or another's—are altered, or shaped, by that sin. Their spiritual hearing and seeing has been crippled.

We are careful about our children's diets because we know the food they consume can affect everything, both now and in the future. We are careful about what they read or see for the same reasons. We become good at those things we habituate and we know that what is habituated has profound consequences. If you practice silence and a blank mind in order to deal with battering over a period of twenty years, then you will not be able to think or articulate clearly just because someone has stepped in to help. If you practice deception for years to cover a pornography addiction, truth, clarity, and faithfulness will not suddenly appear, even if a confession is made and change is desired.

So if simply speaking the truth is not sufficient alone, how can we respond to those who are suffering so that they are helped and ultimately transformed? We can learn from our Lord. He stepped into the alarm moments of our lives. He entered the chaos and noise. He encountered the suffering and the sin of this world and had staying power. He has called us to be like him. Let us consider what that was like for him so that we might follow him into the lives he brings before us.

I. He Left Glory

The first thing one must do to enter into the alarm moments of others' lives is leave glory. Jesus left his world, its beauty, its comfort, its safety, and its "undisturbedness" (John 6:38). He left what was rightfully his and entered what was foreign to him. He left perfect love for hatred, order for chaos, beauty for ugliness, and light for darkness. He left behind functioning as the "self" he is in heaven so that he might function as a self like us. He put on the cloak of humanity.

You must leave glory if you are to help those in crisis. You too must leave that which is familiar, ordered, predictable, and comfortable for you in order to help those in crisis. You must enter into foreign territory where you do not know the way. You must go and encounter things that have never been in your life. You leave your safety and enter a life wrecked by an assault. You leave your health and sit at the bedside of someone with cancer. You leave your order and walk alongside an addict. You will be forever changed by the sufferings and sin of others.

2. He Became Little

Second, in leaving glory, Jesus became little. He is the Creator and Sustainer of the universe. He is eternal, immortal, and infinite. He became unlike himself. He reduced himself in size, power, impact, words, and potential to help (Philippians 2:6–7). He became little for our sakes. He became like us so we could receive him. His becoming like us is a kind of listening unlike any the world has ever seen. He allowed himself to be "taught" by us about what it is like to be human.

When you enter a life in crisis, you must become little. You will not help if you swoop in, tell people what to do, and take over. You need to leave glory and enter in, in small doses so you can truly listen and understand and be touched by their infirmities. If you have never been chronically sexually abused, you do not know what that kind of life is like. If you have been, you only know your experience, not theirs. Enter in, listen, live with, observe, and learn. Be little; it is about them, not you. You will need to be little for victims of rape and abuse, or for those in chronic pain whose minds cannot easily grasp truth. You will put yourself or your thoughts into the mix by eyedropper amounts, just the way the Lord of the Universe has done with you. If he poured everything in his mind into yours, then yours would blow up. You could not hold it, organize it, understand it, or use it.

3. He Entered Darkness

Third, in leaving glory he entered darkness. Jesus dwelt in the unfamiliar. He who is the beginning and the end could not see tomorrow. He who is the light of the world was eclipsed. He who is the Word became silent. He who is perfection was scarred. His life was touched by many things that were foreign to him, things that were an assault on him.

Typically, when we enter into another's suffering we try to drag them into our world. We want them to think what we think, choose what we would choose, understand what we see, and live more like we do. We want them to leave their depression, sorrow, or grief behind and "get over it." Those are not necessarily bad goals, but you can only get people there by entering into their darkness. You must go in and get them *so that* you can bring them out. You cannot call or talk people out of suffering or trauma or addiction or great grief. You must go in to them and sit with them and listen and understand, and then little by little you can begin to walk with them toward a new and different place. You cannot help if you do not enter the darkness.

4. He Did Not Get Lost in the Darkness

Fourth, Jesus was not lost in the darkness (John 1:5). He brought the character of the Father with him when he became little and entered our darkness. He brought truth and love manifest in the flesh when he came and sat with us. He came into the darkness and sat down bearing the character of the Father, full of grace and truth. He lived out that character while he walked with us and ate with us and talked with us. Who he was explained the Father to us. Light began to dawn for us because it was lived out in front of us.

Often we think we need techniques, programs, plans, or the right words—and those can be helpful things. However, people do not just need knowledge *about* the character of God but the actual demonstration of it in the flesh, *in you*. They will know his truth, his love, his mercy, and his grace as we sit with them and live with them. They will know of his infinite grace and patience as those qualities are evidenced in you. People who have been abused have been saturated with evil, lies, manipulation, humiliation, and rage. Oh how they need to sit with the loving and truthful character of the Father in you! They do not just need to hear about it. They need to experience it in you, in the flesh. People who are depressed do not need statements about hope; they need you to hope for them when they cannot lift their head.

5. He Did Not Abandon Us

Fifth, our Lord did not abandon us. He left glory, entered our darkness, and did not run, even when facing the cross. He felt like running. He was overwhelmed by what he faced, but he did not abandon humanity (Luke 22:42, 44). He did not leave us alone in our mess, our alarm moments. He does not leave us now. Had he abandoned us, we would have never found our way out. We could not see, we could not think, we could not walk upright. He stays and waits and calls us to come to him.

You will want to abandon. There will be one phone call too many, one mistake too many, one bad choice too many. You will get weary and it will feel heavy. You will want a life free of crises and alarms. But the love of the Father does not abandon his own. I see many times how we in the body of Christ start off well with a crisis but do not have staying power. We find it difficult to maintain connection with crises, especially chronic ones, so we abandon those who have no choice about suffering in their lives. They cannot abandon the suffering and so must endure it alone. Our Head who entered in also does not abandon.

6. He Did Not Catch Our Disease

Sixth, our Lord left glory and entered the darkness, but he did not catch the disease from which we suffer. It is easy when working with alarm moments to get caught up in the crisis and lose perspective. He did not. He did not sin, even when he suffered with our sufferings (Hebrews 4:15). He did not allow the chaos, darkness, evil, and noise to destroy him. He entered into the darkness, but stayed light. He entered into the sickness, but did not get sick. We work with chaos and failure and get impatient or angry; we work with slowness and react with frustration; we sit with deafness and think if we speak louder it will be heard. The suffering can shape us in twisted ways until we look nothing like our Lord in that place. How can we work with those who are suffering and not catch the soul diseases around us?

How do *we* become those with staying power in the alarm moments of others' lives? How do *we* keep from catching the diseases with which we are working? How do *we* maintain life in ourselves so we do not become twisted up, crippled by an ongoing exposure to suffering, sin, and evil?

Staying power means having the ability to endure. To endure is to hold out against; sustain without impairment; to bear with patience. If we are to truly help those in crisis, then clearly we need a place to stand. We will abandon them or end up impaired without that place. We will become cynical, bitter, or despairing.

Handley C. Moule, Bishop of Durham said, "If you would deal aright with suffering people, earnest Christian of the church, live at the Center. Dwell deep. From the person back evermore to Jesus Christ, that from Jesus Christ you may the better go back to the person, bringing the peace and power of the Lord Himself upon you" (adapted quote).[20] In other words, it is only as we come to him and drink deeply that we can endure in carrying living water to dry and thirsty places.

I would have you remember three things if you are to minister to suffering people in the body of Christ. First, you are doing *God's* work *with* him. Do not make the mistake of thinking of this as *your* work. It is his work, the people are his people, and you are not your own. You are not the Redeemer, merely his servant. If you remember that it is his work, you will continually run to him about what piece of that work he has for you to do. If it is his work, the results are in his hands and you will not need to demand certain outcomes by a certain time, thereby pressuring hurting people to get better so that you feel successful.

It is not only his work to do *with* him, but it is his work done *for* him. You are not working for the ones suffering. You are not working for anyone else looking for their approval or certain status in the church or your community. You are *his* worker. If you work as if it is for the suffering, then you will be governed by them. Their needs will be your ruler and you will end up in their noise and chaos. They are considered and they must be understood, but the work is done *in* their life but *for* your God. *He* says this, not that; these limits, not those; this response, not that one. The needs of others are not the call nor are they your governance. If their suffering rules you, then the outcome is simply double of the problem. The call is from God, the governance is God's alone, and from *that* place in him you enter into the suffering of another.

Third, you can only do this work *by* God and *through* him. You cannot do the work of God in suffering lives, nor will you please God with your work, unless he himself works redemptively in and through you. The work of the Redeemer in this world is a difficult work. He was a Man of Sorrows and acquainted with grief. I prefer to be familiar with comfort. He was despised and rejected. I prefer to be honored and accepted. He took up our sickness, frailties, and disabilities. I prefer health, strength, and wholeness. He was pierced and crushed and oppressed. I prefer no injuries, no smashing, and no injustice. I do not like alarm moment work, and I cannot do it. God has taught me through the lives of many suffering people that I cannot do his work. Yet he has called me to that work. The resolution of that dilemma has only come as I have allowed God to alter me for his work. If I would bend down to bear the burdens of my brothers and sisters, then I must first be made a fit burden-bearer like Jesus. His *first* call on our life is to allow him into our own dungeons in order to sit with us and bring us out into his light and love.

Bending down to bear the burdens of suffering people will expose you to yourself. You can tell yourself you are very patient but unless that patience is tested, you will not know the truth of your belief. As I said early on, crises are separating. You will have a time of "this is what I thought I was" and "this is who I turned out to be." God is always working both sides. He has not just called you to care for the person who is suffering. He is also creating a crisis in you so that he might show you areas of yourself where you are in desperate need of his work. It is only as we bow to the work of his Spirit, exposing and calling us to repentance, that we will truly be able to go out to the circumferences and carry his grace to those in need.

If you will do this work of bending down to bear the burdens of others, you will find that many aspects of your world will be disrupted. Tragedy and suffering turn schedules upside down. Those who have been traumatized are frightened even of their helpers. Freeing people from evil involves great risk, for the Enemy of our souls lets no one loose from his grasp without a fight. Entering into the suffering also means struggling with questions that cannot be answered—tortured, tormented questions. Such things as these do not fit into schedules driven by what is successful, efficient, reasonable, and proper. You are entering relationships centered on suffering. And here, in the place of the cross is the joy of this strange brand of fellowship. An invitation into the fellowship of his sufferings is also an invitation to Calvary. Will we accept?

The Crucified is the One most traumatized, most grieved. He bore the holocausts and genocides. He has carried the massacres, the starving, the crushing poverty, and debilitating illnesses. He has carried every child who has been trafficked, tortured, abused, and thrown away. He was wounded for the sins of those who have perpetrated such horrors. And he has borne our selfishness, our complacency, our love of success, our self-righteousness, and our pride. He has also borne our grief and our pain over the sights and sounds of evil that we ourselves have endured. He has been in the darkness. He has known the loss of all things. He has been abandoned by his Father. He has been to hell. There is no part of any tragedy that he has not known and carried. You will never enter an urban war zone, you will never face a perpetrator, you will never hear a victim's story, you will never sit by a deathbed, and you will never look in a child's frightened face that you are not encountering something your Lord has carried. He has done this so that none of us need face tragedy alone, for he has been there before us and will go with us and will work through us. For what he has done for us in Gethsemane and at Calvary he asks us to do as well.

You cannot partner with the Crucified One without the message of the cross being applied to your own heart and life. His finger will gently press on your pride, your superiority, your complacency, your impatience, your own addictions or mistreatment of others, your love of order, your desire for success, your love of reputation, and your faith in your own works. Suffering will either lead you to quit or harden your heart or it will drive you to God begging for more of him. Isaiah says, "I will give you the treasures of darkness and hidden wealth of secret places, so that you may know that it is I, the LORD, the God of Israel, who calls you by your name" (45:3).

As you go out into this world of suffering and death, take with you the words of the Crucified One, who calls himself the resurrection and the life. Hate what he hates, not just in this world but in yourselves as well. Hate terrorism, violence, abuse, trafficking, disease, trauma, and sin. Not just theirs but yours too. Enter into relationships centered on suffering and find there the beauty of your crucified Savior who awaits you as the treasure in the darkness. Count everything else garbage—everything—and resolve to know nothing except Jesus Christ, and him crucified. And on that day when his kingdom comes and he makes all things new, you and I will gather together with the angels, the elders, and the living creatures to sing: "Worthy is the Lamb that was slain to receive power and riches and wisdom and might and honor and glory and blessing! To Him who sits on the throne, and to the Lamb, be blessing and honor and glory and dominion forever and ever! Amen" (Revelation 5:12–13).

CHAPTER 8

Shame and Trauma

Another aspect of trauma and suffering is shame. The study of shame has broken my heart. To delve deeply into how shame came to be, what it does to humanity, and how we inflict it is to swim in the waters of ruined creatures—ruined though still God-imaging creatures. It can also push you deep into the heart of our God, his ownership of shame (ours) and his great glory bestowed on us through his death on one of mankind's most humiliating instruments of torture.

There is much to cover, and even then we will have only begun. We'll look at a few stories illustrating the experience of shame, and then we will consider the difference between shame and guilt, the impact of shame, and our responses to shame. We will look at cultural expressions and experiences of shame, proper versus destructive shame, and the theological pinnings that need to undergird our thinking and our responses. First, go with me and look into some lives where shame has wrapped itself around the identities and souls of human beings.

* * *

Pakistan: Once the specter of shame begins to loom, some families see killing as the only choice. It is, of course, the ultimate way of hiding, something we all want to do when we feel ashamed. The family of Amal, a seventeen-year-old Jordanian, discovered that she was pregnant. She told the family she had been raped by a friend of her father's while he was staying in the family home. Her sister-in-law sold her gold jewelry to pay for an abortion. But the doctor refused to perform the procedure, which is illegal in Jordan. Instead, Amal said, her father used the money to buy a gun.[1]

The next day, he sent her mother and younger siblings from the house, closed the windows and curtains, and turned the music loud. As Amal lay on a mattress in her room, her father and her twenty-two-year-old brother took turns with the revolver, shooting her eight times and leaving her for dead. Amal did not die.

"When a man's daughter does a wrong [keep in mind we are referring to the rape of a seventeen-year-old], he cannot sit amongst men," a member of Parliament and a prominent tribal leader told a visitor to his home, atop Amman's highest hill. "He will be ostracized. They will not even give him coffee. Who would like to kill his wife or daughter? But if he does not, in a village or among a tribe, they will look down on him."

* * *

Ghetto of a US city: We did not always live on Mango Street. It is on the other side of town. Mama and Papa had told us that one day we would move into a real house that would always be ours. It would have running water and pipes that worked. But the house on Mango was not as they promised at all. One day a nun from my school saw me playing out front. The bottom of the building was boarded up. "Where do you live?" she asked. "There," I said, pointing to the second floor. "You live *there* she asked?"

There. I had to look. The paint was peeling, and there were the wooden bars papa had put in so we would not fall out. You live *there*? The way she said it made me feel like nothing. *There.* I lived *there*.[2]

* * *

Deep South in the US: The first time I heard, "They're different from us and don't value human life the way we do" I was in grade school. "Don't play with her. I don't want you talking to them." Me and my family we had always been "they" . . . I pressed my bony white trash fists to my mouth. The rage was a good feeling, stronger and purer than the shame that followed it, the fear and the sudden urge to run and hide, to deny, to pretend I did not know who I was and what the world would do to me . . . I grew up poor, hated, the victim of physical, emotional, and sexual violence, and I know that such suffering and shame do not ennoble. They destroy.[3]

* * *

Native American Education, Second Grade: Betty Towle, missionary teacher, redheaded and so ugly that no one ever had a crush on her, made me stay in for recess fourteen days straight. "Tell me you're sorry," she said. "Sorry for what?" I asked. "Everything."

Once she gave the class a spelling test but set me aside and gave me a test designed for junior high students. When I spelled all the words right, she crumpled up the paper and made me eat it. "You'll learn respect," she said. She sent a letter home with me that told my parents to either cut my braids or keep me home from school. "Indians, Indians, Indians," she always said.

In third grade I stood alone in the corner, faced the wall, and waited for the punishment and shame to end. I am still waiting.

Wally Jim killed himself by driving his car into a pine tree. No traces of alcohol in his blood, good job, wife, and two kids. "Why'd he do it?" asked the trooper. All the Indians shrugged their shoulders and looked at the ground. "Don't know," we all said, but when we look in the mirror, we see the history of our tribe in our eyes, taste failure in the tap water, and shake with old tears. We understand completely.[4]

* * *

Israel under King David: Tamar, virgin daughter of King David, was summoned to her half-brother's room. He was obsessed with her. He pretended to be ill and through deception called his sister to his room to fix food for him. He grabbed her and forced her to lay with him. She cried out, "Do not violate me, for such a thing is not done in Israel" (2 Samuel 13:12). She cried, knowing her helplessness. "Where could I carry my shame?" (13:13, ESV). She left, tearing her robes with ashes on her head and her hands on her head as well, signifying shame.

※ ※ ※

Stories of shame, individual human stories, all of them true. When we speak of shame, what exactly are we referring to? And how is it different from guilt? In the Western world we are more aware of guilt and speak about it more readily. I do not think that is because we have less shame, or even that it is less important to us, but because we deal with it by hiding it from ourselves—we want to be independent, self-sufficient, and competent. When we speak of guilt, we generally refer to something to do with moral action (thought, word, or deed). In Western culture it is about whether or not I, as an individual, have done the right or wrong thing. I have chosen an action; I am responsible for that action; it can be measured objectively; and it is either right or wrong. If it is wrong, I am guilty. The opposite of guilt is moral purity or innocence, and the search for innocence is immediate when guilt is exposed, even if we have to lie to find it.

Shame, on the other hand, seems to be subjective and affective. It is who I am, not about an action taken. Dr. Silvan Tomkins, psychologist and developer of Affect Theory defined shame this way:

> If distress is the affect of suffering, shame is the affect of indignity and alienation. Though terror speaks to life and death and distress makes the world a vale of tears, yet shame

strikes deepest into the heart of man . . . While terror and distress hurt, they are wounds inflicted from the outside which penetrate the smooth surface of the ego; but shame is felt as an inner torment, a sickness of the soul. It does not matter whether the humiliated one has been shamed by derisive laughter or whether he mocks himself. In either event he feels himself naked, defeated, alienated and lacking in dignity or worth.[5]

Lawrence Langer, in *Holocaust Testimonies: The Ruins of Memory,* says "humiliated memory recalls an utter distress that shatters all molds designed to contain a unified and irreproachable image of the self. Its voice represents pure misery, even decades after the events that it narrates. Neither time nor amnesia soothes its gnawing."[6] Carl Jung called shame "the swampland of the soul" and "a soul-eating emotion."

The opposite of shame is not moral purity but rather glory or honor. Both shame and guilt are about falling short of some standard, but guilt is about violating the rule and shame has more to do with being the kind of person (bad, weak, dishonorable) who failed to be strong enough to keep it or to prove invincible to the humiliation it brought.

Impact of Shame

What is the impact of shame on a person or a soul? I do not think we can answer such a question without going back to the beginning— a familiar story for us all. Adam and Eve were living in perfect harmony with God, themselves, each other, and God's world— all open and transparent; all of one piece; no hidden corners; no breaks in integrity. Humans disrobed, exposed, fully known, and full of glory. In that place they were given moral choice, to eat or not to eat. There was a moral dimension to life in the garden. In that context a crafty, beguiling shining one appeared and seductively lured them to use that moral choice to pursue what appeared real and good and desirable but was in fact false and evil and soul-damaging.

"*Then* the eyes of both of them were opened, and they knew they were naked; and they sewed fig leaves together and made themselves loin coverings" (Genesis 3:7). The immediate consequence was fear and shame and hiding. They saw themselves stripped and deprived of all honor. They saw themselves degraded, disgraced, and desolate. They were, in their wrongdoing, guilty and exposed before God and one another. They made coverings as a solution to save their esteem. It is a way of saying, "I am defective but honor me still." They ran from the presence of God and hid from each other as well.

There is both guilt and shame in this story of course. Guilt because Adam and Eve made an objective moral choice to defy God. They were no longer morally pure. Innocence was gone. They were guilty before God, and as a result they were afraid and they ran and hid from him. Shame because they were exposed in their wrongdoing, their defectiveness, their new "less than." They were dishonored, disgraced, and so they covered. They did not run just because of their wrongdoing; they also ran and hid because they did not want to be seen in their shameful state. As noted in C. S. Lewis's *Prince Caspian*, Lord Adam and Lady Eve possess honor and glory enough to lift the head of any beggar and shame enough to bow the shoulder of any emperor on earth.[7] They hid because they who had been glorious were now ruined creatures. When we feel defective, we shun exposure.

God's response is astounding. He comes and asks, *Where are you?* He is in essence saying, *I want to see you.* The response is *I was afraid because I could be seen, so I hid. I do not want you to see me.* When we feel shamed, we cannot tolerate being seen. We hide behind, we cover, we work to prevent exposure. We do not want the eyes of others upon us, and we work to hide from our own eyes as well. The man from Amman said, "They will not even give you coffee" (i.e., they want you to be invisible, to disappear, or to make the shame disappear). In my work with victims of sexual abuse I have often encountered those who have not looked at themselves in a mirror for many years due to the burden of shame they carry.

Adam and Eve used two things: wearing fig leaves and hiding among the trees. People who are full of shame use any number of things. The purpose of the covering is to hide the shamed self so that honor can be given anyway, from the self or from others. I am guilty, dishonored, defective, inadequate, and humiliated, and I will hide those things so I can still find honor. Honor and being seen have become mutually exclusive. How do people hide? They hide in pride and arrogance—intellectual, economic, performance, status, or power. They hide in substances such as drugs and alcohol and in rage, thereby shaming others. The ultimate hiddenness is suicide or death of the shamed one.

Shame is not just a feeling, though it is profoundly that. Shame is a sense of the self—the "I am"—as defective, empty, worthless, and trashed. It causes the self to curl in on itself, hidden and unreachable so as not to be seen. Shame also threatens the relational bond, heightening the need to hide the shamed self. Shame damaged the relational bond between Adam and Eve—instead of continuing to bare themselves to each other, they covered themselves with fig leaves—as well as between them and God when they ran and hid. So hiding is preferred to the feared relational break, but of course hiding is no solution at all, as the break has already occurred internally, and hiding merely reinforces both the shame and the resulting breakdown of connection.

Response to Shame

What kinds of responses do humans have to their sense of shame? Dr. Donald Nathanson, clinical professor of psychiatry at Jefferson Medical College, wrote *Shame and Pride* in 1992, in which he discusses the Cognitive Phase of Shame. When something shameful occurs, memory tends to search for previous similar experiences. There may arise immediate associations to old events such as the following:

1. Matters of personal size, strength, ability, or skill (I am weak, incompetent, stupid)
2. Dependence/independence (sense of helplessness)
3. Competition (I am a loser)
4. Sense of self (I am unique only to the extent I am defective)
5. Personal attractiveness (I am ugly, deformed)
6. Sexuality (there is something wrong with me sexually)

It is not hard to see how many kinds of trauma might instill such thoughts that can wrap around the self tightly like a mantle until it becomes who the self is. In the context of trauma I was weak, stupid, and helpless, then set apart as defective as a result. The effect and cognitions of shame then bundle over time and produce what Silvan Tomkins called Scripts, which are deeply habituated. Scripts include the beliefs and feelings we form about ourselves in the places of shame. Over time they become deeply entrenched and life-shaping. We in essence accumulate a library of feelings and beliefs as well as defenses (such as drugs) against them, and we end up controlled by those scripts.

Dr. Nathanson also talks about the Compass of Shame.[8] He takes Silvan Tomkins's work, quoted above, and attempts to translate it into more accessible language. He says that those of us with more resources and affirming history process shame differently than those who have no inner resources. Those who have led relatively safe lives and come from stable homes and communities have a reserve from which to draw, such that even when shamed, that experience does not swallow up the self and utterly define it. Those with few resources who have come from chaotic and broken families, violence-ridden communities, and previously suffered

from trauma and/or shaming experiences tend to respond in one
of four defensive directions.

The north end is running from shame with *Withdrawal*—hid-

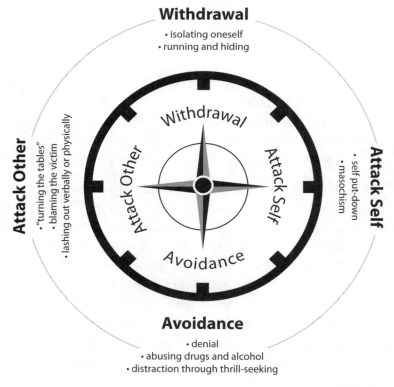

Copyright © 1992 by Dr. Donald Nathanson

ing from others and living in fear of exposure regarding what we
see as defective. This is a place of alienation. East on the compass
is *Attack Self.* We diminish ourselves in the presence of others. We
stay connected, unlike in *Withdrawal* but usually to those who
feed off losers "so they can feel like winners." The south end of
the compass is *Avoidance.* This is the attempt to hide the feelings of shame entirely from ourselves—alcohol, narcotics, or other
addictions. A variation of *Avoidance* is to draw attention to the
self through exhibitionistic behaviors, showing off. It is not unlike

narcissistic personality disorder where self-aggrandizement is a way of avoiding shame to the extent that there is no conscious awareness of the shame anymore. Connection is maintained but without intimacy. Finally, the west end of the compass is *Attack Others*. This is the bully, those who prey on the vulnerable and dole out their own sense of shame onto others, externalizing it and often scarring their victims for life. Their victims are buried under the shame of others and the scathing rage the bullies carry for themselves. It is easy to see, hearing about these likely responses to shame, that the damage to humans, both self and others, is profound.

Systemic Expressions of Shame

We should be keenly aware of the fact that there are different cultural ways of dealing with shame. I want to consider some of these with the up-front disclaimer that I am no culture expert in general and of those areas of the world we refer to as shame/honor cultures, even less so. My perspective is obviously more psychological, which does however include a knowledge of systems.

Shame is a disorder of the self; the identity. It is foundational. It is not a self with a disorder; it is a disordered self. Shame resides on the level of "I am . . ." not on the level of "I did, said, or thought . . ." though it can certainly permeate all those arenas.

In the Western world in general, the self is the individual: alone, capable, and responsible. What happens or fails to happen resides firmly in the power of that individual. If you try hard, you will succeed. If you work hard, you will climb. It is up to you, and you are expected to make it happen. If it does not happen, well then literally, shame on you. And if you fail, you fail alone. It is no one else's fault but yours. You are somehow flawed because we all know if you work hard and do it right success will come. Our identity is singular, ours alone.

In the Western world, we use the threat of guilt and fear of punishment to manage others—children, students, lawbreakers, etc. If you do wrong, you are punished. The guilt and shame are yours and no one else's, and retribution is to be feared. The concept of sin has much more power in Western society and is understood more readily than the concept of shame. In the West, innocence is desired and guilt is to be avoided. The Western world has a great deal of difficulty understanding what we might call "choiceless" choices and situations that are quite unclear, e.g., the starving child who steals. We want to assign blame. If you steal, it is because you are bad, period. Starving is irrelevant. We have often said, if you were raped, it was because you were seductive. We seem not to be able to tolerate the idea of powerlessness.

In many other parts of the world the self is the community, the family, the tribe. Everything is measured on an honor/dishonor continuum and anything dishonorable is to the whole not to the individual alone. Shame of the corporate self is to be avoided at all costs. The individual is subservient to the community honor. Honor is the driving force of the Arab psyche, and the honor of all interlocks to surround the community like a coat of armor. The smallest chink is a threat and shame is the greatest of all threats. It would seem that Eastern shame is a far more overtly powerful force than shame in the Western world because in the East it sits on the whole group not just the individual. Failure to conform is shameful for the entire community. It is more shameful to be exposed than to do wrong. So, for example, lying about something may be deemed honorable if it hides something shameful. Murder is more honorable than shame. Public censure is most feared.

Honor is, of course, the absence of shame. Strength is honored and there is little to no compassion for weakness. Violence is a way of demonstrating honor and removing shame from the family or tribe. You cannot give honor to yourself; it is bestowed. Such societies perceive violated women not as victims but as someone who debased the family honor, and they will undo the shame by taking her life. To fail in that is to further dishonor the family. In a grotesque example, an Egyptian strangled his unmarried pregnant daughter to death and cut her up and put her in the toilet. He said this, "Shame kept following me wherever I went (before he murdered her). The village people had no mercy on me. They were making jokes and mocking me. I could not bear it and decided to put an end to this shame."[9] He literally flushed it away. We are horrified—and we should be—but we have city streets full of heroin and crack addicts flushing away their own lives bit by bit because of a deep sense of shame they find intolerable.

In a poignant example that carries strains of the truth in a twisted way, a twenty-five-year-old Palestinian hanged his sister with a rope. "I did not kill her, but rather helped her to commit suicide and to carry out the death penalty she sentenced herself to. I did it to wash with her blood the family honor that was violated because of her and in response to the will of society that would not have mercy on me if I didn't. . . . Society taught us from childhood that blood is the only solution to wash the honor."[10]

These societies see those who refrain from washing shame with blood as cowards not worthy of living. Many would describe such an Arab as less than a man. We find these horrifying though we do need to recognize that in Western society leniency for murderers of females is not unknown. In 1989 a New York City judge sentenced a man to five years on probation for murdering his wife because of the great shame and humiliation he felt over her adultery.[11] In 1994 a Maryland judge sentenced a man to eighteen months with apologies for the harsh sentence given the stress he was under due to the shame of his wife's adultery.[12]

Other Kinds of Shame

We have considered the faces of shame with which most of us are familiar. We understand individual shame; we have all experienced it. We understand—some much more than others—the concept of

communal shame; if one brings dishonor, then one must be elimi-
nated in order to restore honor. There are other kinds or causes of
shame I would like to touch on. This is not an exhaustive list, but
this area is far more profound and complex than I think we have
usually realized. Let us briefly consider four other types of shame:

The first I call "inverted shame." By that I mean everything
is turned upside down and what we might ordinarily consider
shameful brings pride and esteem. If you have read the Simon
and Burns book, *The Corner: A Year in the Life of an Inner City
Neighborhood,* or watched the HBO series *The Wire,* you have
an idea of what I mean by inverted shame. Words we consider
shameful are used with pride. Actions so appalling you cannot
describe them are done with flair and applauded. The selling of
drugs by children, the using of females, the killing of young lives
are badges of honor in a hellish place where the corner, the spots of
sidewalk where these things occur, are considered a refuge to the
lost and disowned of society. Shame only occurs when one tries to
lift someone out and the one being helped does not have any idea
how to navigate in society. Then they feel shame.

We would say the words they use are shameful, and we would
be right. We would call the actions shameful, and we would be
right. We would say the degrading and dishonoring of fellow humans is beyond shameful, and we would be right. We would express horror when we see cops or teachers or ministers adapt to
the evil and begin to mimic the inversions and get honor for it.
Shame is to be avoided on the corner just like everywhere else, but
someone mixed all the labels up. And so that which is honoring is
shameful and that which is shameful has become honor. Human
beings, created in the image of God, given dignity and honor and
glory enough to walk freely and openly with God in the garden,
become twisted, distorted, and shamed to the extent that words
meant to humiliate and degrade have become badges of honor.

It is a full-blown example of what the Enemy did in the garden: good is evil and evil is good. Shame for shameful things can

be good and lead to restoration of dignity and healing. Pride in shameful things—in degradation, death, and dishonor—is diabolical. But human beings dishonored and discarded by society will scramble for honor wherever they can find it.

A second kind of shame, which has a great deal to do with trauma, is what I would call "inflicted shame." That is, the shame of one person inflicted on the self of the other. It is the shame belonging to the perpetrator but carried by the victim. It is the litter of Amnon carried by Tamar. It is the Congolese rape victim, bearing the shame of the rapist or the so-called witch in Ghana, alienated, shamed, and presumed cursed because her mother died. It is the child who has been sexually abused and called a whore for most of her adolescent years. None of these have behaved shamefully, but they are labelled and bear the shame of perpetrators who have no shame. Inflicted shame is when one human being uses, humiliates, and degrades another, leaving behind a profound and often lifelong sense of shame. Elie Wiesel in his novel *The Accident* says, "That's the way it is: shame tortures not the executioners but their victims. The greatest shame is to have been chosen . . ."[13] Many of my patients throughout the decades who have been victims of incest and child sexual abuse carry great shame over having been "chosen," as if somehow that "choosing" by the perpetrator reveals something inherently shameful in them. They will often ask me, "But why did he choose [to rape or abuse] me? What does that say about me?"

A third type of shame we might call the shame of deprivation. It is the shame of being reduced to less than human, deprived of necessities to the point where so much of what it means to be human seems destroyed—no initiative, no creativity, no connection, no voice—an empty shell who cannot care for self or loved ones and in fact, no longer sees them. Elie Wiesel wrote about the shame of hunger. He said "it is the easiest way for a tormentor to dehumanize another human being. . . . Poor men and women who yesterday were proud members of their tribes, bearers of ancient traditions and cultures, and who are now wandering among corpses. What is so horrifying in hunger is that it makes the individual death an anonymous death."[14]

I think it is also not just physical deprivation that shames, but the depriving of voice, of choice, of power to impact or change something. It is described again and again in the Holocaust literature. The shame of being there, yet not—not seen, not heard, not able, not choosing—one becomes utterly diminished. Those things that are meant to resound with the image of God in man, those things that bring dignity and honor, are gone and what is left is a shell. Writers talk about the loss of moral dimension, moral choice, because of the utter absence of control. In other words, humans deprived of all that constitutes human yet still living and breathing. Genocide, torture, starvation/famine, and many aspects of war produce the shame of deprivation.

One stunning story was told by a survivor of Auschwitz about the day the allied troops came to the camp to set them free. It was a day they had longed for, talked about, and waited for, but when it arrived he was so empty, diminished, and starved that when he heard all he could do was roll out of his bunk and lay on the floor. He had nothing left with which to respond to freedom. Good no longer affected him. He could not choose.

The fourth type of shame is the "shame of survival." This kind of shame runs through a great deal of the Holocaust literature and of course has been evident in many of the veterans I have seen through the years. We have often spoken of survivor's guilt in the context of war, but I am not sure that is accurate or at least it is not adequate. I think we need to consider the place of shame in surviving as well as in our thinking about moral injury.

Auschwitz survivor Primo Levi talks about the feeling of shame that coincided with reacquired freedom. "Coming out of the darkness, one suffered because of the reacquired consciousness of having been diminished. Not by our will, cowardice or fault, yet nevertheless we had lived . . . at the animal level. . . . We endured filth, promiscuity, and destitution, suffering much less than we would have suffered from such things in normal life, because our moral yardstick had changed. . . . I believe that it is was *precisely this turning to look back . . .* that gave rise to so many suicides."[15] With freedom and regained strength and a different context, shame comes when the thoughts come: *you should have; you could have; you should never have,* etc. Levi also talks about the shame of being alive instead of another, and particularly someone who was more kind, generous, or courageous than yourself. In his book, *The Drowned and the Saved,* he talks about the permanent search of a justification in his own eyes and those of others for still being alive.

Many veterans struggle with acts commanded and obeyed or committed voluntarily in war that are measured differently when people look back. Confusion and shame rise up and judgment by a post-war moral measure cannot be endured. The self has been redefined as the one who could and did commit horrors. It cannot be undone. Suicide is preferable.

If you have seen *Saving Private Ryan,* you remember the poignant scene where the old soldier in the cemetery basically asks, "Was I worth it?" Was saving me and the loss of others it cost worthwhile? Do I measure up to that? Anyone who works with vets needs to read *The Drowned and the Saved,* paying particular attention to Primo Levi's chapter on shame and his comments about suicide.[16] To consider moral injury and the suicide rate among vets and not talk about shame is to miss something significant. The burden of shame can be crushing for a vet when he turns back and measures his combat actions by a moral yardstick not present in war or feel that he survived while the "best" did not.

Responses to Shame

Most of us are familiar with the three standard responses to trauma: fight, flight, or freeze. I believe we can use these as a way to think about shame responses as well. Some of us, when shamed, fight. We attack others—sometimes those who shame us and often those who are weaker or vulnerable to us in some way. Some of you may have seen or read Peter Shaffer's play *Equus* (1973) about a young man with a pathological fascination with horses. It is a complicated plot with the usual Freudian sexual themes. The point is that at the end when Alan confuses the horses with God and screams, "He sees you; He sees you forever! God sees." Alan says, "No more; I will not be seen."[17] And so he blinds the horses with a hoof pick so they see him no more.

Obviously this is a fight response to shame. We get rid of shame by "blinding," by silencing, whoever sees us. We kill the raped sister, we destroy with words the one who knows something shameful about us; we murder the adulterous wife; we diminish ourselves by starvation so as to render ourselves invisible to ourselves; we avoid and abandon those who remind us of things we cannot bear to face. We, as it were, fight by putting out their eyes.

The second response is to flee. We flee into suicide, drugs, alcohol, wealth, success, promiscuity, and religious ritual. Anything to numb the pain of shame or counteract it by weighing the balance in favor of what we deem to be "the good." In doing so, we hurt the self: with death, drugs, food, sex, overwork, terrible pressure, and relentless judgment.

The third response is to freeze. Freezing is dissociative—paralysis, passivity—it is as if no one is home because if no one is home, then there can be no shame. Freezing means it is not mine; I do not own it; I can do nothing about what is not mine.

How Are We to Carry the Great Burden of Shame?

Shame is a crushing burden and must be carried by frail human beings who were originally intended for glory. Where has the glory gone? Can we ever get it back? Or must we drown in this swampland of shame?

When you look into the various Hebrew words in Scripture that refer to shame, you get a list like this: whispered about by harmful spectators, taunted, insulted, disgraced, rebuked, reproached, disfigured, dried up, blemished, considered with contempt. It is enough to make anyone curl up in a corner and cover themselves. It sounds like your worst nightmare come true. No wonder Adam and Eve covered and hid from the All-Seeing God. Shame is the complete loss of glory.

They ran and fled. Their eyes were opened to see themselves as creatures who had forsaken the One who is himself Glory. The shame was overpowering and they covered and ran and hid. Creatures meant to see God and reflect his glory were now groveling in trash dumps, pumping veins full of heroin, selling bodies, torturing, maiming, screaming insults, and cursing. They saw themselves apart from God and so they hid. We understand that. We do not want to see either, whether it is a view of ourselves we cannot bear or the sight of others shamed and destroyed. We want to hide or turn away.

What is God's response? Pursuit—the very thing we do not want when we feel ashamed. He came for them. *I want to see you*, he said. In doing so, God laid bare what Adam had attempted to wrap together and cover up. The Enemy was forced to crawl on his belly eating dirt, he who was a shining angel of light. But God's shamed and ruined creatures (who often think God will treat them like he treated the Enemy) are gently covered by God himself and promised redemption. That covering required that blood be shed. Remember the Palestinian who said "I did it (hung my sister) to wash with her blood the family honor . . . we are taught that blood is the only solution to wash the honor." That Palestinian spoke truth but he did not know whose blood would wash honor clean. Truly God is our glory and the lifter of our heads (Psalm 3:3).

And so the centuries go on—wars, rapes, hate, fear, children thrown to Moloch, the people of God abandoning him and shaming themselves and each other over and over again. Glory lost and seemingly irretrievable.

And then a baby born to an unwed mother—shameful. A child of Nazareth—shameful. A man who walked the roads with women in his company—shameful. He touched lepers, demoniacs, and bothered with children—shameful.

Sold for the price of a slave—shameful. Arrested by religious leaders and publicly insulted—shameful. Dragged to the front of jeering crowds—shameful. And then dragged through the streets—shameful. Set on high for all to see—naked, struck, beard plucked out, spit upon, humiliated, and erected on one of the most shaming and torturous instruments of death in the history of the world. He was shamed by the world he had made. He became shame, embodied it. All could see—he did not hide.

We who are shamed creatures, whether by our own doing or due to the torment of others, are called to look, to fix our eyes on this Jesus, this utterly exposed and shamed Jesus. He did not hide when he was shamed, and we are called to see. Watch him endure this torture, the jeering, the pain, the insults, the naked-ness, the spit running down. The author of Hebrews calls us to fix our eyes on *this* Jesus, the one we would naturally turn our eyes away from. We do not want to see. He says watch with me. Stare down my shame with me. And then we are told he despised that shame. Despised? Not feared, not diminished by, not wasted from, not curled up and hiding. It means to hate, loathe, abhor, consider worthless. He considered worthless the very thing that leads us to feel utterly worthless.

In 1 John we are told to love one another and that if we hate our brother the love of God is not in us. The Greek there for hate means literally, "to spit on someone in your heart." Jesus says, "I hid not my face from shame and spitting." Hiding our faces is ex-actly what we want to do when we feel shame. Children know this instinctively. They run, they hide in a closet, or they cover their faces when they feel shame. He did not hide; he despised it, hated it. In essence, Jesus spit on the shame, considered it worthless, it carried no weight, no value. Jesus spit on being spit on. He scorned scorn. He diminished shame itself, one of the most diminishing agents of human beings. He shamed shame. He did not hide; he did not cover; he did not shrink. He hated shame and stared it straight in the face. And then he sat down at the right hand of the throne of God full of glory.

He despised shame and sat in glory. We are shamed and glory disappears. He faced shame and transformed it into glory. On the cross Jesus spits back, not on shameful humans, those warped, ruined, and twisted but still created in his image. No, he spits on the shame they spilled all over him, and he refused to let it define him, diminish him, or destroy his work and purpose. And what was that work and purpose? To change our shame into glory.

We are there with him, all of us bearing the shame of our own sin and of the sins of others against us. He did not hide from that shame and rather than despising us, he despised the shame. In doing so, he has carried shameful creatures back to glory. He transforms shame into glory. "We all, with unveiled face [not hidden], beholding as in a mirror the glory of the Lord, are being transformed into the same image from glory to glory" (2 Corinthians 3:18). We who hid our faces from him can now behold him, see him and be seen by him without shame. And as we do we are changed into glory.

So here we are, formerly shamed creatures fixed on Jesus and being changed from glory to glory. We are scattered all over the world. We work with traumatized humans who bear great burdens of shame often inflicted on them by others. We have been called, in this work, to fix our eyes on Jesus, the great despiser of shame, the All-Glorious One. This Jesus, that he might make a shamed people holy, suffered outside the gate—in a place of shame. Therefore, let us who can look at him with open face and have been given glory, go to him outside the camp bearing *his reproach.*

Go and bear his reproach. Be chided; be reproached by others as he was for lifting the fallen, strengthening the faint, touching the lepers, and bringing life to dead places. Go to the shamed and bend down and lift them up. Go to the shamed of this world and bring them a taste of his glory, the glory he has given you by his blood. And God forbid that we should glory except in the cross, that shaming instrument of torture that brings glory to ruined humans.

CHAPTER 9

Living with Trauma Memories

Anyone who has trauma memories knows that they want them to go away. If they cannot get them to disappear, they at least want to forget them; they want to hide them from themselves. Those who try to hide or forget them also know the experience of having them continue to break through into their conscious mind.

Listen to a quote from a trauma survivor. "I live beside it. It is right there, fixed, unchangeable, wrapped in the tough skin of memory that separates itself from the present me. I wish the skin to become tougher, for I fear it will grow thinner and crack, permitting the trauma to spill out and capture me."[1] Here is one more: "My head is filled with garbage, all these images you know, and sounds, and my nostrils filled with smells . . . you can't excise it . . . it's like another skin beneath this skin and you cannot shed it . . . I am not like you. You have one vision of life and I have two . . . I have a double life."[2]

This woman, a survivor of the Nazi Holocaust, has described a common experience—though she tries to forget or hide the memory from herself, it continues to live beside her and she is always fearful that it will reach out and grab her. You cannot erase trauma memories. One psychologist says, "What cannot be talked about can also not be put to rest, and if it is not, the wounds continue to fester from generation to generation."[3]

In his book, *Holocaust Testimonies: The Ruins of Memory*, Lawrence Langer addresses the reasons survivors of the Nazi death camps experience such difficulty in reporting their memories. Langer collected detailed testimonies from camp survivors and noted the particular difficulty they had in recounting their experiences. According to his understanding, those experiences are so discrepant from everyday life that the survivor is left with a "dual existence." That is, everyday life versus the "co-temporal" recollections of the trauma. The traumatic memories are discontinuous from everyday narrative memory. They do not fit into everyday schemas. So you have the narrative story of a life with a segment that never quite gets integrated into that story because it simply does not fit the categories.

I have found Langer's work to be helpful in my work with survivors of trauma. One of the things that Langer's work clearly demonstrates is how trauma divides the self and keeps it from being whole. It divides into "me and not-me" or "my life and not-my-life." There is a very basic split that occurs due to the trauma. "I was born, raised, went to school, got married, had a job, had children, then got a job in New York at the World Trade Center (WTC), *and then more than 5,000 people were killed?* And then I worked . . ." Or, "my family lived in India and my father was a fisherman, like his father before him. Every morning he would go fishing and my mother and I would make rice cakes, and then a wave came and destroyed everything and killed my parents and my siblings." It simply does not fit with the storyline. It would sound bizarre to hear someone tell such a story as if one line led to the next and nothing extraordinary had been stated. The vocabulary doesn't work. The categories are inadequate.

Deep Memory (Buried Self)

This occurs when efforts to leave the memory behind prove futile. "I live a double existence. The double of Auschwitz does not mingle with my present life. As if it weren't me at all."[4] Do you hear the splitting, the surreal quality? Those who survive an earthquake will find themselves in a business meeting or at a dinner party and suddenly experience that double existence, desperately wanting the images of crushed bodies, death, and tragedy to go away, trying to make sure the skin that holds the trauma separate will prove strong enough because they are supposed to be having a dinner conversation.

Another death camp survivor: "Sometimes it bursts and gives out its contents. Then I feel it again physically. I feel it again through my whole body . . . it takes days for everything to return to normal, for the skin of memory to heal itself."[5] A survivor of chronic childhood abuse will see an image on television and suddenly find themselves physically reacting as if they are being abused. A combat veteran hears a helicopter and suddenly thinks he is in a war zone and acts accordingly.

Langer uses two terms here. *Deep memory* is the old, isolated memory of the trauma. It burrows beneath. When it spills out, it corrodes the comforts of the *common memory*. Common memory is the present memory that restores the self to normal and offers detached portraits of what was. With its talk of normalcy, it mediates the atrocity and says that in spite of evil, some things are okay. Common and deep memory function as two adjacent worlds that occasionally intrude upon each other.

Langer also talks about a common occurrence when a trauma survivor tries to tell another what happened. "Do you understand what I am trying to tell you?" The question acknowledges the limited power of words. Those who listen must also acknowledge that limitation. Words must be used, but they cannot convey all. A vast sphere separates what was endured from our capacity to absorb it. The survivor is remembering what was. The hearer is imagining what was. That calls for ongoing humility in the listener. As we listen to memories of trauma from others, we must do so with respect and humility, knowing that no vocabulary is sufficient for communicating the whole experience. We will never respond by reducing trauma to an experience you can simply get over with the push of a mental button.

Anguished Memory (Divided Self)

This term is used to refer to memory that assaults and finally divides the self. Survivors talk about the inability to link the past and the future. "I split myself. It wasn't me there. I was somebody else."[6] You will hear survivors of the WTC trauma or the tsunami or Hurricane Katrina or an earthquake speak with "before the event" or "after the event" language. Rape victims do the same. The event divides their lives in two. In order to live in the present, the memories of trauma have to be blocked from the conscious mind. In clinical terms we call this dissociation. Who I was in the trauma experience is and must be foreign to who I am now, and there is no apparent bridge. Think for example of a competent, successful professional woman who has a history of chronic sexual abuse in childhood. Many of those memories are of searing physical pain, blood, utter abandonment by her mother, rage, and name-calling, all of which occurred again and again. How does such a woman maintain herself at a business meeting, a church gathering, or in a business or personal relationship with any man, if those anguished memories are not separated from her present-day self?

From another concentration camp survivor: ". . . in order to survive I had to die first. To me, I was dead. I died and I didn't want to know nothing and I didn't want to hear nothing. I didn't want to talk about it, and I didn't want to admit that this happened to me. . . . There is a sort of division, you know, a compartmentalization of what happened, and it's kept tightly separated, and yet it isn't . . . it must not interfere, the other must not become so overwhelming that it will make so-called normal life unable to function."[7]

The traumatized self must "die" so the present-day self can live. However, we know that the memories are not gone, dead, or silenced and they can burst into memory at any moment, causing the survivor to live a life always vulnerable to being overwhelmed by anguish.

Humiliated Memory (Besieged Self)

One more form of memory referred to by Langer is humiliated memory, which recalls an utter distress that shatters all molds designed to contain a unified and irreproachable image of the self. It is the memory of things that make death preferable to life. The shame and humiliation inherent in sexual abuse and rape fall into this category. People who acted during the trauma in ways that are diametrically opposed to their views of themselves will experience humiliated memory. Those present on September 11 or the earthquake or during Katrina who acted less than heroically or altruistically will experience this kind of memory. The impact of such memories is not limited to those who endured the events but is also felt by those who hear about the events. Just as we are impacted by hearing of heroics and bravery, so we are impacted by hearing of the cold-blooded murder of thousands of civilians or the leaving behind of the sick and the elderly. Such knowledge leads to unflattering images of human nature, and we are tempted to interpret the past so as to reclaim our positive beliefs rather than confront their undoing. We long to erase the contrast between what we hear and what we wish to know.

Another way to express this is that the concept of helplessness is alien to those who have a strong sense of responsibility and so survivors may judge themselves harshly when they reflect back on their choices and behavior. "I should have . . . I could have . . . why didn't I?" Many adults judge themselves as child victims as if they had the knowledge and resources of the adult. They see themselves as weak, stupid, bad, or something that resulted in the abuse occurring. It is a belief with long tentacles, and it takes much time for freedom to come.

To walk into memories of trauma is to encounter anguished and humiliated memory. It means dealing with content and searching for forms because such memories defy all normal categories. It requires a suspension of normal categories for life if one is to tell, hear, and/or absorb the reality of the trauma. Thought categories and words die in us in the face of unspeakable brutality. Yet words are necessary and it becomes about speaking the unspeakable, explaining the unexplainable, and bearing the unbearable.

Trauma memories do not disappear. Our brains are made so that they do not forget anything. We sometimes have the experience of not being able to find something in our brains or forgetting something, but that is not the same as it disappearing. Since that is the case, it would seem that we must learn how to live with them so that they are not destructive to our present life. I want to focus on things that help those with trauma memories to live with them, to honor them, and yet to still live their present lives in productive and creative ways. We are going to do this in two ways. The first thing we will do is discuss three ways human beings can respond to trauma memories to help themselves toward recovery. The second part will be three ways for traumatized people to take a stand against the trauma and for life. I will discuss two of those in this segment and the third in the following segment as I think it needs extra discussion.

First Phase of Trauma Recovery

Following a traumatic experience every human being must make the heartbreaking adjustment to a new world full of losses. Trauma involves an event that threatens life or physical safety, that takes away choice, and that results in overwhelming fear. This is includes things like war, violence, rape, sexual abuse, and physical abuse. When these things happen to humans, they feel alone, helpless, humiliated, and hopeless. Following trauma, people turn inward, away from life, because the memories and the feelings are all that they can handle. This is not wrong; it is necessary for awhile. However, eventually if life is to go on, the person must return to the outside world. What kinds of things are needed to help people face what is inside, to remember well, and yet be able to return to life in a good way?

Recovery involves a reversal of the experience of trauma. Trauma brings silence because it feels like there are no words to really describe what happened. Trauma brings emotional darkness and aloneness because it feels like no one cares and no one could possibly understand. Trauma makes time stand still because we get so lost in what happened we cannot see forward and we lose hope. There are three main things that must occur to reverse this and bring about recovery. All three must happen. Just one of them will not be enough. The three things are: talking, tears, and time. Let's look at each one.

Talking

How many of you in this room know how to talk? How many of you do talk? Does anyone know someone who does not or never has talked? It would seem that talking is part of being human. It is how God made us. He meant for us to talk, to express ourselves, to dialogue together with him and with each other. When someone does not talk, something is broken. There may be something physically wrong. Or there may be something emotionally wounded. Sometimes when people do not talk at all or do not talk about a particular event, it is because the pain is so great they cannot find the words at all, or they just keep saying the same thing trying to find the right words and get relief.

Talking is absolutely necessary for recovery. Even though words are inadequate, they must be spoken. To remain silent is to fail to honor the event and memory. By honoring the memory, I mean speaking the truth about it, saying it really happened, saying it was really evil, and saying that it really did damage. It dishonors victims when we are silent about their experience or pretend it did not occur or was not important. Talking says *I am here, what happened was wrong, I am damaged by it, justice is needed, and so is care for my broken heart.* At the beginning talking might not be done using words. Sometimes people only moan or sigh or cry or scream. It is the beginning of giving voice to that which cannot be spoken. Many times people need us to sit with them in silence. It is a way of joining with them so they are not alone in their experience of struggling to find words. Eventually words must come. Sometimes people need help with that. It can be helpful to say to someone, "I am going to say one word and if it describes what you felt or saw just nod your head." You might use words such as *horrifying, dark, alone, grief, fear, overwhelming, hopeless,* or *pain.* Little by little you help them find words until they can give you pieces of the story. Trauma stories do not first come out with a beginning, middle, and an end. They come out in broken pieces, disordered, and perhaps unclear.

Talking is about telling the truth. It connects the survivor to another person. It restores dignity because their story matters. It gives them choice because they can decide when to speak or be silent, and victims get to choose their own words. Again it is the reversal of what happened during the trauma. Injustice, violence, and abuse teach us lies. Such events suggest we are worthless and do not matter. Trauma tells the truth and gives dignity because the story matters as does its impact. Violence and abuse disconnect us from caring relationships. We are alone, and we are not considered. Telling the trauma story gives a place of caring connection that helps the soul. Trauma recovery requires talking, and as the story is repeated, strength to say and grasp the truth grows.

Tears

How many of you have ever shed tears? How many have had the experience of wanting to cry but feeling like you cannot? How many have had the experience of someone telling you that you should not cry?

Trauma recovery also requires tears. Facing a new world full of losses brings grief. Many emotions are the companions of trauma: fear, sadness, aloneness, humiliation, despair, anger, and grief are some of them. These are strong emotions, and they are hard to experience. These are not feelings any of us want in our lives, however like words, they must be expressed. Feelings tell the story as much as words tell the story. Feelings express what the trauma did to the victim just like blood shows what a cut did to the skin. It is like seeing and acknowledging the physical wounds on the body after an accident. Feelings are the expression of the wounds of the heart, and they too need to be seen and heard.

For some people words tend to come first. That is actually good because choosing words, saying words, and having someone listen and honor them helps to strengthen the survivor to face his/her feelings. It also connects them to a caring person they can trust to bear the terrifying feelings with them. Many survivors try hard not to feel and will often say things like, "If I start crying, I will never stop," or "If I feel the grief or hopelessness, I will fall into a black hole and never get out."

Many will try hard not to feel anything, and oftentimes people will use alcohol or drugs to help them feel numb. They think if they stay drunk or use drugs they can keep the memories and feelings away. When people do such things, they spend their lives controlled by the trauma because everything they are doing is about running from it. It is as much in charge of their lives as when it was occurring.

At the same time, it is important for all of us to remember that telling a trauma story—facing the truth and expressing the deep and painful emotions that keep company with trauma—takes tremendous courage. Most people cannot do it alone. They need connection with a caring and patient person to help them have the courage to face the truth of what happened and how it hurt them. A companion in tragedy or difficulty always helps us have courage.

Many emotions cannot be adequately expressed in words and so nonverbal ways are important. I have often asked people to draw or paint me a picture of their sadness or fear or grief. Many years ago I saw a woman who created a dance that told the story of what happened to her and how she felt. Sometimes people write stories or poems or songs. People create jewelry or other art objects to symbolize the trauma and its pain. We often express deep feelings through creative avenues, including good feelings like joy or love. So I think it is helpful to encourage trauma survivors to use such means for their pain as well. Use traditions in your own culture to assist this process.

Psalm 56:8 says, "You [meaning God] have taken account of my wanderings; put my tears in Your bottle. Are they not in Your book?" This is important because often we are uncomfortable with strong emotions. Culture may say such feelings are not proper, religious teachings may say it shows unbelief to have such feelings, or family teachings may suggest we should be tough and not have feelings (or that feelings are alright for women but not for men, or for children but not for adults), that somehow they are a sign of weakness. This verse says that the God who created us considers our pain. He pays attention to it, and he collects our tears in a bottle and writes them in his book because we matter. What happened matters and our feelings about it matter to him also. He is recording our story and our tears for us. We will help others in their recovery if we learn to be like him in the way we treat feelings. We honor others and help them record the story of their trauma by listening to their words and their tears. Tears require strength and courage because they mean facing pain.

Many of those who are traumatized will be afraid to face and feel the feelings related to the trauma. They fear losing control of themselves and the pain and suffering they will endure. These fears are understandable for the feelings surrounding the trauma are powerful and such emotions can quickly re-create the trauma in which the survivor felt overwhelmed and helpless. Dealing with and healing from such feelings will never occur easily. Feeling will alternate with numbness and exhaustion. Those breaks are necessary and must not be rushed. It feels much safer to experience the emotions of trauma with someone who will listen, assure them their feelings are normal, and not condemn them. Grief is one of the most intense emotions that accompanies trauma, so we will spend an entire chapter on that.

You will find that for many trauma survivors one or two specific memories have become symbolic for the whole experience. Sometimes we can figure that out by listening well and hearing what memory or part of a memory the survivor keeps returning to. Those segments represent the whole in some way and also carry intense emotion.

I remember a man who grew up in the inner city and witnessed much violence on the street and in the home. He was repeatedly raped by his stepfather. He vividly remembers looking through the venetian blinds one day and watching his mother walk down the sidewalk. He talked about seeing life through the blinds. It was, though he did not know it at the time, the great moment of his utter abandonment to that stepfather for his mother never returned. Seeing life through the blinds meant people cannot be trusted; they always leave and your safety is up to you alone. He was eight years old. Such symbolic memories tell the larger story as for example, the death of a child may also be how the survivor tells you about the death of any hope or being traumatized by a religious person may also tell the story of the death of faith for someone.

As you listen to the story and see and experience the emotions, it is also important to follow the most intense emotions and listen for the larger story as well—often one the survivor does not hear herself saying.

Time

There is a third thing that must occur for trauma recovery to begin and grow—time—and this we have no control over. Trauma recovery needs talking, tears, and time and it must have all three. If you do not tell the story, there will be no recovery. People will stay stuck in the past and controlled by the trauma. It must be spoken over and over again. Trauma recovery needs tears. Tears honor the victim and the awfulness of what occurred. They express buried emotions that haunt sleep and disturb life. Expressing emotions, finding words for them, is also a way of gaining mastery over them. In both talking and tears the victim is staring down the trauma as one might stare down an enemy and say, "I will speak of you; you will not silence me." Clearly it takes time for these things to happen. It takes time for words to come. It takes time to listen and understand. It takes time for feelings to be expressed and understood.

Recovery from anything takes time. If you fall off some steps and break a bone, it will take time for the doctor to understand which bone is broken and what needs to happen to heal it. He will need to sit with and listen and explore so he understands exactly what the problem is. You will hurt. You will be in pain. Even after the doctor does some things to help the bone reset, it will still hurt.

You may want your leg to be better tomorrow. You may want the pain to be over. It will not change the pace at which time proceeds. It always goes by one minute at a time, and there is nothing you can do about it. Time is needed for recovery. It is not the same amount for each trauma survivor. Some take longer and some do not. But no matter how strong someone is, no matter how hard they work to tell their story and express their feelings, it will take time. And I can tell you two things for sure about time: 1) there is nothing we can do to make it go faster, and 2) when we are in pain, that is exactly what we want it to do!

We also know from research that as time passes trauma survivors end up carrying a smaller piece of the whole, especially if the story has been told. As life goes on around the survivor, new experiences and new relationships affect them and they can learn new responses to their past instead of those the trauma taught them. Over time survivors can choose what they want to do with their suffering.

So to recap, there are three things we need in order to begin recovering from trauma—talking, tears, and time. Remember it has to be all three. Talking once will not do it—repetition over time is necessary. Talking can also be done in a way that does not include the heart. Tears alone are not enough for healing, as no mastery will come—words are necessary too and again need to be repeated over time. Time alone is not enough either, as the truth is not stated or owned or actively managed, and the victim remains at the mercy of the memories just as they were at the mercy of the trauma.

Second Phase of Trauma Recovery

Talking, tears, and time are instruments the survivor can use to help herself toward recovery. More is needed. The things we have mentioned are all focused back toward the trauma. Again, it is like the broken leg. Initially all energy is focused on the brokenness, the pain, and what needs to be done for that leg to heal. However, if that is all that the patient does, he will never walk right again. This stage is about learning all over again how to walk through life.

Also remember that recovery from trauma requires a reversal of the experience of the trauma, which was a threat to life, without choice, and full of fear. Trauma silences us, isolates us, and we are helpless to stop it. Trauma destroys love, dignity, and purpose. Our second phase speaks to those same three things in different ways. The next stage involves loving relationship, work or purpose, and faith. Let us look at each one in turn.

Loving Relationship

First, what do I mean by loving relationship? Returning to relationship after the shattering of trauma starts with the person we tell our story to. When we speak, we are heard. We are heard by someone who seeks to understand and feel with us. We are no longer isolated and alone in our suffering. However, we must eventually choose whether we will love again, care again, reach for another human being again. Trauma took away choice. Surviving and then telling our story returns that to us. We must choose what we will do with humans. We can hide, hate, or run from them, but then the trauma still has mastery.

Every act of kindness, every act of helpfulness, every act of forgiveness, and every act of love defies the trauma. It is as though you are standing and facing what tried to destroy you and putting your hands on your hips and saying, "No, you will not own me. You will not make me less than human. You will not create me in your own image of darkness, helplessness, aloneness, and fear. I choose to be kind; I choose to love again; I choose to forgive; I choose to be connected to my fellow human beings." Perpetrators of violence destroy trust and care. Survivors can reclaim what was lost little by little and choose those things again. Part of what giving good or giving care to others does is to reverse the terrible feelings of humiliation. Violence makes us feel degraded, less than human, full of shame. Every small act of caring for others reminds all of our humanity, and there is dignity in that.

Work or Purpose

The second thing is purpose, something that is often found in work but can be found in other ways as well. Some years ago I went to the Dominican Republic and remember walking through the slums of the capital and seeing men sitting around doing nothing with little expression in their faces and eyes that looked dead.

There was no work. They could not provide anything for their families. They were depressed and had no self-respect. They felt less than men. Many of them coped by drinking, and there was a lot of violence in the homes. They had no sense of purpose, and they could not see any reason to exist.

We are meant to have purpose. When God first made the world and it was still good, men and women worked. He made us to work. It gives us dignity, meaning, and purpose. We can see the impact we make. When you can provide for your family through a job, growing food and selling it, fishing, or caring for children, you feel a sense of value and strength. You can see the results of your hard work. When you can create goods or things of beauty— a basket, jewelry, music, or a good meal—you can point and say, "Look, that is what I did. That is here because I am here." It is not only proof of your existence, but it also shows that you are producing good.

Work can be paid or not. It simply means you are using your strength, your abilities, or your brains to be productive and creative. You can do it every day, in small ways and affecting many lives. You will feel yourself making choices. It will give you dignity, honor, and respect. You are doing good in this world. It has been noted that in refugee camps where people have purpose and work to produce, create or help others, they do much better and become stronger. It reverses the trauma, which brought helplessness, evil, and shame. Traumatized people who are given work recover and reconnect with life much more quickly than those without work. Work provides purpose, a schedule, a focus, and a familiar place, all of which is connected to the present and the future.

Faith

Finally, we need to consider how trauma affects faith, and how to think about that in terms of recovery. First let us notice a couple of things about faith. Trauma freezes thinking. Someone who has experienced trauma thinks about herself, her life, her relationships, and her future through the frame of the trauma. She gets stuck. Trauma stops growth because it shuts everything down. It is a kind of death. The thinking that grows out of the traumatic experience controls the input from new experiences. That means after trauma, rather than faith being foundational, the traumatic experience becomes foundational. The trauma will serve as the framework. The more aspects of a person involved in what was learned, the stronger the lesson. In the trauma of sexual abuse, every sense was involved (touch, taste, smell, sound, and sight) and it was involved during a state of hyperawareness because of the fear. The lessons taught, right or wrong (such as, I am worthless), will not be forgotten.

Think about a couple in China who lost a child in the collapse of a school during the earthquake there. What do you think might happen if some years from now they have another child and send him to school? How do you think they will feel the first day they see him go into the school building? Do you think they will feel afraid?

Second, you and I learn about the unseen or the things of faith through the seen world. We are of the earth, and we learn through our five senses—hearing, seeing, touching, tasting, and smelling. God knows how he created us to be and so he teaches us truths through the world around us. Whether it's catching a glimpse of eternity through the seemingly endless horizon over the sea or learning the holiest of mysteries through the partaking of bread and wine, God uses this method to teach us about his character so we don't have to guess what he is like. He takes on flesh and bone and skin so we can look at Jesus and know him. God explains himself to us through the things we can understand.

When people are traumatized, instead of learning from God who he is, they learn from the trauma and believe that God is behind the evil. For many, God is viewed through the frame of that trauma. Violence and humiliation means God does not care. He does not love me or those I love. He has abandoned us. It is quite common for people to lose their faith in God after they have experienced trauma. It is another loss.

I have only found one response to this difficult problem and that is the cross of Jesus Christ, for it is there that trauma and God come together. Christ has endured all fears, powerlessness, helplessness, destruction, alienation, silence, loss, and hell. He understands trauma. He willingly entered into trauma for us. He endured humiliation, betrayal, abandonment, nakedness, aloneness, darkness, the silence of God, helplessness, shame, grief, and the loss of all things, including his life. He did that for us. First, he endured trauma so that we would know we have a God who understands. Think about things you have experienced, and see if they are on this list: he bore our grief, carried our sorrow, was hit, full of pain, cut, crushed, and beaten. He was taken away. He was removed from the living. He was despised and abandoned. God was silent. Have you felt some of these things? Have they been part of your life too? When you speak with him, remember that he knows.

He has promised to make all things new. Why he allows these things now I do not know. Why we must wait for those promises to be fulfilled I do not know. But I do know who he is because of how he lived and died, and if he can conquer death and hell, then I will struggle to have faith that he will finish that job someday.

Suffering and faith are difficult to hold together, aren't they? One without the other we can do. When things are going well, we can have faith. When we are suffering, it is easy for faith to die. But faith is about believing in things we hope for that are not here yet. Faith is about trusting that what we cannot yet see will become real someday. Evil always wants to destroy faith. It wants to swallow up hope. It says, "Look at the destruction I have brought; there is no good and there is no hope of good." But remember, trauma brings helplessness, and recovery brings choice. Do we choose life or death, evil or good, love or hate, faith or denial of God? Those things that are evil are the choice of death, hatred, and the denial of God. To choose such things is to look like the evil that tried to destroy us.

Faith in God is a struggle in ordinary life. Faith in God when we have seen tragedy and trauma is a massive struggle. But it is a good fight because it is a fight against those things that tried to destroy us and make us like themselves. Rather than bearing the image of the evil that was done to us, we can choose to look to Jesus, who bears the scars of evil as well, but is also its conqueror and refused to bow while it did its worst to him. God is alive and still reigns on his throne, and he will indeed come someday and make all things new. Our question is what to do: how will we live while we wait?

CHAPTER 10

Living with Ongoing Trauma

I once sat in a supervisory session with a therapist who was working with a woman who lived with a relentlessly violent husband. The client had asked her, "What is wrong with me that I cannot get over the trauma of his abuse?" The therapist asked me, "What do I tell her?" My answer was, "You cannot 'get over' something that is still happening." This is true on a physiological level as well. If you have the flu, a temperature of 103, chills, and bronchial symptoms, you cannot recover until it is over. You are fighting it, enduring it, protecting yourself in any way you can from worsening your condition. You might talk about it, but your talk is largely focused on your symptoms, on what you are doing to keep it from getting worse and how you are eager for it to pass *so that* you can begin the recovery work of little by little regaining your strength. It is critical that the alleviating of symptoms *does not* mean full recovery.

It seems to me that an attempt to do typical trauma recovery, in the midst of ongoing trauma is the equivalent of undressing someone who is still standing in a life-threatening blizzard. You simply put the traumatized at greater risk of harm.

Healing from trauma requires safety and stabilization. They are necessary ingredients for forming an alliance, a safe connection, with the trauma survivor so that they can look back at what was overwhelming and traumatic and begin to speak and feel and integrate those memories into life without being swallowed up again and working destruction in their present lives.

What happens when there is little to no safety? What do we do when life continues to be danger-filled, uncertain, and unstable? A great number of people live in such circumstances. Women in the Democratic Republic of the Congo (DRC) are at risk of being raped merely because they want to feed their children. Those in Southern Sudan are living with bombing and instability and cannot go home again. Those in Syria live with constant war, inadequate supplies, and destruction. In oppressive regimes people live with constant vigilance and fear and restricted movement and words. As any inner city pastor will tell you, those who live in our urban ghettos live with ongoing trauma. Many around the world live in so-called tent cities with constant instability and unpredictability on the most basic of levels.

How are we to think about these situations, the people who live in them, and trauma? What kind of responses are helpful and resilience building *and* avoid additional overwhelming for traumatized people who live daily in crushing circumstances?

Years ago in a counseling session, a combat vet who had recently returned from Iraq talked about how they had tried programs on the ground in Iraq to help the soldiers deal with the trauma they were experiencing as it was happening. The idea behind it was that if they dealt with it immediately they would have less severe struggles after returning home. He said it was not working and the soldiers did not like it or trust it. He said, "They want us to put our guard down and tell them how we feel about killing people and then they want us to pick up our guns and go back out there and kill some more? They're crazy." He also said, "I do not even know if I can face this stuff now that I am home, it is over, and I am safe. What makes them think we can do it while we are getting shot at?" The soldier's comments are worthy of attention and, I think, very astute.

Think with me about the diagnosis of post-traumatic stress disorder. It is critical to note that it is called *post* (meaning after) traumatic stress disorder. The trauma has occurred; now the trauma is over. As we look a bit at the definition, note the use of past tense words. The first criterion is that the person has been expos*ed* to a traumatic event in which *both* of the following have been present:

1. The person has experienced, witnessed, or been confronted with an event or events that involved actual or threatened death or serious injury, or a threat to the physical integrity of oneself or others.
2. The person's response involved intense fear, helplessness, or horror.

Please note that everything described here is done so in the past tense. In a word, a traumatized human being is an utterly overwhelmed human being due to a *previous* event(s). The definition of overwhelmed is either a) bury or drown beneath a huge mass or b) defeat completely. It includes words like to surge, submerge, engulf or overcome completely in mind or feeling. A trauma is the equivalent of a personal tsunami. Just sit for a minute and absorb the words (surge, submerge, engulf)—even simply on a physical level. Think about being buried or submerged under a huge mass. You cannot breathe; you cannot see; you cannot move. You want to claw your way out. Your heart races; you think you will die. Think of people carried away by a tsunami, buried under a collapsed building in Haiti, or under dead bodies in the Rwanda genocide. Now pretend I come along while you are buried and start talking to you about telling your story and not only the story but what kind of feelings it elicited. You cannot breathe; getting the next breath is what you are thinking about; getting away; finding safety, escape. You are wondering if you will survive or if your loved ones did or will. Your trauma story is in the middle, not at the end. It is not a hard jump to realize how trauma stories and trauma feelings cannot and even perhaps *should not* be looked at in the ways we generally do with those who are still in dangerous and traumatizing situations.

When I was ten years old, my family lived on the southernmost island of Japan. My father was stationed there with the Air Force. When the weather was nice we would often spend a Saturday afternoon at the beach swimming in the Sea of Japan. One afternoon I went out to swim by myself and had an experience where I thought I was going to drown. I can still recall the feelings of trying to find the surface, the overwhelming sensation of water everywhere, and the desperate need for oxygen. It would make no sense to have come alongside at that moment to ask me to tell my story and to put into words how I was feeling and thinking about that experience and its impact on me. If someone had asked and I had tried to answer, I would have simply ingested more of what was overwhelming and threatening me.

That is a picture of trying to do the standard trauma recovery in the midst of ongoing, relentless trauma. You would not ask a rape victim to tell her story *while* she was being raped. You cannot expect a child living with ongoing sexual abuse or a woman living with violence to tell the story, understand its impact, and work toward healing. It would be the equivalent of asking an accident victim to start rehab while still under the car that hit them. An awareness of these things needs to guide our thinking and development of working with those living with ongoing trauma. If we are not careful we will end up encouraging people to ingest even more feelings of being helpless and overwhelmed.

Another aspect of this has to do with vigilance. When we work with trauma survivors they are usually hyper-vigilant, and that often gets in the way of their present-day functioning. We work with them to help them learn to be grounded and manage their anxiety and reduce that constant vigilance. One of the points my soldier client was making was that he *needed* to be hyper-vigilant;

he was in combat, people had guns and wanted to kill him. His safety would be jeopardized if he let down his vigilant stance. He could die. His buddies could die. That would also be true for a woman going out in the field in Congo to get food for her family. At some point a sense of safety lulls us and may in fact put us at greater risk. It would be true for those in the streets of Syria; it is also true for many living in the gang-controlled, violent inner cities of the US. Walking down the street or sitting on your porch or stopping at a red light could get you shot. It is true for women in ongoing domestic violence or children who are chronically abused. To put down your guard and reflect and feel is to fail to see the next abusive event coming. Our assessment powers as humans are tremendously compromised when we are simply trying to dodge the next blow. That takes all of our focus. Safety and respite are needed to assess damage and the accompanying emotions and thoughts. Most of the established trauma work today assumes that the trauma is past; it is gone and now there is safety. What if it is not? What if it may never be over? How do we help when the trauma, or multiple traumas, is ongoing and no end is in sight?

I do not pretend to have the answer. I do know it is an important question and a critical area of study. This is a relatively new idea in the trauma field and more so in the Western world and it needs much thought and work and field-testing. Our ideas must include the voices and input of those who are living in such circumstances. It *must* be a duet. Those living with trauma are, in fact, the only ones who can tell us what is helpful and what is not. We may have vast amounts of knowledge and resources, but that does not mean what we have will work on the ground. We need to ask the people on the ground and respect their resistance to our current modes. The soldier's resistance was not an avoidance of dealing with his trauma per se or some kind of attitude problem or denial of the traumas—he saw the idea as stupid and dangerous to himself and his fellow soldiers for whom he maintained great vigilance and focus. I think he was correct.

I think another piece of this is the need to face the fact that many humans, precious ones created to bear the image of God in this world, are chronically living in situations that are making them sick. They live with constantly high cortisol levels, which we know makes our bodies sick. The circumstances make their brains sick, their emotions twisted, their sense of self shattered, and for many, their souls damaged. I daresay we prefer those who come to us post-trauma, but the truth of the matter is that there are millions of precious people who never get to live post-trauma.

In April I head to Timisoara, Romania. Underground in the sewers of that city live what are called the "rat children." They were dumped in the streets by poverty-stricken parents. These abandoned children have made a home for themselves in the sewers. Trauma levels are ridiculously high. They have been there a few decades and now have born children who live in those same sewers. There is not only chronic trauma, there is also no memory of anything else. There is no post-trauma for the rat children. In fact, for many there was never any pre-trauma either. It requires us to not only be creative in our responses but to also face our own assumptions, preferences and biases, which likely include dealing with traumas that were, not those that are and will be. It will require us to confront ourselves. I have seen many caregivers through the years who unwisely cling to the idea that if they just do it right, or get the sufferer to do it right, everything will be all better—as if it has never been. Children who live in sewers will never become adults who are all better, no matter how much you do. Child soldiers will never grow up to be adults who did not kill people. It is difficult for us to be faithful in such work, never denying that this world does indeed still lie in the power of the Evil One. We can love and build up and support and bring change little by little in the sewers of this world, but there is only one who can make it all better. And he has not promised to do so until he returns, which means we need to face great evil with partial outcomes while remaining faithful. It is a hard school, as most of you know.

Musing about the issues is merely a starting point for dialogue, not the answer. Some of you have more global experience with those in continuous traumatic circumstances; many of you have years of experience with trauma and its impact and what builds resiliency. The work needs global and urban trauma heads, clinical trauma heads and the input of those living in these situations working together if it is to be wise, ethical, and effective. My hope is that out of this will come conversations, ideas, recommendations, and challenges that will benefit those of our brothers and sisters in this world for whom the ideas of safety and stability, let alone the experience of such things, is lost or has never been known.

So, let me muse by returning to some basic concepts that I have used and written about throughout the years. Some of you may be familiar with these concepts from *Counseling Survivors of Sexual Abuse*. The first concept is voice. Trauma is the experience of the self, silenced. The words of the victim, the feelings of the victim, the thoughts of the victim, and the choices of the victim are silenced. When we are overwhelmed we are focused on surviving, living, defending, getting out, or disconnecting. Normally when we hurt we say "ouch" about even small things. The trauma victim's ouch is completely shut down. Their opinions, ideas, thoughts, or feelings are completely disregarded and irrelevant—whether it is a war, a rape, or a tsunami.

The experience of trauma is diametrically opposed to the image of God in man. The voice of God spoke everything into existence. He entered history as *the Word* made flesh. To be created in his image is to have a self that projects itself into the world. To be in his image is to have voice, creative expression, thought, and will brought to bear on this world. When you have been brutally raped or lost everything and/or everyone you love, all of that is crushed. The self is shattered, fractured, and silenced and does not speak who it is into the world.

The second concept is relationship. We were created in relationship to God and to one another—and God entered this world in order to reestablish relationship through his death. His image is reflected in relationship. The voice of the triune God has said aloneness is not good. Humans long for safe relationship. We seek it out even as infants. Trauma violates and shatters relationship. It brings betrayal, fear, humiliation, loss of dignity, shame, and it obliterates safety. In essence trauma removes the components of good relationship. Trauma isolates; it endangers; it creates barriers and destroys bonds. Empathy is destroyed; safety is trashed; connection is severed. It is also true that trauma profoundly impacts our relationship with God as he is often viewed through a powerfully distorted lens that frankly leads to seeing him as the Evil One. The violation and destruction of faith at times of great suffering and loss is one of the greatest tragedies of the traumatic experience.

The third concept is power, and by that I mean impact or choice. God called us to rule and subdue. Those are power words. They mean to go have impact; go make things happen; go grow; go create and change things. Trauma removes and squashes power. The victim is rendered powerless, whether by a tsunami, an earthquake, a rape, or a war. The victim feels useless, powerless, and ineffective, and the loss of dignity and purpose is profound. We were meant to work, to make things happen, to see things change simply because we are there. The other possible outcome is that the victim under threat and duress has had their power harnessed for evil and been forced to exercise it in ways that are morally wounding and shattering to the self.

All of these aspects: voice, relationship, and power are rooted in the character of God and evidenced in the image of God in human beings. Trauma destroys the essence of what it means to be human and to have the dignity of carrying the image of God. Dignity, vibrancy, impacting, creativity, building, producing— all life bearing—are silenced and crushed by trauma, especially chronic trauma. Anything we do in response to trauma needs to be built on the foundation of the image of God in us and work in restorative ways towards the recovery of that image. At the same time, we must not replicate the experience of trauma or destroy that image.

So let us take these three aspects of the image of God (voice, relationship, and power) plus our understanding of the experience of trauma and weave them together as we think through our response to a person living with ongoing and relentless trauma. In brief, we want to restore voice, build relationship, and increase power while not overwhelming the self or increasing fear or helplessness. Those are the parameters of our work. Honor of the other—the image-bearing one—is foundational to the work—their voice, their choices (including refusals), their culture, their current circumstances, their ways of expression, and their need to not be overwhelmed yet again.

The Western model has typically been to make room for the victim's story in the context of a safe, one-on-one therapeutic relationship and strengthened their use of voice and power in the world. Everyone reading this knows that model as it stands can be imminently helpful and redemptive, but cannot and should not be picked up as it is and transplanted around the world. Even if it worked everywhere, which it does not, it would not practically be possible. Everyone reading this knows such a model would not work in a refugee camp or a combat zone. I think, however, we would be unwise to simply trash it because it has components that have been helpful in the West. Those components are helpful because they are based on the nature of human beings who are suffering.

I said in the last chapter that when I teach about living with trauma memories the first stage involves talking, tears, and time. As we typically think about it, to tell the story is to immerse oneself in it, to let down your guard and to face it and feel it again. To do so is to become vulnerable. Vulnerability while under fire is not a wise thing. The story is not told to express or feel or give words to the unspeakable. The story is told for the purpose of protecting.

That is a guiding principle in all ethical trauma work; however, it is ratcheted up considerably in cases of ongoing trauma. When I work with someone in my office and help ground them so they are not overwhelmed by their trauma before they leave, I do not generally have to consider whether or not they will get shot or raped on their return home.

Such care needs to be greatly intensified when the person still lives with trauma. In other words, "I would like you to tell me your story *to whatever degree you choose* for the purpose of working together to think through how you (and your family) can protect your hearts and minds and bodies in the midst of the suffering you are experiencing." The parameters are clear and include containment. The statement restores dignity by giving voice (tell your story), by restoring a sense of power (however you choose), in relationship (we are working together) with a shared work/purpose—with all of that done honoring the truth of a brutal and a painful reality. You are bestowing dignity by partnering with them and honoring both their reality and their potential in the midst of that.

Another vital aspect of "talking" is lament. It is a contained way of telling the truth of your story without getting lost in it. We lament over injustice, trauma, grief, and loss. Lament is spoken to God. Lament is full of emotion. It can be done collectively, which binds people together (see example in Appendix B). Lament can tell the story, express the tears, and connect to God and others. Much is restorative while great grief is made more manageable and contained. Then even when trauma is ongoing, there is a known and safe place to communally express it.

The second piece of dealing with trauma is developing loving relationships, work or purpose, and faith. Those aspects are much more communal in nature. The traditional Western way is more individualistic. Much of the world considers community to be primary in ways the Western mind often fails to grasp. I believe in responding to those living with ongoing trauma that we need to begin with fostering and building community, rather than tending to the individual stories as a prerequisite to that work. Here it is more linear of course—partly due to our culture and perhaps sadly due to the lack of effective community care in the Western church. For example, the church delivers the trauma survivor to the professional, and then after the work is done the survivor returns to the church to be a productive member of the community.

Let's consider a few examples to get our thinking stirred. I think we need to consider this model with our returning vets. They experience a loss of purpose/mission and the loss of their band of brothers. Many have spoken to me of feeling useless and without purpose and as if they have "lost their family." Efforts that bring traumatized vets together on a mission (such as relief work in Haiti) reconnect them to their fellow warriors and a sense of purpose. Doing this in conjunction with the traditional trauma therapy work is much more likely to build their resiliency.

Anyone who has done trauma work in the inner city understands these dynamics. Much of our inner city is communal and divided by ethnicity. That division can be a problem (e.g., gang wars), but it can also be strength. How do single mothers earning minimum wage, having little to no education, and living in a violent neighborhood survive and nurture children so they do not repeat the cycle? A mother cannot do it alone. Her voice needs to be heard (she wants more for her children). Her resources are minimal; she needs others to help her. Her voice and joining with others can have impact. It happens. Someone becomes block captain and organizes things—overseeing what the kids are doing, finding a basketball hoop, getting trash picked up. Adults work together to walk children to school so there is greater safety. They help each other get kids to school, and parents' voices are heard in schools that used to silent parents. Those who can read, read to others' children. Hard? Yes, of course. Discouraging? Absolutely. But such things restore dignity, turn a ship little by little, shape a community, and restore hope.

A few years ago there was a study of a refugee camp where the UN and/or NGOs had made rules that residents could not pick up sticks for firewood. No teachers were brought in because it was a temporary camp, and nothing was organized so everyone felt useless, hopeless, and profoundly depressed. All signs of family and community life were missing. The levels of depression and suicide were high. Fyodor Dostoevsky said this, "Deprived of meaningful work, men and women lose their reason for existence; they go stark raving mad."[1] This is compared to refugee camps that are struggling for food and clean water and whose residents live in extreme poverty but who are organized communally, have tasks to accomplish, teach their children or send them to be taught every day, practice their traditions and celebrations in whatever way they can, and worship as they choose. Are many traumatized? Absolutely, and certainly some cannot function. But, however minimal, there is life there and purpose and hope and the sense of the next generation being given important things.

Such a place is still overwhelmingly sad and lacking in so many things humans need and long for. But nurturing those aspects that are integral to the image of God in us are good, and I believe need to govern our trauma work when the people we are caring for live with relentless trauma.

So when people have safety and stabilization and are living post-trauma I work toward helping them with talking, tears, and understanding that time is a factor. As they give voice to their story, they have power to control how much and when to stop. They do so in the context of a safe and respectful relationship. They express what happened, its impact on their lives, and their deep grief and questions of God in response. We then move toward finding a new purpose, building healthy relationships, and growing their faith.

When trauma is continuous, those factors are still present and needed for healing, but I think they need to be ordered differently and the focus is not so much on recovery or healing as it is on managing, containing, working together, surviving with dignity, and protecting those things which are valued and can be protected (such as pouring into the next generation). That means the talking and tears are far less, and expression alone is not the goal but rather that expression is done so as to build and protect and nurture life in the midst of the things of death that are all around. That process is not linear, which is more the Western model, but has all the factors simultaneously woven together and strengthened.

So the goal of the story is to restore dignity, voice, relationship, and power. Bad storytelling or unregulated telling replicates trauma. The person feels violated by telling—overwhelmed, powerless, and threatened. As with the actual trauma that violation makes a person leave—through substance abuse, violence to others, numbness, or dissociation. This is hard to do under any circumstances, but even more so when the trauma is ongoing because options for respite and stability are little to none. When I work in my office and we look at the trauma story, I always build in recovery time into the session and work with the client regarding respite following the session. Ongoing trauma means facing the truth in much smaller bites with respite running throughout and being the larger portion, not the bookends.

Part of what I gather from some of the research is that those in refugee camps who do nothing exacerbate their trauma and can become morosely depressed. We have said three things are vital in the midst of trauma: 1) ongoing connection and community, a sense of belonging together, ability to share one another's sorrows and even little joys that may arise. Isolation, hiding, not talking will make it worse; 2) a sense of purpose and meaning—sharing together to build the housing, participating in educating the children, gathering wood for a fire, telling stories to each other or sharing rituals. These give dignity and a sense of purpose in the midst of devastation; 3) faith—this includes lamenting together (which I think needs some guidance so as not to be out of control and overwhelm others); singing together; worshiping together—reminders of God when he appears absent and abandoning. These can all be simple, basic things—but they fight against despair, silence, isolation, and meaninglessness—all of which will take trauma and use it to choke their hearts and minds and souls. These things bend toward life and participation in them, even in the midst of trauma, is the bending of the will toward living.

One other point is quite significant when working with Christians in these situations. All of us, no matter what our lives are like, have a difficult time remembering that our God's kingdom is the kingdom of the heart. We tend to be far more concerned about external kingdom building than internal. In the West that takes certain forms—big churches, success, fame, etc., and meanwhile hearts harbor fear, jealousy, greed, and unfaithfulness. I suspect that when externals are snatched from us, we are equally vulnerable in different ways to being focused on externals rather than the heart. I want to be exceedingly careful here because I do not in any way mean to minimize the crushing losses of family, home, food, education, order, and safety that so many in the world suffer on a daily basis. I know there are many who spiritualize everything as if such trauma did not matter. I was, however, quite struck by some comments of Sudanese refugees participating in a workshop on trauma (quoted with permission):

> Before coming to the workshop my heart was not good. I was not happy during that time. I was thinking a lot about my family. But I came to the workshop and my heart has now become better because we have been sharing together in our groups and praying for each other.
>
> Since before coming to the workshop I was having so much pain in myself for what happened to me a long time ago and also to the enemies whom were attacking us everywhere. It was very painful in my heart to think of all of these problems which were going on for many years up until now. Now I am able to express my feelings in my heart about these

things. . . . The pain that was in my heart is less now that I have done this workshop.

When I came to the workshop I thank God through you very much that now I have learned things I never knew before. I pray and hope that God will help me to learn more and more about this trauma healing because it is the most helpful way of solving human problems here in the camp. This is how we can create right relationships between us here as we are healed ourselves. *So you must pray for me as I help others.*

These are people suffering from ongoing trauma but who have focused on their hearts and their relationships with God and others. They have hope. They see change—not in their situation—but in themselves. They sense purpose—telling others, teaching others what they have learned and helping others in their need. These are people whose suffering is excruciating who will bear fruit in the lives of others. They are burdened excessively, but they have hope and love. Trauma turned their lives upside down—and still does—but it has not killed the soul.

There was a remarkable story in *World* magazine titled "War of Northern Aggression" by Mindy Belz. She writes the following about the situation in southern Sudan:

> The spiritual outlook is improving too. Many churches have been planted among the refugee camps. At a recent baptismal Sunday service, pastors set up 25 buckets of water beneath the trees. Three men manned each bucket, two with plastic cups and one with a towel. A choir sang, and a pastor preached, and hundreds came forward to the buckets two by two—men and women, boys and girls. When the service ended, church leaders had baptized more than 1,300 refugees.[2]

There may be no school, but there can be teaching. There may be no church, but there can be preaching. There may be little food, but there can be shared traditions. There may be little of anything, but there can be shared singing. How? When the people come together in communal relationships with shared goals, purpose, lament, and faith while the story of the trauma is yet being lived, while creation is groaning loudly there can be buckets of water to welcome others into the community of faith.

So the concept is this: what can we ease or take from the bucket of fear, the bucket of grief, the bucket of overwhelmed, the bucket of hopeless helplessness? And what can we put in the bucket of voice, the bucket of relationship, the bucket of power? What can we add to the bucket of work or purpose and the bucket of faith? It is little by little work, just as God told Israel about their enemies: "I will drive them out before you little by little, until you become fruitful and take possession of the land" (Exodus 23:30).

In summary, we know that the whole creation does indeed groan, and as we are involved in this work it increases our own groaning. But we also know that the Son of God has come and that we as his people have been planted in the midst of great suffering to bring buckets—buckets for holding small pieces of large traumas, buckets for containing grief beyond measure, buckets of life and dignity to bestow on the crushed ones, and buckets of the Living Water, the One who deals with us all and nourishes us little by little for he knows we are but dust. May we honor the suffering ones who bear his image by our willingness to take small steps of truth and love so they will not be submerged yet again—for the sake of Lord of heaven and earth who took such steps for us.

CHAPTER 11

The Many Faces of Grief

How many of us have experienced grief? It is a universal human experience. All of us go through it many times in our lives. Since we cannot escape it, let us consider what it is and how a journey through grief might look. If you are going on a journey, it is better if you know something of the way: Where am I going? What will I experience? Where might I lodge? How long will it take? And what do I need to help me along the way?

Grief is the result of some kind of death. Death is the unwanted guest in human life. We do not want it; we often fear it; we cannot command it; and we hate our helplessness. Some of us work hard to ignore it. We do not want to talk about it. We work hard so we do not have to face its slow destruction of our physical beings. And yet it relentlessly comes into our lives and the lives of those we love. The experience is universal. It cuts across gender lines, racial lines, cultural lines, national lines, economic lines, and age groups. None of us can escape an encounter with this uninvited guest whose name is Death.

Death is not something we only encounter at the end of our lives, is it? We meet it hundreds of times in a lifetime. We meet it in every ending: the death of a dream, the end of a relationship or a job, the loss of a child who leaves home, a chronic illness, a rape, an abuse, and in war. We even meet death in times of joy—a wedding, the birth of a child, a graduation—all times of great joy, yet they carry within them the death of something else, the nature of a relationship or a season of life.

We often cope by distancing ourselves from this uninvited guest. Our own death is far away. We define death as narrowly as possible in efforts to deny its persistent presence. We consider only our physical end as death so all the little deaths that occur between here and there can be called something else. Yet, if the truth is told, you and I are involved in a continuing process of dealing with death while we still live. That means we are often grieving.

Now none of us likes grieving. It hurts. We want to avoid it. We see it as an enemy. However, let us be clear today as we consider this difficult subject: Grief is not our enemy. We are faced with a formidable foe, but that foe is not grief; it is death itself. Grief is not our enemy. It hurts; the pain can be overwhelming. But grief is also a sign of life and healing and mending. Anything that is of life is not an enemy. We must be careful in our thinking to separate out death from grief. If we do not, we will seriously misunderstand what it is like for us to live in this dying world, and we will respond inappropriately to the grief of others.

Grief is a process that takes time and helps us mend after a loss. It is painful and we want to avoid it, but if we do so, we will get stuck and healthy mending will never occur. We experience many little deaths while we live, and we grieve in response to these deaths. We must confront death in the lives of those we love. They leave us to grieve for them. Ultimately, we must face our own death, grieving as we die and then leaving others to grieve for us. You cannot live in this world and not grieve. To live here and not grieve is to be out of touch with reality. It is a failure to live in truth.

How are we as the people of God to think about the many deaths we must encounter and the resulting process of grieving? How are we to care for ourselves as we grieve? How are we to care well for others as they grieve?

Definition

When we talk about grief, what is it exactly that we are discussing? The dictionary defines grief as "intense emotional suffering caused by loss, misfortune, injury or evil of any kind."[1] It carries with it the idea of great sorrow and of bearing up under a heavy weight or burden. Obviously grief can occur under many circumstances and when it comes, it weighs heavy or pushes down on a life.

Causes of Grief

What kinds of things can cause us to experience grief? I want to make certain we grasp the many faces of loss and do not simplistically assume that grief only occurs when a loved one dies.

1. Death: This is the most obvious reason for grief. The loss of a loved one or the death of a close family member (child, spouse, parent, good friend, or a grandparent), especially due to sudden or tragic death, has been uniformly identified as the most devastating type of loss and the most potent stressor in ordinary life.

2. Health: Chronic illness, waning health, amputation, and the aging process—anything that means the loss of one's body as it has been known—will result in grief. In the case of something like chronic illness the grief can go on for years because one loss is piled on top of another as the illness continues.

3. Place: Loss of either physical place or loss of position or status brings grief. The loss of home, church, community, job, and reputation can all bring on a grief reaction. This is often complex because you may move due to a better job, which is a good thing, and yet grieve the loss of many things and people. It often confuses people.

4. Relationships: Loss of a friend, a romantic attachment, separation or divorce, infertility, miscarriage, a child lost

in a drug addiction, or a loved one lost in a severe mental illness all cause grief that is often complicated because in some of these situations the person is gone—but not gone.

5. Trauma and abuse: These experiences (sexual abuse, rape, domestic abuse, etc.) cause the loss of security, safety, sense of self, faith, and life as we have known it. They alter the way we think about ourselves and others, all of which result in grief.

6. Natural disasters, terrorism, and war: These events produce multiple and devastating losses for individuals and whole communities, and sometimes for an entire nation. The sudden traumatic loss caused by disasters may continue for a significant amount of time, especially when displacement is involved. It is normal for grief to be intensely felt and protracted under such circumstances. An experience of safety, security, and predictability in the world is challenged. Uncertainty, fear, and anxiety become part of everyday life.

7. Things: A precious object, items of great sentimental value. This is especially true when the lost thing is connected to a person or way of life we have lost.

We clearly experience grief due to myriad losses. The Bible says, "For we know that the whole creation groans . . . and not only this, but also we ourselves . . . groan within ourselves" (Romans 8:22–23). It is in part reflecting on the fact that grief is ever-present in this world where things are not as God created them to be because Death has entered. The word *groan* carries in it the sense of many joining together in the experience of communal grieving. In other words, the whole creation, all of us together, grieve under the weight of death. Grief is not African or American or Cambodian—grief is universal.

Scriptures

There is a lot in the Bible about grief. And if you think about it, grief often profoundly impacts someone's faith, threatens it even. Loss and grief raise questions about God and his goodness and trustworthiness for many people. The Bible recognizes grief as something common to humans and frankly speaks about it in ways that might surprise many in the church. It certainly does not suggest we should get over it quickly or that strong grieving is not acceptable to God.

Listen to Jeremiah 31:15: "A voice is heard in Ramah, lamentation and bitter weeping. Rachel weeping for her children; she *refuses to be comforted* for her children, because they are no more" (italics added). Words such as these have been fitting many times throughout the world—in Nazi Germany, in Rwanda, in Congo.

Hannah, grieving her infertility, speaks of pouring out her great anguish and grief (1 Samuel 1).

Jeremiah said, "My eyes fail from weeping, I am in torment within, my heart is poured out on the ground because my people are destroyed" (Lamentations 2:11 NIV). The book of Lamentations is devoted to grief and reflects many of the thoughts and feelings experienced by those who grieve. It expresses deep pain, questions God, and speaks of feelings of abandonment and great sorrow. We will talk more about lamenting a bit later. Such responses to loss, when expressed, are often greeted with criticism or correction from others.

Even Jesus himself felt great grief over the death of his friend Lazarus. He wept and those who witnessed his tears interpreted them as a clear sign of the depth of the friendship.

Journey Through Grief

Grieving takes both time and energy. It is like a journey that takes us through several different villages. People grieve uniquely and so

everyone does not travel through these villages in the same way.
The order may be different or some may find themselves repeating
certain parts and visiting one village many times.

Village 1: This is the village of shock and denial. People often
feel numb when they first experience the loss and they keep
thinking, "Oh no, no; this cannot be true." They cannot absorb the reality and are stunned by the news. They often sit
and stare with no idea of time passing. Denial makes people
disbelieve the loss or sometimes they immediately try to return to normal routines so it can seem like nothing happened
or changed. Denial can feel good. It functions like a drug for
a broken heart. Denial is not always bad because it helps us
accept the loss bit by bit so we are not overwhelmed. We can
only take in the truth little by little.

Village 2: This is the village of the body. Grieving often
has physical manifestations. Chest pains, feeling like you
cannot breathe, a racing heart, hollowness in the stomach,
and sweaty palms are not unusual. Sleeping and eating patterns are often disrupted. The body is involved in the grieving process along with the mind and the emotions. Fear and
anxiety, which often accompany grief, can frequently manifest in physical ways.

Village 3: Anger is typically a part of grief. It is often
our response once the pain of the loss settles in. Initially we
feel overwhelming sadness, disappointment, hurt, and fear.
Anger is a response to our pain. Sometimes it is directed at
the one who is gone and other times it is directed at God.
Sometimes, when we are overwhelmed, we share our anger
with everyone around us! We feel betrayed by God and forsaken. How can we trust the One responsible for our loss?
He could have stopped it and he didn't. Death makes us feel
small, vulnerable, and insecure. Loss brings us face-to-face
with our own mortality and our lack of control. It leaves us
facing our dependency on God, while also facing the reality that he has allowed this difficult thing to occur. Grieving

always challenges our faith. I think part of the reason for this is because no matter how much we trust God, to some degree we all trust not so much in *him* as in what he has given. For example, I trust God is good because certain things in my life remain safe and secure. When those are removed by a death of some kind, the very character of God is thrown into question for us. Anger can also be a way of rejecting the loss. Anger distracts us from the sadness and pain and can energize us. Anger is sometimes preferred over sorrow. Anger can feel stronger, even more alive than sadness.

Village 4: This is the village of no hope. When people get to this village, they feel sad and without hope. They have trouble getting up and running their lives. The griever becomes passive as he/she realizes the loss is real and there is absolutely nothing he/she can do about it. Illusions are gone and it feels like any future has gone with them. Sorrow swallows everything else up, and the griever expects nothing else to follow. This is the darkest place in the grieving process. It is the depths, the pit, and there seems to be no light here. Yet the emptiness of this face of grief has within it the seeds of surrender to the awful truth that is the beginning of acceptance.

Village 5: This is the village of new beginnings. In the hopelessness it somehow begins to slowly dawn on the griever that he/she is still among the living. There has been a death, yes, but it has not been ours. We are still here and will probably be here tomorrow. True, we are not the same and the pain of our loss has left a scar. Something begins to shift, however, and instead of looking down or in we begin to look out and up. We are surprised that life has gone on. We thought all life had stopped. We watch as an observer for awhile and then ever so slowly begin the process of connecting with life again, the loss a part of us but no longer swallowing us up. We reenter life changed, more humble. We are far more aware of our status as creatures, our frailty, and our finiteness. We are aware of the temporary nature of things and that all things here are temporal and will either leave us or be left by us. We also come to see that the very God we thought had abandoned us has come to dwell with us so that this hideous enemy Death, whose attack flattened us, might be destroyed forever. It is a small taste of the resurrection.

Everyone's grief experience is unique. No two people go through the grieving process in the same way or on the same timetable. The aspects of grief do not occur in a linear fashion. Many of these aspects cycle around again and again or even occur simultaneously.

Walter Wangerin in his book *Mourning into Dancing* wrote the following:

> Each griever's experience will be unique. And she can feel, in the event itself, frightfully lonely and bewildered. And pain may persuade her that this grief is the evil. In fact, death is the evil, not grief. And we who are her friends will know this; we who choose to become her comforters, will learn the general pattern of the process, the purposes of each aspect of grief so that we might name her wounds and companion her sorrows till grief has brought her back to life and wholly to us again.[2]

All of the villages in grief have one overarching task: learning to let go, learning to live without what once was, learning to wear something that feels like it does not fit. Perhaps some of you have had the experience of having your dominant hand or arm in a cast. While you wear that cast you repeatedly, hundreds of times a day, go to do something requiring the use of that hand and find it is not there for you. The smallest of tasks cannot be done the way you usually do them. Things you did without thinking, things you did with ease either must be done differently or not at all or with the help of others. Once the throbbing pain wears off, you find yourself constantly confronted with your limitations due to the absence of your hand, and you feel frustrated, angry, and depressed.

However, over time you find new ways, you adapt, and you learn to live with the absence. It is not the same. You certainly want your hand back, but you go on without it. Now the analogy breaks down in many ways, but I use it to give you a small picture of what loss is like, how we might respond to it, and how we learn to live with it.

When we lose someone we love or a way of life is lost to illness or trauma shatters, we find we keep trying to do life as before. We keep looking for the one we have lost. We expect them at every turn. We expect our bodies to function as they used to. We keep being surprised at our limitations. We must learn to live with the absence death has brought, and we bump into that wall over and over and over again. It is a crisis time and the word *crisis* in part means "a separating." We think of a before and an after—before a death and after, before a rape and after, before a job loss and after. Life was one way and now, forever changed, it is another way.

Steps toward Grief Resolution

Step 1: Admitting the loss has taken place and that it is final. Accepting the finality of the loss is a difficult place to reach. It takes a long time. The mind rejects such a thought. We imagine other things that might have happened with other possible outcomes, we attempt to bargain with God, we engage in forms of denial, and we refuse to alter our normal routines and surroundings. Our refusal to accept the finality of the loss softens over time. People often say to us, "You have to just accept it." As if there is a button to push. There is no button. Acceptance takes much time, much time.

Step 2: Experiencing and expressing all the emotions and thoughts accompanying the loss. People often do things to assist themselves in the process. They look at old photographs, they revisit places, they want to talk about their memories, or they write about what they remember or how they feel. Sometimes others respond negatively to such things, as if we are torturing ourselves or making things worse. However, it is actually helpful and necessary in the grieving process. It gives voice to the pain and the loss.

Step 3: Finding a way to let go or say good-bye. Much of the early aspects of grief involve clinging to what was. As the process moves on over time, the clinging is less fierce and little by little the griever's hold on what was lost is relinquished. Obviously, when someone dies, the funeral is part of that process but it occurs at the very beginning stages and often feels unreal as a result. Sometimes people feel the need to do something much later in the process as a memorial or a way of saying good-bye when they have more fully faced the truth of their loss.

Step 4: Learning to reinvest the emotional and mental energy consumed by grieving in new relationships, endeavors, people, and projects. This obviously occurs toward the end of grieving as we begin, little by little, to turn to our present life rather than back toward our past. Sometimes people push us to do this early on as if it will help us "get over it." It is not something that can or should be done early on. It is the latter phase of a long process.

These are basically what we call the "tasks" of grieving, and if they do not happen, it is generally because someone has gotten stuck in the process somehow. There is something called "complicated grief" that can arise from a number of factors. Grief that falls in this category has a greater likelihood of getting stuck. An unresolved relationship with the deceased, especially one involving hostility, estrangement, circumstances that make the loss uncertain (no body can be found), socially unacceptable death (AIDS or suicide), a past history of unresolved grief, or personality characteristics that cause an inability to express feelings or tolerate any emotional distress can all result in complicated grieving. Too many deaths at once or violent deaths are also more difficult to resolve. Most grieving is resolved in a healthy way in two to four years.

The idea that it takes one neat little year is a myth. Certainly, it is most raw during the first year, but it is not completed just because a year has passed. If after several years the intensity and frequency of grieving has not lessened, or if someone is unwilling to deal with the material possessions of the deceased or they develop physical symptoms similar to the deceased or a phobia about illness or death, then it is probably wise to seek professional help.

Mistakes and Myths

I would like to go from here to consider some of the myths we often believe about grieving and some mistakes we make in trying to care for those who are mourning. These errors often lead us to hurt either ourselves or another because we misunderstand what grief is like. Keep in mind what we said earlier, that grief is not the enemy. The enemy is death. Grieving is a process that occurs in response to death, and it is that process that leads to life. If we mistake grief as the enemy, we run the risk of being an obstacle in the work that is necessary for healing to occur.

1. *We often think that grief extends over a set period of time, moves in a linear fashion through certain stages, and should be finished in a year.* Grieving generally takes considerably longer than a year. The faces of grief are many and experienced uniquely, both because of individual factors such as personality or history but also due to the kind of loss experienced. Loss of a child or a spouse differs from each other. Death and divorce differ. Loss of person and place differ. Trauma and physical death differ.

2. *Death that was anticipated is easier to grieve than death that was sudden.* One is not less challenging than the other; they are simply different. Each has difficult aspects peculiar to it. During an extended illness the person is still with you to some degree and yet the loss is continual, little

by little. Sudden death has a shock element that is very difficult. Death is final whether expected or sudden.

3. *Focus on the present; do not talk about your loss; keep busy and distract yourself.* If you do that, you will fail to grieve and you will end up stuck. Grief is work. It takes tremendous energy and is often exhausting. It is a worthwhile task and you will not heal by avoiding it.

4. *If you really had faith in God, grieving would be short or even unnecessary because he is sufficient.* Many well-meaning people believe this. The problem is that the Bible does not agree. Christ himself grieved as we mentioned before. He also has called those of us who follow him to weep with those who weep and to mourn with those who mourn. He has *not* called us to admonish them, to condemn their grieving, or to hurry them along. He has, in fact, called us to join *with them* in their grieving and weeping, not to make them like us. When we choose to "be with" someone that means that the grieving one sets the pace. I do not think he means only at the funeral. I think it means during their grieving process.

5. *Anger expressed in the process of grief should always be shut down.* Some feel it is wrong for a Christian to feel angry about their loss, but read the Psalms. They are often full of anger with the psalmist wondering where God is, what he is doing, and why he has seemingly forsaken one he claims to love. We will use a lament to look at this.

6. *It will make someone feel better to be reminded of what they have not lost or of the fact that it could have been worse.* These are the sentences that begin with "At least you did not . . ." or "They were so sick anyway" or "Aren't you glad you still have three healthy children?" Or "Aren't you glad you were just raped and not killed?" It is as if thinking about what you did not lose will alleviate the pain of what you did lose. You are grieving a real loss. Nothing

will make it other than a real loss. We do not grieve what we have but what we do not have. We compare our loss to the good we had, not to the bad that never happened. Remembering what we have does not fill the empty space.

How to Be a Comforter

People grieve differently. In giving you some of the faces of grief I have given you a way to interpret what you might see when someone grieves. There is not a set, right way to grieve. Part of comforting another is simply recognizing the various aspects of grief and normalizing them. When a mourner fears they are losing their mind as they cycle through various kinds of grieving, the comforter can assure them that they are not insane but this is indeed part of grieving. This reassurance brings stability in the griever's chaos.

Walter Wangerin says this to comforters: "Always take your cues from her. By instinct she is leading, in patience you are serving."[3] The mourner tells you what they feel and think. You do not teach. You listen; you read her and you reassure because you understand the nature of grief.

Expect anger. Do not be surprised by its intensity. Know that even if you are used as the target, it is not about you. As a comforter you have offered yourself to be present with the griever, giving her an opportunity to express what she feels. Keep in mind that connecting with you, even around anger, is a way of connecting with life when it feels like death has swallowed everything. The fact that you are privileged to be present means life has been allowed in place of death.

The role of comforter will expose you. If you have not accepted death or endings as a reality, your own included, the loss you are confronting in another will become a threat to you and you will react wrongly. I believe that one of the reasons we so often criticize another's process or rush them along is because we have not yet really accepted the reality, the finality of trauma, endings, or death ourselves. We want to make it less of a threat, to minimize it, and so we end up minimizing the griever's loss. Surely, it cannot be *that* bad.

The other side of this is to be so overwhelmed by death and the sorrow accompanying it that we get lost in the grief process with the mourner. We have no sense of detachment and cannot offer hope, for we struggle to stay connected with life. You, as comforter, are the bridge for the mourner. You must compassionately and patiently walk through the valley, visit the villages, with the one who grieves. At the same time, you must maintain a solid hold on life and the God of hope or you will provide no bridge out. Comforters must bridge the gap between death and hope.

Comforting is a ministry. You become a servant to the bereaved. The length of her grieving is determined by her, not by how long you can stand to be sad. Your work is to be with her where she is, not drag her out where you are more comfortable. After a funeral, everyone goes back to his or her own life—everyone, that is, except the griever. Six months later the world looks up and says, "Oh, is she *still* mourning?" As comforter, you stay with her.

After a chronic illness is diagnosed, everyone comes around the sick person. But years later it is easy to forget or say surely it is not that bad; it must be in his head. But over time he will watch his life eroded by the disease as it eats away at his body and his capacities. He will struggle with depression. His grief will be relentless. He will grieve his inability to do what his heart longs to do. He may eventually go from a full-orbed life to a bed. If he takes medication, he will suffer from side effects that will debilitate him in additional ways. His sleep will suffer, he will endure pain, and the daily care of his body will absorb more and more of his energy. This could last for decades. What will such a man need from you? How will you handle all of his emotions? Can you allow him to grieve, weep, and ask questions? Can you endure with him what he has no choice to endure? You will get tired of his illness and his limitations—so will he. You can leave; he cannot. Many will leave or forget. Grief does not come in neat packages.

Comforters are not usually explainers. They cannot answer the questions that always arise, nor do they try to. You do not know the purpose or the why. To try to answer such things makes you kin to Job's comforters in the Bible, who were no comforters at all. God was angry with Job's so-called comforters, for in their attempt to explain and answer, they had misrepresented God to the suffering one.

The role of comforter can also be practical. Grief distracts us. We get lost in it. We cannot think. Sometimes we neglect our bodies and need gentle reminders to do things for ourselves. Often we forget basic requirements like paying bills or doing wash. Food is of little interest and may need to be provided for awhile. Loving assistance is often necessary. Anniversaries, holidays, the first time of doing something alone or in a wheelchair, or not being able to do it at all needs the presence of comforters.

Comforters must take care of themselves. You will need to nurture your own connections to life. You need to be with others who are neither grieving nor helping the one who is. Remember, you are the comforter, not the griever. Your life must reflect that truth. You will need support. You will need friends who will do fun or silly things that bring laughter. You are being food for the grieving. It is vital you find places and ways to be fed.

Laments

We make the mistake of trying to hurry the grieving along and manage how much grief they express. We want it short and not too emotional. We want to answer their questions. I am afraid churches often treat grievers as if they are doing something wrong when they grieve, particularly if they seem to question God. The book of Psalms has in it a type of song we call a lament psalm. In a lament, people pour out their complaints to God and ask him to act on their behalf. David says in Psalm 13:1, "How long, O Lord? Will You forget me forever?" Laments encourage people to be honest with God and to speak the truth about their feelings and doubts and questions. They do not try to solve the problem; they simply let God know honestly what they are feeling and thinking. It is interesting to read some of these psalms (3, 4, 5, 6, 11, 13, 16, 17, 22). They express feelings many folks of faith would say show a lack of faith. But the laments are *to God*! Faith is being demonstrated by someone in extreme pain because they are talking to God about that pain and the questions it raises.

When Jesus first began his public ministry, he stood up in the synagogue and read from the prophet Isaiah and said that part of what he came to do was heal the brokenhearted and comfort those who mourn. The Scriptures also say that he has borne our griefs and carried our sorrows. That means we will never encounter any grief, our own or another's, that he has not carried. He is our Great Comforter. He is the expert in sorrow and longs for us to bring him our troubled hearts as we live in this troubled world. He himself bore the sorrows of the soul. He himself bore the crushing of the body. He says to us, *Come. Come to me.* It is like a loving mother would say to her small child, "Come, child. Come to me." He will hear your laments, your questions, your doubts, and your sorrow.

Everyone has known loss—in death, in rape or other trauma, in marriage, in war. All of us have been robbed by death of someone or thing we hold dear. Grieve, dear friends, grieve. Honor those you know who are grieving. But do not grieve as those without hope (1 Thessalonians 4:13). Jesus, the grief-bearer, leads the way in the path of sorrow, and he has promised that one day "He will wipe away every tear from our eyes; and there will no longer be any death; there will no longer be any mourning or crying or pain . . . and he who sits on the throne will make all things new" (Revelation 21:4–5, adapted).

"Therefore, my beloved brethren, be steadfast, immovable, always abounding in the work of the Lord, knowing that your toil is not in vain in the Lord" (1 Corinthians 15:58).

CHAPTER 12

Leadership, Power, and Deception in the Church and the Home

The issues of power and deception have become a topic of discussion in recent years. We read and hear about power and its abuse by individuals within families and churches and certainly within political circles and governments. We hear about deception and how cover-ups have been carried on for years by large institutions, organizations, and churches. These are critical topics for us to consider.

By way of introduction let me say why I think that is so. In addition to my work with trauma victims, I have also spent many years working with those in Christian leadership—pastors, missionaries, elders, professors, and others who have controlled the intellects, hearts, and sex lives of their sheep, using the sheep as food for themselves and their goals, rather than feeding the sheep God called them to serve. Needless to say, I have seen untold damage done to the body and name of Christ, often *in* the name of Christ. It is for the sake of that body and that wonderful name that I believe we need to wrestle with the issues of power and deception.

Many of you are involved in ministry and in positions of leadership. Some of you are Christian leaders around the globe. That means you have relationships where you hold a large amount of power in broken lives. You also minister to many who have been or are being abused and deceived. I believe that you are men and women who care about the body and the name of Christ our Savior. You do not want to hear the word "woe" from the throne of God, which is what he spoke to the shepherds of Israel who fed on the sheep, in the following words: "Those who are sickly you have not strengthened, the diseased you have not healed, the broken you have not bound up, the scattered you have not brought back, nor have you sought for the lost; but with force and with severity you have dominated them" (Ezekiel 34:4). These shepherds misused their God-given power and allowed the flock to become prey. God's response was to remove his flock from their care.

I believe that you desire to care for and protect the sheep of God. You do not want them to become prey to you or anyone else. Out of honor for that desire and concern for both the sheep and the glory of God, I would like to put some thoughts before you about the concepts of power and deception.

Definition of Power

What do we mean when we speak of *power*? The word simply means ability; capacity; ability or strength exercised to influence, impact, shape, or command. All of us have power. We have power because it was given to us by God at creation; it is part of the image of God in us. He told Adam and Eve to subdue the earth and rule over the living creatures on the earth. The words *subdue* and *rule* are power words that mean to make subservient; to prevail over; to dominate. Those are strong words and suggest that humans have the capacity to influence and shape their world.

It is important to note that though all of us have power, many humans feel powerless—some in certain contexts; others all the time. If you have ever lived or traveled in a poverty-stricken area or spoken to a sexual assault victim you have witnessed feelings of

utter powerlessness. Any of you who have parented small children
have had days when you *felt* tired, needy, weak, and powerless
and yet you knew you had power to damage your small children.
In fact, fragilities and weakness do not necessarily remove our
power at all. They do, however, make us more likely to use power
destructively. The weaker and needier we feel, the more dangerous
we are in a position of power because we are far more likely to neglect or use the sheep under our care to feed ourselves. Those who
feel powerless or inadequate often abuse power.

It is also important to note that power is not a fixed trait. An
individual's power varies with the context. For example, I have
power over my grown sons because I am their mother. However,
because they are well over six feet tall they have power over me
physically. A dynamic and brilliant CEO of a huge corporation
may wield tremendous power over many people, but put him in
front of his critical mother with whom he has many unresolved
issues and you will watch his power seemingly vanish, which in
turn may feed his need to abuse power in his home. His sense of
powerlessness in one arena may be the very thing driving his reach
for great power in another.

We cannot talk about power without discussing its flip side,
which is vulnerability. A vulnerable person is susceptible to attack
or injury. The word *vulnerable* comes from the Latin word "to
wound." A woman in a room full of men is physically vulnerable.
A client in a counselor's office is vulnerable. A parishioner in a
pastor's office is vulnerable. A patient in a doctor's office is vulnerable. A child with a parent is vulnerable. Whenever power is used
in a way that wounds the vulnerable, trust is exploited and abuse
has occurred. The word *abuse* basically means to use wrongly or
to mistreat. When a person with power uses another for his own
ends, abuse has occurred. The shepherd has used the sheep for
food.

Kinds of Power

We have said that power is not always a felt thing and that it changes with context. It is also true that there are many different kinds of power. Let me name a few. The most obvious, of course, is *physical power*. The bigger and the stronger have power over the smaller and the weaker—usually a man with a woman, a parent with a child, an older child with a smaller child. Physical power can also be presence rather than size. I am sure you have all known someone whose personality and charisma made them fill a room and dominate it; it gave a sense of largeness even though their physical size was not necessarily great.

Another kind of power is *verbal*. People who have a command of words, or are articulate, can dominate a conversation, a room, a relationship, a group, or a nation. We often use words to sway others or move them toward what we want. Words can be used to influence, shape, and encourage or to humiliate, deceive, maneuver, and control. Words have the power to move large numbers of people. Think of the power of the words of Martin Luther King, Jr. and the tremendous influence he had on people. Think of the power of the words of Adolf Hitler and the tremendous influence he had on people for evil. Think of times when you have used words to titillate, to condemn, or to shock because it met some need in yourself; it served your end in some way. Think of other times when you have used words to lift up, affirm, or give hope. Verbal power is a tremendous power.

A third kind of power is *emotional power*. Spouses have this kind of power over each other. Parents and children wield that kind of power. I have emotional power over my clients. People can wield power by their moodiness or their sensitivity. In essence, they hold everyone around them in bondage to their feelings. People walk on eggshells trying to prevent a particular mood from descending or being aggravated. Spouses that punish by withdrawal, refusing to talk for days or weeks on end, are using emotional power to hurt others. Preachers can use emotional power to sway or convince church members—for good or ill.

Knowledge, intellect, and skill also bring power. If I am smarter or know more or have more skill, then I have more power in those arenas. Those with a theological degree have "theological power" over others. It is assumed that they know more and they are given the right to tell the rest of us what is true. The power of a pastor in the theological realm is intensified by the fact that many see him as speaking for God; indeed, he may tell them that he is doing exactly that.

Some of us have *"psychological power."* Not only do we have knowledge of people that others do not have, it can include knowledge about how to maneuver and manipulate and play on the emotions of others. Many of us experience this imbalance of power regarding knowledge when we are ill and need to rely on physicians to tell us not only what is wrong but also how to fix it.

There is also *power of position.* Position can be literal, such as the position of president, CEO, director, pastor, therapist, or parent. Position also extends to the power of reputation or status. Those others labeled brilliant or godly or successful are accorded power by others on the basis of their reputation. They can simply walk into a room and because of their reputation people give their words and actions a certain weight or power.

It is critical to note that one person often has multiple kinds of power. Think about it. Position, combined with a large and/or dynamic physical presence, verbal skill, knowledge, and the capacity to sway people emotionally is a phenomenal combination. For example, let's take a dynamic physical presence, an articulate voice, emotional sway, and theological knowledge, roll it together in the position of pastor and put it in the room with a female (usually less powerful physically), a parishioner (less power in position), whose struggle or pain has rendered her somewhat inarticulate and who is theologically uncertain or struggling, and you have a set up for an abuse of power. Words, knowledge, skill, position, and emotion can all be used in concert to move or convince another human being who is vulnerable.

Take a teacher or dorm parent at a boarding school—an adult with knowledge in a powerful position—and put them with a child away from home—smaller and emotionally vulnerable—and it is not hard to see how verbal, physical, and sexual abuse can easily occur. Vulnerability, isolation, neediness, ignorance, emotional pain, and a lack of power make any individual extremely susceptible to abuse by another.

The Abuse of Power

Whenever power is used to exploit the vulnerable—to exploit trust—abuse has occurred. There are three components to the abuse of power: self-deception, deception of others, and coercion. Deception of others is inevitably preceded by deception of the self. We as human beings have a seemingly unlimited capacity to hide truths that are painful to us. We have an uncanny ability to suppress knowing what we know. We do so by, at least initially, twisting the truth just a shade. The most powerful lie of all is the lie that contains a likeness to the truth in some way. As a result self-deception can be the root of terrible evil. Self-deception is not the worst thing that you can do, but it is the means by which we do the most terrible things.[1]

The prophet Jeremiah offers us fascinating insight into the mechanisms of self-deception. A deceived person trusts in something human for sustenance until he no longer recognizes when good comes. In other words, he loses his capacity to discern good from evil. The result is that he who feeds himself in this way lives in the wilderness and does not see where he is. In contrast, the one who trusts God for sustenance is not afraid when drought threatens but remains green and bears fruit. The process of deception is subtle, painting a false color on things, cheating those who invest in such things, and finally resulting in their ruin.

The Dynamics of Deception of Self and Others

Self-deception becomes a habit of the mind. It essentially functions as a narcotic because it protects us from seeing or feeling
that which is painful to us. A person who is skilled in deception
is a person who is addicted to deceit. It deeply habituates the soul
to look at things diametrically opposed to the way God sees. It is
about hiding, pretending, ignoring, camouflaging, and covering.
Have you ever seen someone on a sidewalk or in a store that you
did not want to encounter? Have you then had the experience of
suppressing what you know? You turn your head or your eyes; you
go a slightly different route in order to "keep from seeing them."
The deception can be carried even further if you encounter them
in spite of your maneuvering and you respond with "surprise" that
they are there.

Another aspect of self-deception is our ability to justify to ourselves that which we know is wrong. I speed because I am late, I
eat too much chocolate because I worked hard, or I speak harshly
to a family member because I had a bad day. I know speeding, too
much chocolate, and harsh words are wrong, but I use external
things to justify breaking the rules—man or God's. We hear this
when working with domestic abuse. In other words, "I was abusive because he/she. . . . It is painful to me to face my wrongdoing
and so I deceive myself, I administer the narcotic of deceit, in order
to avoid that pain."

We also deceive ourselves by comparing or contrasting. We
compare a bad thing we are doing to a good thing with the implication that the good somehow lessens the evil of the bad. For example, I may cheat on my taxes but at least I go to church, or I hate
my mother but at least I have never told her. We apply the narcotic
of self-deception in order to maintain a good feeling or image of
ourselves, even though what we are doing is wrong.

Another way we often deceive ourselves is by the use of mis-
direction. This occurs in many relationships—it occurs frequently

in marriage. One spouse tells the other something they did wrong and they respond by pointing out something wrong with him or her. A weakness or failure in the person who is correcting you becomes your focus rather than facing the truth about what was said. Again, the narcotic is used to avoid the pain of facing the truth.

George Adam Smith, Scottish theologian and Hebrew scholar, in his reflections on Psalm 36 gives us a biography of deceit. Deception's origin is in the human heart and none of us is exempt. It is there; you and I know its presence in our own hearts and we have heard its whisper. If we are honest, all of us have yielded to its whisper. All of us know the heart experience of temptation and the immediate response of self-deception, seemingly working in concert with the temptation to convince us of its rightness or to justify it in some way. We have mentioned more ordinary examples already, such as speeding because I am late. Do keep in mind the object of our deception can also be a good thing used wrongly, such as verbal skills, theological knowledge, or a ministry goal. It is easy to use God-given gifts to lift ourselves up, to get our way, and render ourselves never wrong or at least unaccountable to anyone. When we have a fear of God in our hearts then another powerful factor is introduced into this battle in the soul. If there is no fear of God or we silence that fear, then we can easily move into thinking by deception that we can engage in the sin without harm to ourselves. This is not unlike what the Enemy told Eve—you will not die; it will not hurt you. We convince ourselves we can stop; one more time will not hurt; one more bite; one more look; one more justification; one more injection—of a substance or getting it our way. If we engage in such self-delusion long enough we will, over time, lose our taste for the good *and* our power to loathe evil. We eventually silence the voice of God and our response of fear to that voice. The problem of course is that sin *will* hurt us; it will lead to death. Once we begin removing our taste for good and our power to hate evil, then we only habituate that which causes our death.

As deception becomes a way of life, evil can be easily practiced by an increasingly dead soul that then becomes presumptuous, planning and actively participating in evil. Over time the possibility for penitence is destroyed and the habit ends in soul death. Smith says the stages are: temptation, delusion, audacity, and habit ending in death.[2] In other words, temptation arises, self-deception or delusion joins in, evil is termed good or at least justified, the choice is habituated, and the prisoner is trapped, actively participating and barreling toward death, no longer able to stop.

When it is laid out like this, it all sounds horrifying and repellent. However, it can show up in our ministries and our lives in subtle ways. I fear many people are suffering terribly because they live with evil and have gone to leadership only to be sent home, disbelieved. Deception and great evil can easily lie below the surface of high position, great theological knowledge, stunning verbal skills, and excellent performance. If the Enemy of our souls can appear as an angel of light, then surely an evil human being who is in fact mimicking him can appear well-clothed, theologically articulate, and beautiful to the human eye.

Suppose a woman comes to her pastor and she is timid and not very articulate, perhaps a bit hysterical and afraid. She tells him that her husband is beating her or sexually molesting her daughter or raging and verbally abusive or emotionally entangled with another woman in the church. She tells it haltingly, without much clarity, nervously pulling on her sleeve. Her husband is a successful businessman who gives large sums of money to the church. He is a fellow elder and well-known to the community. He has a seminary degree and is well-read. He can sway groups when there is conflict in the church. He is quite charismatic and everyone thinks he is a fine man. In such circumstances it is very, very easy for two things to happen. One is to presume outward appearances tell the story of the heart. Surely someone with characteristics such as I have described would not possibly also be someone who beats his wife or molests his daughter or is inappropriately involved with another woman. We think, *I know this man; this is not how he acts.* Two, if any doubt creeps in, it is also easy for the hearer to lean on his/her own capacity for self-deception and talk himself out of considering the truth of what has been told. In other words, I will discredit the wife because of her presentation, and credit the husband because of his success, plus—how can I disrupt the church and community with this. If it were exposed and shown to be true, the church would lose money, reputation and possibly be divided over it.

Of course things get even more complicated. The fact is, the hearer/witness is potentially invested in the truth not being heard and exposed and so the truth-teller is sent away, discredited and unprotected. You see, often we think our positions, places, institutions, and organizations are worth more protection than truth because if we stand with truth—or even exploring the possible truth of something—we risk the loss of what we hold dear. We do not, in fact, believe that sin is the worst thing in the world. And in that we are just as deluded as the one we are hearing about or sitting across from in our office.

It is so easy to get caught up in the externals and believe that *their* destruction would be the worst thing that could happen. When someone comes forward and exposes sin sometimes the first response is to silence the truth-teller and to be concerned about how the truth will damage the marriage, the church, or the institution. The governing force becomes protecting the form at all costs, even if its substance is rotten. Yet our God responded to the Israelites when they were continuously disobedient to him by destroying the forms so the substance could be exposed and cleansed and eventually transformed. He hates evil and nothing is valuable enough to protect it over and above dealing with that evil. Marriage is good and God-ordained, but evil in marriage is never acceptable. Church is good and God-ordained, but evil in the church is never acceptable.

We use all manner of self-deceptions to protect ourselves from information that would cause us to view ourselves in ways we do not like. This mechanism enables us to ignore, commit wrongs, and feel justified or more righteous when in fact we ought to face our failures, abuses, and sins or our complicity with evil in others' lives so as to protect our own image, reputation, organization, or work.

A crisis is a separating time in that it separates the two roads that can be followed and exposes the heart of the chooser. Let's consider what can happen at the point of crisis with someone enslaved to abusive behavior. The crisis comes—sexual abuse is exposed, domestic violence is revealed, the cell phone records expose a sexual relationship with a parishioner. What happens? Usually some kind of deceptive response happens (that is, after all, what has been habituated)—outright denial ("I did not do it") or an admission and a promise ("I did it and I won't do it again") or minimizing ("At least I did not have intercourse with her"). There are many variations of these responses. They all serve the same purpose—they are an attempt to right the boat, to hide the truth, to make things okay, to get things back to how they were prior to the exposure. People will marshal all their resources to that end—they will use tears, pleading, threats, justifications, blame, and even Bible verses.

Why is this? Remember what an abuser is: someone *devoted* to the practice of a particular habit. To be devoted means to give one's self up, to give one's time, energy, thought, and action to something. Devotion is a matter of the will; of giving the self over to something or someone. So an abuser is one who has given him/herself over to the practice of a habit such as victimizing children, or using women to feed appetites. The habit is practiced, repeated, nurtured, and protected. The self will eventually do whatever is necessary to insure ongoing practice of that habit. It seems necessary to, and even good for, life and well-being. Keep in mind that the offender is not just concerned about exposure but also about the loss of the habit. The thought of separating from the habit is frightening because it is thought to bring life, and any threat results in holding one more tightly, i.e., desperately looking for new and better ways to deceive.

It is crucial that we understand the anatomy of deception or we will fall terribly short in our efforts to help those who are so enslaved. You can have a crisis of exposure and as a result a man can quit visiting prostitutes or victimizing children, but if the engine is still running, he will continue to live with deception and simply find other ways to satiate himself that are less obvious to you or even to himself. Underlying addiction is the engine of self-deception. Under the self-deception is a history that is important to explore and understand because it will help us see why the behavior developed and took the forms that it did. Ultimately, underlying both deceptions and history is a human being who has claimed personal ownership of his or her life.

The Use of Coercion

Coercion, another component of the abuse of power, is about restraining or silencing someone or keeping them from acting by the use of force. The word *coerce* literally means "to surround." The force used can be physical, verbal, or emotional. We can coerce by surrounding another with words. The threat of dire consequences from a father to a child he is abusing is enough to force the child into silence. It is some form of force used to take from another. Physical force is the most obvious form of coercion whether it is a fist, a weapon, or brute power used to restrain.

Oppression is a more subtle form of coercion. To oppress is to impose unreasonable burdens or to severely weigh another down. Oppression can be carried out through unreasonable laws and by withholding what should rightfully be given.

You can coerce through emotional avenues—anger is often used. Rage frightens others into obedience or silence. Fear can be used coercively as well, by frightening victims into obedience (in the Rwanda genocide, for example, "If you do not kill your neighbor, we will kill you") or by showing fear about the ruin that will occur if the truth is told ("If you give voice to what I have done to you, my whole ministry will be destroyed").

You can coerce through psychological means (such as the threat of exposure or alienation or isolation). A child can be coerced or oppressed into silence regarding abuse by being told that if he exposes the truth his mother will no longer love him or no one will believe him. A woman can be coerced into silence by a pastor who simply says, "No one will believe you—they will believe me"—which is in fact probably true.

Coercion can also involve good things. The one in power holds the follower or victim close by gifts, affirmations, money, a job, or something valued by the victim. Though it may never be spoken, the threat of withdrawal of those things is inherent in giving them. This is often done by pedophiles who groom children with gifts. We coerce by binding someone in our own web of deception by any means possible.

The abuse of power involves three components: the deception of self, the deception of others, and the coercion of others. It deceives and confuses victims. The one abusing power is also clearly deceived and confused. The abuse of power requires deadening one's ability to discern good and evil. Truth and lies become confused or often even reversed. It is dangerous ground for a Christian.

We said earlier that the weaker and needier we are the more dangerous we are in a position of power. When expectations are placed on us—by self or others—we feel pressured and often anxious to meet those expectations. We fear we are inadequate. Our tendency to abuse power is greatly magnified during times of weariness, neediness, and anxiety. A drive for power is often a cover for terrible anxiety. Research shows that high anxiety occurs in subjects whose actions have no effect in achieving a desired goal. Unmanaged anxiety leads to pathology. The more isolated, insignificant and ineffective one feels the greater the felt need for power. People often seek power in an attempt to overcome deficiencies, but power only aggravates the nature of sin and does not palliate it. In other words, whatever sin tendencies or weakness we have, a position of power will make it worse, not better, as we seem to suppose.

Think about ministry in the church or in a mission organization. The leader is expected to achieve success—larger numbers, financial stability, often a certain personality, spiritual depth, and excellent results in accomplishing the mission. Such things are never a steady diet in any work and so anxiety sets in. Anxiety has to be hidden because it is considered unattractive and wrong in a Christian leader. Once anxiety and fear are hidden a life has become split and it is an easy step to finding ways to silence or control those feelings—such as, alcohol, pornography, or feeding off the sheep. That feeding can be a refusal to hear criticism in order to keep the ego fed, an increasing demand for praise, a hectic work schedule so thinking time is limited, or an abuse of power through an emotional affair or sexual relationship with one of the sheep. The split in the life grows greater, anxiety increases rather than abates, and self-deception is the narcotic used to continue a public image of service to God and a private life that is lacking integrity and the power of the Spirit of God.

One of the insidious things is that all of this can be done in the name of ministry. I overwork, I neglect family, I neglect my personal relationship with God, I demand praise, and I am "helping" needy people by giving them a more personal relationship for the sake of the gospel. We end up using the ministry to justify forsaking love and obedience to the Master.

Let me make one other critical point here. The more obvious temptations to an abuse of power are the things that we know to be wrong, e.g., sex with a parishioner or battering a wife. I do not think that the temptation to abuse our power comes to most of us along such obvious ways, at least not initially. I believe that temptations of any kind are carefully crafted to fit who we are and they reveal something about who we are. The reason is that the temptation to abuse power in one direction or the other is a temptation to take a shortcut toward the realization of an aim I believe to be good.

The temptation to take a shortcut to a good end was what our Enemy presented to Adam and Eve in the garden. It is also what he put before our Lord in the wilderness. *You, the Living Bread, are called to feed the hungry. Here is a quick way. You, the Son of the Father, called to reveal his nature and care for his children. Here is a quick way. You, to whom the kingdoms of this world and our God will be given, here is a quick way.* He was presented with good ends. They were God-ordained ends. Pastors, do you want to build the church, the body of Christ? You want to build a ministry of healing? You want to help release the captives of sexual abuse, sexual addictions? These are good ends. They are God-ordained ends. But if we serve the ends, rather than the Master of the ends, we put ourselves in the place of God, we take the shortcut and disaster will come.

Three Myths

There are many myths about abusers—how they operate and what they're like—but below I've listed what I would consider the top three most harmful.

1. *The presence of good deeds, kind words, and a good reputation means a person could not possibly be an abuser.* Truth: An abuser often cultivates such things for the purpose of deception. Socially responsible behavior in public causes people to drop their guard and allow access to themselves or to their children. The ability to charm, to be nice, to be likeable is critical to gaining access. Author of *The Gift of Fear*, Gavin De Becker said the following:

"Niceness is a decision . . . a strategy of social interaction; it is not a character trait."[3]

Stop for a minute and reflect on the words *sex offender* or *abuser*. What kinds of characteristics come to mind? Pervert? Creep? Monster? It is a misconception to think that those who abuse are somehow different from the rest of us. They can be good friends, loyal employees, or responsible citizens. There are often no telltale signs in their public behavior. There have been several articles about the BTK murderer, Dennis L. Rader, from Kansas, and how many people were so shocked that this man is a family man, a church member, and works with the Cub Scouts.[4] Again, "nice" is not a character trait, nor are "nice" activities any proof of integrity, safety, or morality.

2. *Most abusers are not like us. They are strangers, odd, mean, monsters, and certainly not Christian, let alone in a leadership position.* Truth: Most abuse is done by an intimate. In well over 50 percent of child sexual abuse cases, the child knows and trusts the person who commits the abuse.[5] Abusers are mothers, fathers, stepparents, grandparents, and extended family members. They are neighbors, babysitters, coaches, pastors, missionaries, and teachers. In one survey of survivors, of the 955 abusers identified by the survivors, only 11 were strangers. Sex offenders will tell you they go to church communities on purpose because Christians can be easily deceived by nice behavior and they will easily give you access to their children.[6] And for all the headlines about random violence, most of the violence occurs in homes and is done by those who are intimately acquainted with the victim.

3. *You can usually tell when someone is lying.* Truth: Decades of research show that people cannot reliably tell who is lying and who is not, yet most people believe that they can.[7] We tend to think we know the signs of lying—lack of eye contact, fidgeting, picking at clothes, shifting. All of those behaviors can be suppressed with practice. It is threatening to think that we cannot really know whether or not someone is trustworthy. Christians,

however, should not be surprised because the Scriptures say that the heart is deceitful *above all things* . . . who can understand it? We often seem to prefer living with the delusion that *we* can understand it and even tell who is deceiving and who is not. We are fooling ourselves when we do so—speaking of deception. Those who habituate lying become good liars. Research shows that some people are born good liars; they innately know how to do it well. Finally, there are psychopathic liars—those who lie needlessly because of the thrill of it—they like lying.

There are more myths, but the underlying point is this: like abusers, we prefer deception. We use deception to feel better, to feel safe, or so we can believe our children are fine, even when they are not. We do not want to think about these things. We do not want to feel afraid for our children or the children under our care. We do not want to have to be watchful of others. We do not want our illusions about those in leadership trampled. It is uncomfortable and we prefer our own comfort to awareness. Victims pay the price of that preference.

Scriptural Understanding of Power

We are all frail and sinful. We all have power. Some of us have a great deal of power. We are easily seduced into using that power for ourselves rather than for the glory of God. What does the Scripture tell us about power and how do we use what God has given so that he is well-pleased and so we do not damage that great and holy Name?

Let me give you two Scriptures that will guide our understanding of a scriptural use of power. In Matthew 28:18 Jesus said, "All authority [all power] has been given to Me in heaven and on earth. Go therefore. . . ." And in John 20:21 Jesus showed his hands and his side and said, "As the Father has sent Me, I also send you." Jesus holds all authority. That means any little bit of power you and I have is derivative; we are dispatched *under* his authority.

Jesus does not give authority to us; he retains it. He is sending us out *under* his authority to carry out his enterprises.

Every drop of power you and I hold is power given to us by the One who holds it all. It is not ours. It is his. He has shared what is rightfully his with us. Are you verbally powerful? Then the Word gave that power to you. Are you physically powerful? Then the Mighty God who breaks down strongholds and sustains the universe gave that power to you. Do you have power of position? Then the King of kings and Lord of lords gave that power to you. Do you have power of knowledge or skill? Then the Creator God whose ways are past finding out gave that power to you. Do you hold emotional power with others? Then the Comforter, the Wonderful Counselor gave that power to you. Any power that you and I hold is God's and has been given to us by him. It has been given for the sole purpose of glorifying him.

Second, if all power is derivative then we will hold that power with great humility. We are creatures, no more and no less. We follow the one who became flesh. He who holds all power, while he was here said things like: "The Son can do nothing of Himself; I am come not to do My own will; I do not seek My glory" (John 5:19; 6:38; 8:50). The state of heart manifested by the Son of the Father should abound in those of us who follow him. We tout our own teachings, our own writings, and our own reputations. He did nothing of the sort. We seek a share of the glory and power for ourselves. He humbled himself before both God and man and became a servant. We seek to build our own little kingdoms. He came to build the Father's. God gives power to us as creatures and it is to be held in trust. If we understand the nature of power, its source, and its danger, we will walk humbly before others, for our Master has said that if we would be chief, if we would lead and impact others, if we would have power, then we must serve. Before telling the disciples he was sending them, Jesus said, "Look, see my hands and my side." These are the marks of his great humility; the visible evidence that he came to serve, not to be served. These marks are the insignia of his authority. Those who follow him, endowed with his power are called to go the way of the cross.

Third, we make the mistake of seeing power as an external thing. Power is not about having rule over a spouse or a church or a parishioner or an institution or company. It is not external; it is internal. God's kingdom is the kingdom of the heart—it is not our churches, institutions, missions, or schools. He is building his kingdom—not ours—and he does that by having authority over the human heart to the point that it is full of the Holy Spirit. *That* is godly power, and when we are full of God's power internally we bring life and light and grace and truth and love into all our external enterprises, both great and small, and God's kingdom grows and he is glorified. Any cause or work, no matter how good, that leads us to sin has become an ungodly force in our lives. Any power God has given is to be used in conformity to the Word of God and the character of God.

And how will we serve? We have said that all power is derivative and is to be held with humility. To what end is this done? Power is to be humbly held in love to God and to others. Its sole purpose is to be used for the glory of God and the good of others. Any time we use power to damage or use another we have failed in handling the gift. Any time we use power to simply feed or elevate ourselves we have used the gift poorly. Our use of power is to be governed by the Word of God and the Spirit of God. Any use of power that is not subject to the Word of God is a wrong use. Any use of power based on self-deception, or some area where we have told ourselves that what God calls evil is instead good, is a wrong use.

Using the power of position to drive ministry workers into the ground "for the sake of the gospel" is a wrong use of power. Using emotional and verbal power to achieve glory when God says he will share his glory with no one is a wrong use of power. Using the power of success or financial knowledge to achieve ministry ends without integrity is a wrong use of power. Using the power of theological knowledge to maneuver people to achieve our own ends is a wrong use of power. Using our position in the home, or the church to get our own way, serve our own ends, crush others, silence them, and frighten them is an ungodly use of power. Using our influence or our reputations to manipulate others is a wrong use of power.

You are leaders. You are sinful humans, but you are also creatures God put his honor into. He has sent you to walk the way of the cross, obedient to his Word, serving with humility, governed by his Spirit, and bowing to his authority over every aspect of your life. You follow the one who became a slain Lamb. You follow the one who measures leadership not by the external sphere or kingdom but by the heart. You follow the one who has called you to demonstrate his character in every aspect of your life. He has called you to leadership full of the life of Christ. He would have you intolerant of sin, no matter what it might achieve. He would have you die to your choices, your goals, and your desires if they lead to disobedience in any corner of your life.

Our desire for expansion, for growth, for a kingdom, and for progression is not the problem. Such desires are God-given because those desires mirror his. The path by which we would gain such things is the problem. That ordinary, power-seeking, human path will not lead us to the desired ends. It will not lead to glory but to great loss and dishonor to the name we carry. Human beings aspire to leadership and power in part because they aspire to glory, to honor. They think glory is achievable by expansion, by kingdoms, by taking what they need, and by progression. That is not where you will find glory.

Glory is found by walking the way of the cross. That is the way our Savior went and *only* if we go that way will we find glory. "The Word became *flesh* . . . and we saw His glory . . . full of grace and truth" (John 1:14). You want glory in flesh? In your marriage? In your churches? In your country? Then you must walk the way of the cross. "The glory which You have given to Me I have given to them" (John 17:22). You want the glory given by God into the safe-keeping of Jesus? Then you must go the way of the cross. "Father I want them to be with me so they can see the glory you gave me in loving me before the foundation of the world" (John 17:24, author paraphrase). You want to see the glory given by God to the Lamb slain? Then you must go the way of love and obedience to the Lord Jesus Christ no matter the external consequences.

As pastors, counselors, and leaders in the church, we hold a tremendous amount of verbal power, power of knowledge and po-sition, and influence. It is all God's—not yours or mine. What we have has been gifted to us to use as stewards of his glory on this earth. We are not to use that power to feed our egos, demand our rights from others, build our own little external kingdoms, and establish our reputations. It has been given to us so that the world might see something of the glory of God in the flesh—full of grace and truth. That glory is evidenced in humility, love, sacrifice, and death to anything that is not like Jesus Christ.

It is a hard road. On it you will find faithful footprints. It is a road that requires lack of conformity to the false manners, hab-its, tastes, and principles of this world. The leadership of the Son of Man goes in an opposite direction. It is, however, the road to glory. It is my prayer that we will guard the honor God has put into our keeping, exercising *his* power with a stunning likeness to him until that day when we find ourselves at the foot of the throne where by his grace we will hear "Well done, good and faithful ser-vant" (Matthew 25:21 NIV). On that day, as a faithful servant, you will bow before that throne, inhabited by a Lamb slain and you will sing to that Lamb, "Worthy is the Lamb that was slain . . . to receive power and honor and glory—Amen" (Revelation 5:12, au-thor's paraphrase).

CHAPTER 13

Sexual Abuse in Christian Organizations

"We must oppose every form of alienation, liberate people from every kind of oppression, and denounce evil and injustice wherever they exist."[1] We have heard about global violence against women and both international and domestic sex trafficking. We see those as alienation, oppression, evil, and injustice and resonate with the words from the Lausanne Congress that I just quoted. Do you suppose those same words are applicable to our prized and loved Christian organizations as well?

The title of this chapter—"Sexual Abuse in Christian Organizations"—is appalling. It is horrifying that such words should work together. It is horrifying that such words make sense to us. They should not. Consider the words with me, compliments of Webster:

- *Sexual*—of or pertaining to sex.
- *Abuse*—to use wrongly; misuse; to treat in a harmful or injurious way; to deceive; to commit sexual assault upon.
- *Christian*—pertaining to the teachings of Jesus Christ; living based on the teachings of Jesus Christ; exhibiting a spirit proper to a follower of Jesus Christ, as in having a loving regard for others.

- *Organization*—the state or manner of being organized, i.e., coordinated parts for united action; persons organized for some end or work; conforming completely to the standards set forth for the organization.[2]

So what do we have when we string it all together? We have persons organized as the body of Jesus Christ, doing a work for him in this world, ostensibly for his glory, and rather than demonstrating loving regard for others as one might expect, using or allowing that which is sexual to misuse, injure, or harm others. How can such things be?

Some Examples

Michael was eight years old when he first went to Christian summer camp. He was scared and did not know anybody. He was homesick. His counselor paid him special attention and that helped a lot. Then the counselor started taking him for walks in the woods after devotions at night. He started touching him in weird ways and doing other things Michael did not understand. He tried to tell the nurse that something was not right, but she told him he was saying bad things and that his counselor was "a great kid and the son of the camp director and he would not ever do anything to hurt one of the kids."

Sara's parents were missionaries in Asia. When she was seven they took her by airplane to another country and left her at a boarding school. She missed her parents and her home very much. She lived in a dorm with lots of other girls and a man and his wife who took care of them. The man came in the room she shared with another girl at night to pray with them. They had to kneel next to him, and he would touch them on their bottoms for a long time. He told them after prayers that if they told their parents it would force them to leave the school and prevent their parents from telling people about Jesus.

Melissa went to see her pastor about her marriage. Her husband was an abusive alcoholic. He would keep her up at night sitting in a chair while he screamed and cursed at her, and then he would fall asleep until the afternoon. She would pull herself together, get the kids to school, and go to work because they desperately needed the income. She haltingly told the pastor some things about the marriage. He was kind and invited her to return. He wondered if maybe her husband was abusive because their sex life was not great and said he thought he could help her with that. Her husband often said things about her failures in that area so she thought maybe that would help. It began slowly and subtly at first—just a hug at the end of the session. Then longer hugs. Then a kiss. Then he began touching her, undressing her, telling her he would teach her how to do things right. She could not think; she was so confused. He started having sex with her. Eventually she told one of the church leaders' wives, who told her husband. Then some of the men in leadership told her what she was doing was immoral, and the pastor had said she was very seductive. She was not to tell anyone else because it would hurt the church and his ministry and people would leave. Perhaps it was best if she just quietly went away. That would be best for the church.

Sexual abuse in Christian organizations—such a phrase should be the king of oxymorons. Sexual abuse covered up in Christian organizations in order to protect "God's work." Sadly, though the examples are adapted and tweaked, they are all basically true stories. I have spent several decades working with such devastated lives. Many lives have been sacrificed on the altar of secrecy "for the sake of the church or the mission."

Also sadly, there are those who have been placed in positions of power in the Christian world—pastors, missionaries, teachers, professors, camp counselors, coaches, and counselors—whose job was that of shepherding the sheep, but who instead have fed off the vulnerable sheep in their care. Compounding that, some of those ravaged sheep have tried to tell the truth of that abuse, while so-called "Christian" organizations have closed ranks and protected the organizational structure rather than the sheep. People in power are protected because they are gifted, important, and successful, or considered necessary to the furtherance of the work of the kingdom of God. Vulnerable sheep, who have not found it safe to graze, have been thrown out, silenced, slandered, and frankly, abused yet again by the power structure of the body that is clearly not following its Head.

Review of Facts

We have already discussed some of the facts about sexual abuse. We know that at least one in four girls and one in six boys are sexually abused in this country prior to the age of eighteen. One in five women in the US experiences rape or attempted rape.

Sexual abuse can take many forms: verbal, visual, and physical. Verbal sexual abuse includes sexual remarks about a person's body or sexual comments. Visual sexual abuse includes being forced to watch pornography, exhibitionism, or voyeurism and using manipulation or coercion to photograph someone in sexual poses. Physical sexual abuse includes touching sexual parts of the body, being forced to touch another, or putting objects or body parts in another's orifices. Most sexual abuse of both children and adults is committed by someone known to the victim. We are all appalled at the news reports of serial rapists or stranger rape on a city street, however, most of the time the offender is known to the child or the adult who is victimized.

Impact of Sexual Abuse on the Victim

Sexual abuse can have many long-term effects in the life of a victim. The intensity, duration, and range of effects is dependent on many factors: age of the victim, previous experiences of abuse, frequency, the violence level of the abuse, response to a cry for help, personality, support system for the victim, and so on. Victims experience depression, anxiety, post-traumatic stress disorder, substance abuse, self-injury, alienation, sleep disturbance, distorted thinking ("I am evil; I am trash; it is my fault"), and loss of faith. Studies have documented that when the abuser is a leader in the faith community the damage is particularly pronounced. Needless to say, the victim's understanding of God and many precious truths in his Word is twisted and frightening.

Listen to some thoughts written by a survivor of clergy sexual abuse in response to words written to her by a well-meaning friend about God's love:

> I do not believe you intended to inflict any hurt on me, and to the contrary, I expect you intended to offer some comfort and hope. But from my perspective, it is as though your email brandished in front of me the very weapon that was used against me. It is as though you are telling me that I should pick up that very same sword that was once used to eviscerate me and should fall on it all over again. I can't do that. My love of God, my faith, my extraordinary desire to live the will of God . . . those are the very parts of me that were transformed into weapons that savaged and destroyed me. As a result, that part of my brain, that part of me that was once able to turn to God, to surrender to God, to pour out my heart to God, to put things in God's hands, to believe God would take care of me . . . all that part of my brain is inaccessible. It is electrically charged and it is the land of the predator . . . it is a ravaged land that is there within my own head.[3]

How Does It Happen?

How can these things be? How does the sexual abuse of a child or adult occur in a *Christian* home, church, school, or camp? And if it occurs, how is it that the victims are not protected but in fact, often revictimized by the larger system in order to preserve what is typically called God's work? How is it that a woman is told by church leaders not to tell her husband that the pastor raped her? How is it that eleven-year-old girls are forced to sign a confession of *their* sin of seduction for causing a thirty-five-year-old missionary to molest them? How is it that a high school athlete has his college possibilities threatened if he tells on his Christian school coach? More importantly, how is it that God's name and honor and work and yes, even God's Word, are used as weapons to silence victims, first by the predator and second by the system, as if somehow our God was actually invested in protecting structure and form regardless of substance; or as if his work required protection by stepping on the necks of the oppressed, the victims, and rendering them mute?

There are many factors contributing to this heinous problem. I want to consider a few of them with you. We will consider the culture of systems, deception, the abuse of power, response to an offender, and a few governing principles.

The Culture of Systems

A system consists of things or people so closely connected as to make an organic whole. A system has power significantly greater than any one of its parts. All of that power is brought to bear when the system is threatened. That is a good and often lifesaving response when a system is threatened by disease or injury. It is life-endangering when all that force is used to hide something wrong or poisonous to the system.

Think of the system of the physical body for example. If I experience pain in one of my eyes, it gets immediate attention. It waters automatically. I close it and my other eye takes over seeing for me. My hands participate by getting water to flush it out. My brain processes what is happening and makes the decision of whether or not to call an ophthalmologist. Something is wrong and the system unites all its power to make it right and protect the injured part in a healing way.

Conversely, suppose I find a lump on my body and decide to ignore it. I am fearful of what it might mean. I do not want to go through all the appointments and tests and possibly treatment that could be required. I know if it is cancerous the treatment is likely to make me sick or even cause some damage to my body. So I hide it and even attempt to "hide" it from myself. You would tell me my response is foolish and that my efforts at denial could cost me my health or my life. You would, of course, be correct, but do not systems of many kinds hide signs of potential illness all the time? Families of addicts regularly cover for the alcoholic or drug abuser. Families with incest do the same. The system uses its power so that the victim knows not to speak and even works hard to present a healthy face to the world.

Those of you who are counselors work with sick systems that revolve around addiction, sexual abuse, or domestic violence. You have felt the power that rears its head when anyone from within or without the system tries to drag the truth to the light by naming the real problem and asking for help. An entire family will deny the truth and alienate a victim or truth-teller rather than face the fact that there is a cancerous lump metastasizing and destroying the system from within.

We also know that this occurs with regularity in much larger systems—systems that bear the name of Christ. We have seen it in the church, in missions, in Christian organizations, or communities around the world. There is the cancer of immorality, theft, corruption, or sexual abuse, and all the energy of that system goes to maintaining itself and a good appearance while ignoring the disease. Thinking they are preserving the system they call God's, they fail to see and deal with the disease hidden within. They actually think that if they acknowledge the presence of disease and work to stop it, they will in fact, destroy the work of God. However, it is not a step toward the recovery of a sickly system to disguise the worst symptoms of that system to itself.

We *say* it is the work of the Lord and that we are using the power of the system to protect that work. In Jeremiah we read that the Israelites used to say, "The temple of Jehovah" while they were worshiping idols. God's response to them was a call to righteousness. He called them to make healthy their ways and their doings and not to tolerate sin in their midst. We are told in Jeremiah 26 that the prophet spoke to the sick, sinful system all that God had commanded him to speak, and the system's response was to say he must die. They wanted to render him mute. Go back to our examples of Michael and Melissa. The camp nurse and the church leadership wanted to render them mute.

No system—family, church, community, or institution—is truly God's work unless it is full of truth and love. Toleration of sin, pretense, disease, crookedness, or deviation from the truth means the system is in fact *not* the work of God, no matter the words used to describe it. I fear we have a tendency to submit ourselves to some command or idea of men—of the past, of tradition, of a systemic culture—and in so doing refuse to listen to and obey the living and ever-present God.

Some of us have faced the power of systems that name God's name yet look nothing like him. That power can be formidable. It is hard to fight an organic whole, particularly when that system is full of people you love or those important to you and your future. We have seen in large, bold letters the power of such systems in Nazi Germany, Rwanda, Burma, and Bosnia. The system seems to easily sweep others into participation in its corrupt ways. How much easier it is to keep quiet or be swept along, especially when the system has been about good work done in the name of God. We forget that anything done in the name of God that does not bear his character throughout is actually not of him at all. In our forgetting we are more loyal to the commandments of men than the commandments of God.

God thought up systems. He created family; the people of Israel; the church. He intends for them to be vibrant and healthy with likeness to him. They are to bless this world and be a force for righteousness, which is simply Christlikeness, among men. When they are not, his people who are called by his name are to humble themselves and seek his face and give the call to repentance and righteousness that he might be truly glorified in his work, even in its hidden, folded corners.

Deception

Sexual abuse requires both deception and coercion or an abuse of power. The deception must first be of the self and then of the victim and the community. If it is to be covered up, then that deception and coercion must be continued by the system, which then is mimicking the perpetrator. The camp nurse and the church leadership were mimicking the perpetrators in their choice of deception and coercion of the victims. Sexual abuse cannot exist without these components.

Deception is clearly involved in the perpetrator's relationship with the victim, but first and foremost, the perpetrator is *self*-deceived. Deception of others is inevitably preceded by deception of the self. As we discussed, we have a seemingly unlimited capacity to hide truths that are painful. This extends to the organizations and systems we create.

In the last chapter we talked about how the abuser, having deceived himself, now uses deception to lure and control his victims. Then deception and silence is urged or forced on the victim through lies and threats. These are classic tactics for a pedophile, but they are also used by pastors, missionaries, and counselors who engage in sexual behavior with parishioners and clients. They are also used by leadership when it attempts to silence a victim and protect the system. There are also the more subtle deceptions: "I never had intercourse with her" (i.e., it was not *really* sex) or "it would be so hard on the church to expose this" or "I was seduced into giving him/her what they said they wanted" or "We really need to consider the impact on the organization if this gets out" (ignoring their own failure to do just that). Sadly, one of the most powerful weapons of deception is the use of spiritual language. It does, after all, carry the seeming weight of God behind it.

Whenever sin is exposed, it creates a crisis and crises do two things: they reveal character and they are also what we might call "separating" times. A crisis reveals character because in the moments of crisis we do what we have been practicing. We display what we have habituated. We demonstrate what or who we live in obedience to.

That was clearly demonstrated when Hurricane Katrina hit the Gulf States. The poor and the disenfranchised were left behind and forgotten because that was what had been practiced over the decades preceding the storm. They were always there and always in need and others had not practiced going back to care for them. When the crisis came, people simply did what was practiced and did not go back. How people habitually responded to the poor in their midst was revealed in the crisis. A crisis is a revealing time. It reveals what is in the person who has come to you; it will reveal the heart of the one who is accused; it will reveal your heart to you; and it will reveal the heart of the structure or organization that is threatened by the truth. It is absolutely crucial that what is being revealed be seen and understood and responded to in obedience to the Word of God.

Power

A second aspect of sexual abuse is the abuse of power. Power is simply the ability to make something happen. It is the capacity to have impact or influence. All of us have power. As we have noted previously, the one who has power does not always feel powerful. You can hold tremendous power and not *feel* powerful. You can feel tired, needy, weak, and even powerless and yet wield tremendous power. Fragilities and weakness do not necessarily remove our power. They do, however, make us more likely to use our power destructively.

The weaker and needier we feel, the more dangerous we are in our use of power because we are far more likely to use the vulnerable to feed ourselves. In other words, people in power who are compelled by their own anxieties, fears, and weaknesses, all too often abuse the power they have been entrusted with. Sadly, power used in conjunction with deception results in people using their power destructively while telling themselves that it is for the good of those under them. Melissa's pastor told himself and her that he was "helping" her marriage. However, Scripture says *all* power has been given to Christ and so any power we hold is derivative. We are called to the stewardship of any gift we have been given, and power is no exception. We are to steward power for the glory of God, never for the glory or feeding of ourselves.

It is always the responsibility of the shepherd or the one with power to maintain the integrity of the relationship—the boss, the counselor, the pastor. You also know without question that no pastor-parishioner, teacher-student, coach-player, counselor-counselee, adult-child relationship is to have a sexual dynamic. The *world* says it is unethical to do so. The Word of God says a shepherd should *never* feed off the sheep. The Word of God is clear that vulnerable, sickly, or broken sheep are to be fed, protected, healed, and bound up. When the shepherd feeds himself rather than the sheep under his care God says, "Behold, I am against the shepherds, and I will demand My sheep from them. . . . So the shepherds will not feed themselves anymore, but I will deliver My flock from their mouth" (Ezekiel 34:10).

When a shepherd feeds off one of the sheep, the Word of God is honored *when the shepherd is removed*. God is also honored when we call things by their right name—clergy sexual abuse is *not* an affair; pedophilia is not about struggling with difficult circumstances; molesting adolescents is not about a struggling marriage. Such things need to be called by their right names, and the abusive person needs to be held responsible for his/her abusive behavior. God's Word calls us to open our mouths for the silenced; to rescue the oppressed; to care for the afflicted and needy.

Offenders and Repentance

Repentance is a complex and important topic. I can only skim it. Listen to a quote from a youth pastor who abused about one hundred boys before he was caught: "I considered church people easy to fool . . . they have a trust that comes from being Christians . . . they seem to want to believe in the good that exists in all people . . . I think they want to believe in people. And because of that, you can easily convince, with or without convincing words."[4] As Christians we love words like *forgiveness, redemption*, and *transformation*. The use of such words does not make a transformed soul. Nor are such things accomplished by a few words, tears, and a little time.

One thing that has always puzzled me about the Christian community's response to sexual abuse in its midst is its naïveté about sin. The Scripture is clear that our capacity for deception is incomprehensible to us. It is clear that when we keep sinning we actually become a slave of that sin, and slaves cannot free themselves. It is clear that we hate the exposure of sin and will deny, justify, and blame in order to escape responsibility. The Scripture is also clear that *sin* is the worst thing in the world—not exposure, not getting caught, not the loss of all things.

It seems we do not believe what we teach. If we did, we would know that an abuser is a slave and cannot simply stop. We would understand that the narcotic of self-deception has become so powerful in his life that he not only cannot stop lying; he does not even know when he is and has lost his capacity to tell truth from lies, good from evil. We would know that habituated sin has roots and tentacles and has long done damage to the soul so it is not easily routed out. And we would know that exposure, consequences, and treatment are necessary if there is ever to be freedom from the cancer that has sent tentacles throughout his life.

A second thing we need to understand is that neither grace nor forgiveness means letting people do what they want, giving them what they feel they must have, or what will immediately alleviate their suffering. Grace is not a lack of restrictions. In fact, sometimes the thing that is most grace-filled *is* restriction. When our God says, *Do not murder, do not commit adultery*—is he not being full of grace to try and prevent us from engaging in those things that will eat us alive? We do so with our own children when we say do not play in the street. The restriction is full of love and grace. Abusers need that grace extended to them. They have spent years playing in the street of deception, evil and abuse damaging both their victims and themselves. To say to the abuser, "No, you cannot stay in the pulpit; no, you cannot simply transfer to a different ministry" is not an assault on their dignity; it is not an accusation; it is not even a failure to trust (though not trusting them is wise)—it is a keen awareness that their sensibility to sin has been so deadened that they cannot see clearly and are in great danger of further destroying their own soul, not to mention other vulnerable sheep. Of course, we need to protect the vulnerable—our God calls us to that, but we are also protecting the abuser from his own habituated sin and deadness.

Thirdly, *repentance of habituated sin is never immediate*. It is not possible for it to be immediate. Discernment of good and evil, conscience, or any desire to obey God have all been trampled and killed. Such things are not awakened and strong and consistent simply because someone has been caught. Repentance is not seen in tears; it is not seen in words; it is not seen in emotion. Repentance is long, slow, consistent change over an extended period of time because it is from the heart outward. Heart change is supernatural work. We all know that sinful humans do not turn into godly ones quickly—our own lives attest to that. The bottom line is that you *cannot* tell if repentance is genuine for a long, long time. If you think you can you will have not only fooled yourself, but you will risk vulnerable people.

Any abuser who insists he is fine and needs no oversight is not safe because he still has no awareness of his capacity for self-deception. Any abuser who insists he is trustworthy has not understood the scriptural teaching about self-deception and how it results in being unable to tell good from evil. Any abuser who thinks saying "I'm sorry" readies him for a return to ministry has no grasp of his heart's capacity for deceit, his abuse of power, his assault on the sheep, and his tragic dishonor of the name of Christ.

Finally, we think we know people. God says we do not. He says we do not know ourselves. We tend to believe the externals. We believe success, and we believe growth in Christian organizations means godliness in hidden places. Think about it: A man who is the head of a multi-million dollar global Christian organization you believe in is accused by a child who simply says, "That man touched me." Or, closer to home—the child says it about someone on the pastoral staff of your church, about someone who has eaten in your home. Who do you want to believe? A simple, little, confused child whose four words, unbeknownst to the child, have the capacity to bring down a leader or even a system? Or the leader—the one you "know" and respect and give money and allegiance to? Instinctively we will move to protect (or so we think) our family, our organization, or our community. We move to protect the system. God would have his people instinctively follow him in ways that are full of truth and holiness and give honor to his name, which means being willing to follow the trail and discover what is true before the eyes of God, not before the eyes of man.

Some Governing Principles

It can be difficult to know how best to respond to situations of abuse when they arise, when deception and power cause confusion and doubt. Here are some principles to keep in mind when navigating a response:

1. Sexual abuse of a minor, sexual assault, and rape are illegal. They are felonies in all fifty states. There are authorities and professionals trained to handle such things. When Christian organizations think they are wise enough, discerning enough, knowledgeable enough, or skilled enough to manage such complicated issues in-house, they are disobeying the law of the land, further hurting the victims, colluding with the perpetrators, and acting arrogantly. They are also giving credence to the perpetrator who said that church people are easy to fool. Many tend to think they should first determine the truth of the accusation. Christian organizations are not trained to determine such things. It is outside their purview and needs to be done by trained law enforcement, lawyers, and mental health professionals.

2. The treatment of sex offenders is still not well understood and is highly specialized. Many well-meaning Christian organizations have extracted a confession, seen tears and apologies, read Scripture, and given counsel only to release a predator back into the body of Christ. Sexual assault is a crime. The one who committed it is a criminal. Crimes need to be tried in courts and followed up with treatment that considers the complexities and difficulties of helping offenders truly change and understands how to protect the vulnerable when they do not.

3. Clergy sexual abuse is not a crime in many states.[5] Let us be clear, however, it is an abuse of power and a desecration of the name of Christ. It is *not* an affair, nor is the

victim equally culpable. The safety of God's sheep results from *his character* not theirs. And so it should be for the broken, confused, wounded sheep in our communities. They should be safe because of the shepherd's character, and where they are not, a shepherd's character is exposed as being abusive of power, deceptive, and clearly unlike the character of the one he calls Master.

4. Our God demonstrates again and again in his Word that his kingdom is the kingdom of the heart, not the kingdom of institutional structure. He makes utterly clear that he does not desire form over substance. When Israel was following the Temple rituals while worshiping other gods—when they followed form and the substance was rotten—God destroyed them. God hates sin wherever he finds it and has gone to death to destroy it. Do we really think he wants us to avoid the death of an organization or institution by hiding sin, by failing to drag it into the light? He would rather see every human organization and institution fall than see such things preserved while full of sin.

5. What is the primary call of the church today? Is it to evangelize, to hold to pure doctrine, to increase in numbers, to be big and successful, to help the sick and suffering of the world? When Jesus first called his disciples, to what did he call them—a profession, a creed, a task? No, he first and foremost called them to himself. I fear sometimes we have lost that call. Our ears have been seduced away by other things, carrying our hearts with them. We are not only hurting the sheep as a result, we are breaking the heart of the Shepherd. He desires our primary allegiance to be love and obedience to him no matter the cost. He does not want primary allegiance to ministry or service or to institution, system, or organization. He does not want our goal to be knowledge, growth, money, reputation, success, or

tradition. When we pursue him above all else, the body of Christ will be the safest place on earth for the most vulnerable sheep.

Our Head puts before us a choice: the preservation of our systems—our families, churches, organizations, and cultures—or love and obedience to Jesus Christ no matter the cost. Ask yourself, will I be complicit with the sin of abuse, and in so doing align myself with the abuser and with darkness in order to preserve my world? Will I say I do so for the sake of the mission, the church, and God's work? Or will I ever and always be faithful to the name and character of the Head I follow, though the earth shake and the mountains fall into the sea? May we, who are already in positions of power and influence, lead the way by falling on our faces, imploring God to make us like himself no matter the cost to our positions, our programs, our organizations, our ministries, or our traditions.

MINISTRY
IN THE CLINICIAN'S OFFICE

CHAPTER 14

Complex Trauma

Historically, when someone has endured a traumatic event, they have often been diagnosed with post-traumatic stress disorder. In recent years, as our understanding of trauma has grown, there has been discussion of a different diagnosis for a sub-population of trauma survivors. Complex psychological trauma involves stressors that are repetitive and chronic; involve direct harm or neglect by those who should have been caregivers; often occur at developmentally vulnerable times; and have the potential to severely compromise human development.

Post-traumatic stress disorder was originally identified in combat situations and then found to be applicable to things like accidents and natural disasters. It is, however, not really a sufficient diagnosis for those incubated in abuse and terror over a long period of time. The current literature is focused on this new category called complex trauma. In complex trauma, traumatic stressors are interpersonal, premeditated, chronic, planned, and caused by humans. Due to their nature, these stressors cause a more severe and lasting reaction. Complex trauma involves interpersonal violence that is usually repeated and chronic over time. Thus, the individual is shaped over time by the trauma. It includes child abuse of any kind (physical, sexual, and emotional abuse, as well as chronic neglect). It can also include those whose lives have layers of trauma, e.g., someone physically abused growing up; raped as a teen; then in combat as a young adult.

Think about some of the factors involved in ongoing child abuse. It results in insecure, disorganized attachments that have a profound, lifelong impact. So-called "caregivers" exploit the physical and emotional immaturity and dependent status of the child as they meet their own needs or react due to their own inadequacies or histories. The child is used to feed the ego or lust or power hunger of an adult on an ongoing basis. The relationship, which should be a source of comfort, safety, and nurture, is instead a cause of constant distress from which there is no escape, gross insecurity, negligence, instability, and pain. In such an environment the child never regains emotional equilibrium after the abuse, due to its chronic nature.

As a result of chronic, interpersonal trauma, the child develops vigilance, constant anticipation of danger, chronic anxiety, and terror. All of the child's psychological energy is bent by necessity toward coping, not learning or growing. The child has been utterly betrayed by those who should be caring and nurturing and cannot find or seek assistance and safety because there is no safe person or there are ongoing threats if the abuse is disclosed.

Contrary to popular belief, children are not resilient, a word which simply means they can return to their original state. They do not "bounce back" from abuse. Children are instead malleable, which means they are shaped by the forces in their lives, and in the case of ongoing interpersonal trauma they are being shaped by evil, neglect, rage, and abandonment. Such forces do not shape a child in normal ways.

Sexual abuse involves the persuasion or coercion of a child to engage in or assist any other person to engage in sexually explicit conduct. In the majority of child sexual abuse cases, the child knows and trusts the person who commits the abuse. Abusers are mothers, fathers, stepparents, grandparents, and extended family members. They are neighbors, babysitters, coaches, religious leaders, and teachers.

Children learn concretely, through their five senses. They are learning how to think about their bodies, relationships, emotions, choice, identity of the self, and their relationship with God through those concrete experiences. Chronic sexual abuse shapes all of these areas in the child's life and results in distorted thinking, confusion about the self and others, and gross misunderstanding about God. Lifelong patterns are established in all these arenas, so the abuse has long tentacles that continue to strangle a life.

Many survivors hate their bodies and cope with life self-destructively through addictions to food, alcohol, sex, and drugs. Suicidal thoughts and self-mutilation can occur. Eating disorders and sleep disorders are not uncommon. Feelings of shame about the body are often strong. Emotional aftereffects can include anger, fear, and overwhelming grief, shame, and guilt. Another possibility is emotional numbness. Repeated abuse often causes a child to learn how to turn off emotions. This profoundly impacts relationships.

Abuse also damages a survivor's thinking, for it has been shaped throughout childhood by lies and deceit. Such beliefs as "I am worthless, God is not good, love does not exist, and no one can be trusted" are very strong. The work of discerning truth from the lies taught repeatedly through the abuse is a tremendous job.

Dissociation is another thinking process that is often used for coping with chronic abuse. It is a defensive adaptation that allows the child to remove itself from the abuse. The child wants to believe the abuse did not occur so she looks for ways to keep it a secret from herself. When the body is trapped in unbearable circumstances, the mind leaves by way of imaginative and trance-like states.

Problems stemming from the abuse can reverberate throughout a victim's relationships. Childhood sexual abuse involves betrayal, rejection, humiliation, abandonment, and deceit. Trust seems impossible or foolhardy. Relationships are invaded by fear. Control is paramount.

Spiritually the effects of abuse are profound as well. A distorted image of God, coupled with a distorted image of the self, create many barriers to experiencing God's love and grace. God is seen as punitive, capricious, indifferent, or dead. Abuse attributes false things to God and mangles the truths of Scripture for children. When children are abused they repeatedly see in the flesh a series of lies about their heavenly Father. Undoing the damage spiritually, relationally, and emotionally will take a long time and much hard work. That is one of the reasons God's Word says that those who so confuse children would be better off dead.

Diagnostic Categories

Those exposed to such chronic interpersonal trauma exhibit symptoms not covered under the DSM category of PTSD. Judith Herman in her book *Trauma and Recovery* suggested a broader category she called Complex Trauma.[1] Lenore Terr referred to Type I or single incident trauma versus Type II, which was complex or repetitive trauma.[2] Bessel van der Kolk and others at The Trauma Center have developed a diagnostic category called Disorder of Extreme Stress (DESNOS).[3] These authors have linked DESNOS with interpersonal histories of traumatic victimization, multiple traumatic events and/or traumatic exposure of extended duration. This category was also developed based on the research that those diagnosed with PTSD have been found to be eight times more likely to have additional disorders than people not diagnosed with PTSD. Clinicians began to wonder if perhaps another category needed to be developed rather than seeing this pattern as comorbidity.

We will briefly consider the major categories for the diagnosis of Complex Trauma or DESNOS. There are various aspects of a person that are altered when someone endures chronic, complex trauma. First, alteration in regulation of affect and impulses: these patients tend to overreact to stresses, become easily overwhelmed, exhibit intense anger, have difficulty calming themselves, and are often self-destructive. They find it difficult to modulate anger and manage impulses of suicide, sexual acting out, and risk-taking behavior. This category also includes attempts at self-modulating such as addictions and self-harm—self-destructive coping mechanisms that have also ironically been life-saving *at times* because they channel intensely destructive impulses into non-life-threatening behaviors.

Second, we see alterations in attention and consciousness. Trauma is inescapable, extremely distressing, and overwhelms the coping mechanisms people usually find effective—you get away, you fight back, you tell someone to stop. When coping mechanisms are overwhelmed and there is no escape, the result is a strong relationship between trauma and dissociation. There have been several studies suggesting that having dissociative experiences at the moment of trauma is the most significant long-term predictor for the development of a trauma disorder. Victims who suffer interpersonal abuse prior to age fourteen develop significantly more dissociative problems. Those who experience interpersonal trauma beginning in the early years can develop dissociative identity disorder. Trauma has its most pervasive impact when it occurs in childhood or adolescence.

In dissociation, information is not integrated and traumatic experiences are relegated to separate aspects of consciousness. Trauma cannot be effectively catalogued in the brain; labeled or understood. Trauma defies normal categories. There are essentially no files in the brain of a child where the whole of their abusive experience can be put and understood. Think about it—you are a five-year-old girl and you live in a house where you are chronically neglected, beaten, and raped. To absorb the memory—the sensations (voice, smells, pain), the visual, the cognitive twisting, and the emotional aspects—of all that at once would likely lead to insanity. If you cannot escape physically, then one possible coping mechanism is to divide the parts of the experience and store them separately in your mind, even to the point of rendering them inaccessible—hence amnesia. So the abuse from certain ages, the abuse in certain places, the emotional responses, etc. are all filed separately in the computer of the brain.

In the book *Holocaust Testimonies: The Ruins of Memory* by Lawrence Langer, the author studies the memories of those who survived the Nazi Holocaust. He sees memory that is not integrated but split up and hidden in the mind. Langer says that memory functions, or continues on, with or without speech. He says that since memory cannot be silenced in the mind, it might as well be heard. The point is that whether memory is spoken internally or externally, it continues to impact a life. It often speaks through symptoms even when one does not consciously remember the cause of those symptoms.

Langer uses the term *anguished memory* to refer to memory that assaults and finally divides the self. Holocaust survivors talk about the inability to link the past and the future. We have heard some of these in previous chapters, but they bear repeating. "I split myself. It wasn't me there. It just wasn't me. I was somebody else."

"My head is filled with garbage, all these images, you know, and sounds, and my nostrils filled with smells . . . you can't excise it . . . it's like there is another skin beneath this skin and you cannot shed it . . . I am not like you. You have one vision of life and I have two . . . I have a double life."

"There is a sort of division, you know, a compartmentalization of what happened, and it's kept tightly separated, and yet it isn't. . . . It must not interfere, the other must not become so overwhelming that it will make so-called normal life unable to function."

"I live a double existence. The double of Auschwitz doesn't mingle with my present life. It is as if it weren't me at all."[4]

You can, I am sure, hear very similar descriptions to adult survivors who struggle to articulate their trauma and who coped in part by means of splitting, by dissociation. The descriptions of these survivors are uncannily similar to those of our clients who have endured chronic, childhood abuse. The highest levels of dissociation occur in those who experienced multiple or chronic trauma, especially as children. Dissociation in its extreme form is of course found in Dissociative Identity Disorder (DID), which occurs in approximately 1 percent of the general population. However, as counselors, it is critical that we understand that many individuals with trauma histories can experience significant amounts of dissociation and in fact, not be DID. Dissociation as a coping mechanism occurs on a continuum. Research shows that many continue to use dissociation after symptoms of PTSD or DID have been largely resolved. This category regarding alterations in consciousness includes intrusive memories, which may be the more familiar flashbacks and nightmares.

The third category for complex trauma or DESNOS is alterations in self-perception including views of the self as damaged, ineffective, undesirable, and helpless. Victims blame themselves for the abuse, believe they cannot be understood, and minimize the abuse. They carry a great sense of shame not just about what was done to them, thinking it says who they are, but also shame regarding their current symptoms.

Fourth, Herman includes a category not present in the DESNOS literature that focuses on alterations in perceptions of the perpetrator. Many victims are constantly thinking about their abuser—fearful he will appear, planning revenge, feeling still controlled by him even if he is long dead. They also will take the perpetrator's view of themselves. They attribute great or total power to the abuser, though Herman cautions us here because oftentimes a clinician wants to downplay the current level of power the abuser holds. The fact is there are some very evil and powerful people in the world, and extreme fear in a patient should not simply be seen as an old, childhood reaction. You could be working with someone whose family was involved in organized crime, trafficking, or something like that. Their seemingly excessive fear may be based in solid reality.

Fifth, we see alterations in relationships. Obviously, repetitive and premeditated abuse can result in all kinds of attachment disorders. To be chronically mistreated and abused as a child leads to recurring victimization, inability to trust, or in a minority of victims, victimizing of others. They are unable to feel intimate with others. These clients have no model for healthy relationships and so cannot make good and wise judgments. They miss warning signs and so are re-victimized. Or they see the warning signs and feel helpless to deal with them or immediately dissociate, rendering themselves helpless. These struggles will impact the therapy relationship as they struggle to trust and may respond aggressively to the therapist, be overly dependent, or feel victimized in treatment. They feel significantly isolated from others and often live in a withdrawn fashion. They may present as perennially looking for a rescuer and if so, you can be sure they hope you are the one.

The sixth category in diagnosing complex trauma is somatization, a new area not often understood by either the therapeutic or the medical community. There is growing research that shows that chronic trauma has an impact on the body and the brain. Chronic exposure to stress compromises the stress response system of the body, the capacity to evaluate stimuli and encode verbal memory, and it hinders information processing. Traumatized individuals have overactive nervous systems, the exaggerated startle response being one example. Overproduction of certain chemicals results in constant anxiety, hyper-arousal, and difficulty sleeping—all of which have a great impact on health. Current research has found immune system dysfunction in many women with histories of chronic childhood abuse. These physical issues do not generally respond well to conventional medical treatment and such patients often end up being treated with disbelief and even hostility by the medical system. Others have undergone years of unnecessary surgeries.

The final category involves alterations in meaning resulting in despair and hopelessness or the loss of former beliefs. These clients have great difficulty making sense out of life and find the God who allows such abuse confusing at best. To process a history of chronic trauma often threatens every belief formerly or currently held.

Treatment

Therapy with clients who have experienced complex trauma must begin and continue throughout with safety and stabilization as foundational. It is often the longest phase of treatment and is vital to a successful therapeutic outcome. Without this, treatment can easily become re-traumatizing for the client and in some sense merely a reenactment of the abuse. Safety and stabilization include establishing a therapeutic alliance, ongoing psycho-education regarding trauma, its impact and symptoms, how to manage flashbacks, affect, suicidal ideation and risk-taking behaviors. The focus initially is more behavioral, rather than interpretive. Patients have usually sought treatment because they are in crisis. They have no idea how to stabilize themselves. They only know to continually react to their own hyper-arousal state.

Phase One—Safety and Stabilization

The initial phase of treatment is focused on physical safety, building trust, learning how to self-soothe, and developing a support network. You will primarily focus on doing reparative work so that the foundation is laid for the explorative work. All of these are building blocks for the later stages of treatment. You are giving them tools for looking back at the trauma memories and dealing with the pain and unspeakable atrocities.

This first phase usually requires multiple interventions. If substance abuse or an eating disorder is present, adjunctive treatment will be needed. If that treatment is not pursued, these problems will be exacerbated by later memory work and safety can become threatened. Assessment of current levels of safety is needed, as many times clients are living in chaotic or abusive relationships or may be self-harming with addictions, cutting, or suicidal tendencies. The client *cannot* progress in treatment unless a relative degree of safety is acquired. Not only that, dealing with the trauma without safety is merely a repetition of the original dynamic, which is clearly not therapeutic! As long as the client is unsafe, the therapist should focus on giving education, support, and safety plans or options. This needs to continually be a collaborative effort in order to treat the client with respect and to help them develop a sense of power and self-capacity, again a reversal of the old dynamic.

A second key component to the first phase involves assisting the client in understanding and managing bodily and affective states, triggers, and avoidance. If this is not done, the client remains at the mercy of their own hyper-arousal and affective states without any understanding of what might be happening or how to respond in a way that gives them a sense of control. Development of a new self-reflective capacity that involves awareness of internal responses to external stimuli, the capacity to label emotional responses, and a range of choices for responding to those stimuli yields a growing sense of competence in managing the self.

A third aspect to this early phase of treatment is education. The client needs to be told clearly what therapy is and is not, what boundaries exist, how the therapist will respond in emergencies, and what the therapeutic process generally looks like when dealing with trauma. The client also needs to be taught about trauma and how it impacts people, so they can make sense of their own reactions and begin to develop compassion and care toward themselves.

It is also critical for the client to develop a support network. Education about how the trauma shaped their understanding of attachment and how relationships work is important. Chronic mistrust impacts all their relationships and the therapeutic relationship becomes a safe place to express those feelings and understand their origin. Basic education about boundaries and how to discern safe versus unsafe people is also important. An addictions group, group survivor therapy, or a small group in a church are all potential networks for the client to connect with and begin to test their growing interpersonal skills. Such groups offer a support system larger than the individual therapist.

Many therapists get pulled into the history of the trauma too soon, and they want to focus on the traumatic memories. All that will do is destabilize an already chaotic life and the client will again feel at the mercy of those memories, which is not unlike being at the mercy of the original abuse. This first phase can take a long time, even years, especially if someone is abusing a substance, actively self-mutilating, or suicidal. This phase must often be revisited throughout treatment as the eventual memory work involved can lead the client back into chaos and self-destructive choices. When this happens, memory work is put aside until stabilization has been achieved once again. All the while, the therapist is teaching the client how to recognize, label, and manage internal states that feel intolerable, how to be safe, how not to be their own abuser, and how to make choices and combat their relentless feeling of helplessness.

The importance of this to the success of treatment cannot be overemphasized. A lack of safety in the client's life means that they will, and must, continue to use defensive and protective strategies or they will once again be overwhelmed and made vulnerable to further victimization by others or themselves. This segment of treatment helps clients identify arousal states and label emotions, as well as giving skills training so they are not stuck in reactive or dissociative responses.

It is critical during this work that the counselor not end up as governed by the emotional dysregulation as the client is. Two dysregulated people are *not* a good outcome! Treatment must ever and always be unremittingly ethical and have clearly articulated boundaries. You as the therapist need to be as predictable as possible. Concrete safety plans for clients need to be jointly developed, written down, and agreed upon. Given that trauma narrows consciousness, you cannot trust such things to the patient's memory, especially given that these ideas will be needed by them when the system is flooded with hyper-arousal. Write it down, go over it, and actively involve them. Boundaries for out-of-session contact need to be clear as well. These clients live with many ongoing crises, so they will want in-between session contact and it is easy for a therapist to get caught up in the crises with the client and change boundaries. I know therapists who have ended up on the phone daily and nightly, including weekends, or who have gone to the patient's house in an attempt to stop some growing crisis. Counselors need to be clear at the beginning of treatment about their limits and communicate those to the client. Such things as out-of-office contact by phone, how emergencies are to be handled, evening and weekend rules, e-mail rules (is it allowed, is a response to be expected), and the use of hospitalization. Keep in mind that you want the client to eventually learn how to manage themselves.

If you continually rescue them, you are communicating that you do not see them as capable and that you are always available. You will not last, you will begin to feel resentful, and you will interfere with or derail the client's capacity to develop competence. Everything you do with your client is to be governed by what is clinically and ethically best *for them* in their work toward a whole mind, an adult mind, and the capacity to manage themselves.

This first phase focuses primarily on the impact of traumatic experience and education about that impact. As some level of mastery over frightening and reactive responses is attained, then the work can proceed in phase two of treatment.

Phase Two—Processing Memory

The second phase of treatment focuses on the processing of traumatic memories. Safe disclosure of these memories and the shaping impact of those events will eventually lead to a narrative of the client's whole life. Considering these memories must be carefully timed and managed so the client can continue to exercise the knowledge and skills learned during the first phase. This is not about plowing through the memories because again that would repeat the dynamic of the abuse. All good care reverses the dynamic of the original experience. In the trauma the person is overwhelmed and has no say. In retelling their story they can stop, take a break, or leave it for a while in order not to replicate overwhelming fear and pain. It is a little-by-little process always allowing the victim to set the pace and assisting them in stabilizing their agitation.

This phase also deals with all the trauma-related emotions. Unlike PTSD the focus is not primarily on anxiety, though that is a component of the work, but rather on grief and loss as well as shame and rage. The emotional processing can easily be overwhelming and must be paced so the client can maintain an adequate level of functioning. Returning to phase one may periodically be necessary. The process of telling a story that has been lost or silenced and experiencing the hidden, dissociated, and feared emotions can ultimately bring a sense of mastery, competency, and closure to a trauma-ravaged person.

As you proceed through treatment with your patient, keep in mind that ultimately chronic trauma results in continual attempts at leaving, getting away. Keep in mind that it is about getting away from intolerable evil and abuse accompanied by intense, overwhelming affect. It is one of, if not the, fundamental governing forces in the life full of complex trauma. Your client goes away by dissociating, by zoning or numbing out, by abusing a substance, by an eating disorder, by excessive sleep, by erratically terminating relationships—including treatment—and even by standard withdrawal measures we all engage in. Inevitably, leaving is tied to affect, but because affect was always intense, full of pain, and unbearable, the minute it hits it is experienced as frightening and leaving is the single coping mechanism. Do not lose sight of the fact that there are multiple ways of leaving, and all of them need to be recognized for what they are so they can be treated and new coping skills acquired. Even when the story has been told and many symptoms abated, the impulse to leave whenever there is pain or uncertainty or intensity will remain. Leaving the story and its accompanying pain has been habituated. It will take time to solidify the newly learned coping mechanisms and practice them until a new way of life is gained.

Caution: do not get swept up in drama. Complex trauma is a compelling diagnosis to work with. Many trauma patients have compelling stories. Keep ever in mind that the drama was created and nurtured by evil. It was created in the context of chaos and chronic tragedy. The intensity leads some counselors to push the story, compelled to hear what happened, often thinking that just getting through the story will bring relief. The telling is not sufficient, catharsis alone will not heal, and it opens up a floodgate of emotions that require a constant returning to safety and stabilization. Watch yourself. Know your tendencies in the face of intensity and drama—push, get swept up, or withdraw? Monitor those so they are made subject to the good of your client and do not lead the treatment. It is not about your comfort.

Another caution is in order here. Engage in this kind of work only if you have training for dealing with traumatic memories and the intense affect that will occur. Many a counselor has begun this work well-intended but not trained or prepared for the force of it. It is easy for a client to start to lose control of their affect and their self-destructive behaviors. That can be overwhelming for a therapist as well and many either end up tossing ethical guidelines and boundaries out the window or emotionally withdrawing or unethically terminating a client because they do not know how to handle the intensity. Allowing a client to be continually overwhelmed in session will increase their need/use of dissociation, which means the memory and its attendant emotions cannot be processed. Assisting them in learning how to handle their own affect is a critical part of the therapy. Understanding how to clinically manage the client's affect and your own reaction to it is vital for successful treatment.

This second phase is ultimately about the truthful telling of a silenced narrative, with all its accompanying emotions, in the context of a safe, ethical relationship that exists for the good of the client. The telling of the story needs to be carefully timed and structured, keeping in mind the client's ability to tolerate trauma memories and the accompanying affect. The pace also must be handled so that the client develops a sense of self-efficacy. These things reverse the dynamic of the original trauma where the feelings, voice, and choices of the client were considered irrelevant. Another critical component to this process is that the story includes all of the truth—not just truth about the trauma, but of the whole person—the client's accomplishments, goals met, growth, and success. Doing this also reverses the dynamic and states loudly and clearly that the client was and is far more than the traumatic events they endured. This is also someone who has great strength or they would not have survived or reengaged the trauma in treatment. Those strengths should be highlighted and affirmed.

As the second phase progresses it often encompasses issues such as the confrontation of an abuser, a negotiating of a relationship with a former abuser or family system, and questions about forgiveness. I consider all of these in detail in my book, *Counseling Survivors of Sexual Abuse.*[5]

Grief and mourning are also integral parts of the second phase. The grief is deep and intense and frequently frightening to the client. Many fear weeping because they experience their grief as bottomless and believe that if they start grieving they will never stop. There are many laments in the Psalms and prophets such as Jeremiah that can be helpful here, as many Christian clients mistakenly believe their grief and questions and anger are ungodly. To see their own feelings mirrored in the Scriptures and not condemned encourages them to lament the evil and suffering they have endured at the hands of their oppressors. We will return to this a bit later.

Additionally, many spiritual questions and struggles emerge. As suggested earlier, the spiritual impact of such chronic trauma is profound. God is viewed through the lens of abuse. Who he is and what he thinks about the survivor is understood based on who daddy was, or grandfather, or youth pastor, or whoever. They have learned about love, trust, hope, and faith through the experience of abuse. They have also learned about the unseen through the seen. The ins and outs of ordinary life have taught them many lessons about who God is. That is why a therapist or pastor may have the experience of speaking the truths of Scripture to a victim, truths desperately needed, and yet finding that they seem to have no impact. Many times I find that survivors can speak eloquently to me of the truths of Scripture, but on an experiential level their lives are lived out in the context of what the abuse taught them, rather than the truths of the Word of God. Intellectually, truth is rooted in the Word of God. Experientially or personally applied, the truth is rooted in the lessons of abuse.

The survivor is struggling with questions about God: "Who is he? What does he think? What does he think about me? Am I forgivable? Does his patience run out? Why should I have hope?" In the context of therapy the therapist becomes the representative of the character God in the flesh to the client. The work of the therapist is to teach in the seen that which is true in the unseen. The therapist's words, tone of voice, actions, body movements, responses to rage, fear, failure all become ways that the survivor learns about God. I believe that the reputation of God himself is at stake in the life of the therapist. We are called to represent him well. Working through memories and the lies they hold is arduous and slow. It requires tremendous patience. The rewards are wonderful for you begin to see light dawn in a darkened and confused mind. It is quite different, however, from simply telling someone God loves them and having them believe it. Speak it; live it; be it;

repeat again. As you live out God's character in your flesh over time you will begin to see the truths we hold precious come alive in the mind and heart of your client as the reality is observed in you.

The third phase of treatment is a time of connection and growth. It can also be somewhat frightening as clients enter into a more normal life—a long-desired but previously unknown place. This phase includes work on marriage, parenting, intimacy and other life decisions. It often includes finding a way to "give back" as it were. Clients fine tune conflict resolution skills, develop further clarity about safe boundaries and increase in their self-regulatory skills. They learn how to maintain a healthy relationship with their own bodies. The clinician continues to provide a secure base from which the client can explore and grow.

Ending treatment can be a cause for celebration and certainly satisfaction of goals accomplished. It should be a collaborative effort. I recommend scaling down treatment over time so termination is not abrupt. This again ought to be a joint decision, but often going from once a week to every two, to once a month, then three, six, and a year checkup works well. At each juncture the client has the say in whether or not they are ready to proceed to the next stage. Having a scheduled appointment a year out continues to provide the sense of a secure base.

Be careful with this work; move slowly. You will need great wisdom for the diagnostic process and for the treatment process. Consult, consult, consult. Study, read, and attend training sessions. There is good solid research and training going on. There have been some popular, somewhat dramatic writings about working with trauma—quick fixes. Be careful of such things. The Trauma Center at the Justice Resource Institute at Harvard has good research. You will need to grasp the neurobiology of trauma and its effect on brain development. You will need to grasp dissociation in all its complexity. You will need to stay alert, grounded, and clear about the process of treatment. There is much to understand as complex trauma is a complex disorder. Work with humility, patience and a learning, listening attitude.

The God you serve knows the mind of the one before you. You and I are working with what we cannot see nor presume to understand. He longs for that mind to find healing and wholeness. He wants us to be grounded in him who is truth so we are not pulled around and overwhelmed by hideous evil, chaos, and intense pain. He wants us to learn and experience in our relationship with him what he then desires us to patiently model and teach our clients— to live rooted and grounded in him, not tossed around by the evils of this world, having the mind of Christ—a mind that is sound and disciplined. You do this work with him. He is allowing you to have a front-row seat to how he patiently, slowly over time teaches and leads and heals what evil human beings and the Enemy of our souls have shattered. I call this "on your face" work, meaning on your face before God. Frankly, all counseling is such work.

Here we are dealing with evil, fragility, complexity, and we cannot see. I have found that he works with me through this process as intensely and patiently as he calls me to work with the broken life before me. It is a great privilege to do so, and I owe a great debt to those who have brought me their histories and fragmented minds, along with courage and willingness to teach me. I have learned much at their feet and even more about sitting at the feet of God himself, who alone can do the healing that is needed.

CHAPTER 15

Understanding Domestic Violence

It is a sad thing to have to speak about domestic violence in Christian circles. We are talking about violence in homes where God is said to dwell and rule. It should be unthinkable; grievously, it is not. Such a thing cannot be discussed without keeping in mind what God declares about marriage.

Marriage is designed and intended by God to be a union that bears fruit of many kinds and changes the world. Marriage is a living parable; an illustration in the flesh telling the world how much God loves his people and giving them a clear picture of how that love is demonstrated. Marriage is also to mirror for all how God's people are to love him back. Paul tells us that Christ's love for his church is a great mystery and that it has its most glorious, earthly revelation in marriage. It is the best earthly symbol of the existing relationship between Christ and his bride. The love of a husband for a wife is to be a picture of Christ's love for his church. The love of a wife for her husband is to typify the love of the church for Jesus Christ.

Think briefly with me of the love of Christ for his church. It is unselfish love. It is a pure love. It is a serving, nourishing, beautifying love. What then is the church's love for Christ? It is the response of love to the mystery of love, the submission of love to perfect love. Marriage then is to be the response of love to love, the subjection of a great love to a great love, the submission of a self-denying love to a love that denies self. Christ longs for his bride to return his love.

Let that picture sink into your mind and remember that is God's design, his illustration. Let it become clear in your thoughts and picture that symphony of love, two in concert together. And then suddenly picture screaming, name-calling, throwing, cursing, shaking, battering. What has happened? Hell has come into God's artwork. It has torn asunder what God has called to live in harmony. It has brought discord, ugliness, betrayal, and destruction. It is not unlike what happened when the Enemy of our souls brought such things into the garden and into Adam and Eve's lives. The picture of eternal things is hideously marred. It teaches lies about our God. It breeds more wrongdoing, for marriage breeds seed after its own kind, and when violence reigns, its fruit is poisonous. It is unthinkable that such things should be in the illustration of our Savior's love for his body and bride. We will consider that destruction, and as we do, please try to hold to the image of what God has intended.

For the sake of clarity I will talk much of the time as if men are the only abusers, but they are not alone in wreaking havoc on their marriages. Women can scream and taunt and manipulate and control as well as men. They can also be physically abusive. However, because of many power issues (physically and often economically), the wife is often the victim. Most of the research I have looked at suggests that women account for 85 percent of the reports, and men are about 15 percent of the victims in cases of physical assault. I suspect, though I do not have statistics on it, that the percentages are more even when considering verbal and emotional abuse. We do not know how often a woman's assault of a man is in response to his battering. That would certainly be true in some, but not all, cases.

Secondly, I do not even remotely think that all men are abusers. As we discuss this area it could be easy to think the assumption is that men are abusive as a rule, or to think I do not believe there are loving men. I happen to have been married to such a man for more than forty years. I also have two grown sons who are loving and thoughtful men. All three treat me with respect and gentleness and have great integrity. I have worked and continue to work with many male colleagues that I love, respect, and trust. I am not here to speak against men. However, I do want to speak strongly and clearly about sins that I believe are real, and which the church has often been silent about or condoned.

Most of us cling tenaciously to an image of the family that includes tranquility, happiness, love and above all else, safety. We think of violence and crime as things belonging to the street. Sadly, statistics suggest that our images are often an illusion. Violence behind closed doors is a reality and, it could be argued, is epidemic globally. It is also not an "out there" problem. It exists within the body of Christ. Sadly, my work in this area has been within the Christian community, and the examples that I give today come from that work.

For centuries (and in many places still today) wife-beating has been accepted as a natural, though unfortunate consequence of a woman's status as her husband's property. Because of my travels I am keenly aware that there are many places around this world where such abuse is the norm and occurs unquestioned by the church. I was in the car with a gentleman, an elder in his church, in an unnamed country, when this topic arose. I asked him about the frequency of abuse in the homes represented in his church. "Oh, it is very common. It is in most homes." I asked him if the pastor and elders of that church knew it was wrong. "Well, it is in many of their homes. We are just beginning to see that it is wrong." I asked him if they were teaching the men in the congregation that it is wrong. "We are talking about doing that."

Throughout much of history, male violence toward women and children has been socially, legally, and religiously endorsed. Roman law granted the father absolute authority. He had the right to sell his children and the power of life and death over them. He had lifelong absolute authority over all members of his household. In ancient Greece, the wife and children were also the man's absolute property. The order of priority was father, cattle, mother, and children. It is easy to see how custom could dictate violence toward and abuse of women and children if they had less status than a cow.

History has given us a legacy of attitudes toward women and children that is clearly anti-scriptural. Women and children are not possessions to be owned, but persons created in God's image to be loved, nurtured, and treated as creatures that are responsible before him. Men are not owners of others, nor may they dispense with any other human in whatever manner they like.

Kinds of Domestic Abuse

Let's begin with a definition of *abuse*. The English word for *abuse* comes from the Latin word *abutor,* which means, "to use wrongly." Other definitions include "to insult, to consume, to violate, to defile, to tread underfoot, sully or tarnish." Abuse occurs whenever one person uses another person for wrong purposes. Anytime someone uses another as a punching bag, a depository for rage, a thing to be controlled or used for their own gratification, abuse has occurred. Anytime words are used that demean, tarnish, insult, or degrade, abuse has occurred. Anytime intimidation, threats, deriding, sneering, name calling, or humiliation is used, abuse has occurred.

In the US, it is estimated that between one and three million women are physically assaulted by an intimate partner annually.[1] Statistically, 25 percent of the women in my country will experience at least one episode of violence from a husband or a partner. More than three women are murdered daily by their husbands or boyfriends.[2] Pregnant women are more likely to be victims of homicide than to die of any other cause. It is the leading cause of injury in women ages 15–44—more than rape, mugging, and car accidents combined.[3] Statistically, it is far more dangerous for women to go home than to walk city streets alone at night. International statistics report women experiencing physical and sexual assault in their own homes in the range from about 20 percent to 70 percent.

Sadly, in most countries, the numbers for domestic violence do not change when you survey the body of Christ. One conservative denomination's survey found that close to 30 percent of women had experienced at least one episode. Sadly, many Christian women have been beaten, kicked, bruised, and returned home in the name of submission. Often when confronted with a man's abuse of his wife, the standard response has been instruction *to the wife*, which entails doing her duty and suffering for Jesus's sake. Many women have been sent home by church leaders to be beaten, taunted, screamed at, humiliated, and used wrongly, sometimes to death. Your husband may break your bones, smash in your face, call you a slut, break things in your home, terrify your children, forbid you any access to the money and isolate you from others, but you are to submit without a word, glad for the privilege of suffering for Jesus.

Why is this? Are we unsure about whether or not issues of violence and justice are really theological issues? Do we believe that resistance to or exposure of injustice or violence is somehow unbiblical? Is it possible to use Scripture to justify abuse of one's spouse? When did we start thinking that tolerating grievous sin in the home was godly?

Think about the following scenarios and do so remembering the picture we painted of marriage as God designed:

- Would you call it abuse if a man pummeled his wife or grabbed her hair and banged her head into a wall or sofa arm?
- Is it abuse when a man or woman so threatens and intimidates his or her spouse that they will never voice a different opinion?

- Is it abuse when a man ties his wife to the four posters of the marital bed and forces sex on her?
- Is it abuse when a husband so maneuvers for power and control that his wife is prevented from having any knowledge about their finances or any access to money?
- Is it abuse when a man curses at his wife, or calls her a slut, a whore, a bitch, an idiot, or a tub of lard?
- Is it abuse when a husband or wife criticizes everything his/her spouse does day after day—appearance, parenting, housekeeping, friends, work, or relationship to God?
- Are people in these situations being used wrongly, insulted, tread underfoot, or tarnished?

Are they abused? Yes.

What is physical abuse? Hitting, burning, pushing, biting, restraining, scratching, blocking, and beating with an object, using the body to threaten (such as slamming a fist or breaking something). It is using physical power to control, manipulate, or intimidate.

What is verbal abuse? Name-calling, demeaning, humiliating, and sneering are all abusive. It is using words, or using verbal power, to control, manipulate, or intimidate.

What is emotional abuse? It is the systematic tearing down of another person by rejecting, ignoring, terrorizing, isolating, or corrupting. It is the use of emotional power to control, manipulate, or intimidate.

What about financial abuse? This can include no access or knowledge of finances, doling out meager amounts of money at will, or forcing a spouse to ask and using that to control them in other ways. It is the use of money and its associated power to isolate, control, and demean another person.

What about spiritual abuse? Many abusers use the Scriptures and the principles that are in them to manipulate, demean, and control their spouses. Verses on submission are used to demand participation in sinful things, e.g., group sex, strip clubs, justification of sexual assault, or to prevent dialogue. Spiritual abuse is the use of Scripture and spiritual language and principles to control, humiliate, demean, and silence another person.

Domestic abuse is essentially a *pattern* of assaulting, coercing behavior or a pattern of obsessive, controlling behavior. It often builds and becomes increasingly severe. Initially, words are used to threaten and create fear and confusion. Then restricting, isolating, and withholding behaviors are added. Physically acting out is another level, which is essentially doing damage to things (punching a hole in the wall, breaking things). Physical violence to the person is the next level, and finally, weapons of some kind may be added to the abuse. You can understand how the fear and terror build in the home.

You can wound or kill a soul by any of these means. The lack of physical scars does not mean abuse is not occurring. All you have to do is read the accounts of torture in international prisons to get some idea of how humans can be hideously abused without ever touching them. Isolation, deprivation, threats, and words used to control and confuse can have devastating effects. Women who have been physically abused *one time* become easy prey to being managed by verbal and emotional abuse alone because the line has already been crossed and they know it could easily be crossed again. Do not dismiss the power or destructive capacity of either verbal or emotional abuse. Do not think you cannot kill a soul with words alone. Many a child's soul has been killed in this manner. Do not think, "Well, at least he didn't hit her." Yes, he did. He just didn't use his fists.

Look at God's response to oppression and abuse.

"He pled the cause of the afflicted and needy. . . . Is that not what it means to know Me?" (Jeremiah 22:16)

The LORD is a stronghold for the oppressed, a stronghold in times of trouble. . . . He does not forget the cry of the afflicted. (Psalm 9:9, 12 ESV)

"Because the poor are plundered, because the needy groan, I will now arise," says the LORD. "I will place him in the safety for which he longs [protect them from those who verbally abuse them]." (Psalm 12:5 ESV)

Speak up for those who cannot speak for themselves, for the rights of all who are destitute. Speak up and judge fairly; defend the rights of the poor and needy. (Proverbs 31:8–9 NIV)

"What do you mean by crushing my people and grinding the faces of the poor?" (Isaiah 3:15 NIV)

They deprive the poor of justice and deny the rights of the needy. (Isaiah 10:2 NLT)

"Do justice and righteousness and deliver the one who has been robbed from the power of her oppressor. Also do not mistreat or do violence . . ." (Jeremiah 22:3)

David says a righteous king (i.e., one who has power) vindicates the afflicted, crushes the oppressor, and rescues the needy from oppression and violence (Psalm 72). In other words, he uses his power redemptively.

Our God is characterized by justice, care, and concern for the oppressed and defenseless. Jesus came to the brokenhearted, captive, imprisoned, and afflicted. His gentle care for the downtrodden revealed the character of God to us.

Is the church of Jesus Christ called to look like him? Are we not to manifest his character in this dark world? Should not the sheep that are oppressed, afflicted, and maligned within the walls of their own homes find a refuge in the body of Christ?

Oppression, injustice, cruelty, and abuse are not of God. Those who are righteous will *not* be oppressive or abusive. They will *not* use others for wrong purposes. They will not use others for themselves, they will not say insulting things, and they will not tread others underfoot. God is not abusive, and we who name his name are not to be abusive either. God condemns abuse. He speaks out against it and he protects the abused. So must his church if she is to be like him. When God's people are obedient to him, they reprove abusers and defend the helpless. Unfortunately, we have often reproved the helpless and protected and defended abusers.

Scripture gives us a basis for holding abusers accountable for their behavior. The law that is to govern the marital relationship is the law of love, and wife abuse of any sort is a profound abuse of that law. God says, "Husbands, love your wives, just as Christ also loved . . ." (Ephesians 5:25). That statement alone shatters any rationalization or minimization of a screaming fit or an insulting remark, a demeaning name or maneuvering for power in the relationship.

Would the love of Christ pin a woman's arms to the wall and rage at her?

Would the love of Jesus call another person names?

Would the love of Christ drip criticism all over someone's life?

God says, "Husbands, love your wife as your own body, nourish her, cherish her . . ."

Is it nourishing for a woman to be isolated from others, forbidden outside contact?

Is it cherishing to leave bruise marks in the shape of one's fingers on her arm?

Is it cherishing to scream, "I hate you" or "I want a divorce"?

Is it nourishing to make fun of her, to tell jokes that put down women, to refuse to speak to her for days on end?

Is it nourishing and cherishing to spend minutes, hours, years buried in pornography, preferring the feeding of one's own lust to the loving of one's wife?

God says, "Husbands live with your wives in an understanding way . . . show her honor as a fellow heir of the grace of life" (1 Peter 3:7).

Is a man living with his wife in an understanding way when he constantly criticizes her choices, her opinions?

Does he understand her when he insists she do everything around the house because, after all, that is women's work?

Does he grant her honor when he refuses her access to money?

Does he grant her honor when he makes fun of her in front of others?

Does he grant her honor when he grabs her by the shoulders and shakes her or throws her on the bed?

Does he grant her honor when he only allows his viewpoint to stand?

Any abuse that a husband perpetrates against his wife is a betrayal of his oath to love, honor, and cherish her. *Any* abuse that a husband perpetrates against his wife is a manifestation of unfaithfulness to the covenant he made with her. *Any* abuse that a husband perpetrates against his wife is sin, not only against her, but against a holy God. God says, "The deeds of the flesh are . . . enmities, strife, jealousy, outbursts of anger, disputes, dissensions, factions, envying, drunkenness, carousing . . ." (Galatians 5:19–21).

Why, when confronted with violence or abuse in a home, have we often placed the burden on the victim to justify her actions, to somehow prove that she did not "make" him do it, rather than on the abuser to confess his sins and demonstrate change? We have frequently overemphasized the response of the abused to the exclusion of confronting the behavior of the abuser. Are we afraid he will turn his anger on us? Do we fear confrontation? Do we fear we will be accused of not holding the marriage covenant sacred? Do we really think protecting a home full of sin is keeping that sacred covenant? Do we fear standing with the oppressed?

Now I am perfectly aware that all wives are sinners. Some wives are abusive as we saw from the statistics. They are abusive with their tongues or they manipulate and control or they demean and insult. However, let us be clear that *no failure in a wife justifies abuse and violence in a marriage.* Certainly a wife is responsible before God for her words and her actions in the home. She is called to obedience to God's Word no matter what. But *no failure* on the part of the wife, no matter how bad a wife she may be, justifies violence as a response. There is *nothing* in Scripture that justifies abuse, oppression, or violence. Scripture is clear that those things that proceed out of a person proceed from the heart. The cause of abuse is not external but internal in origin. Whatever comes out in relationships says something about what is *inside* us, not about what is outside us.

The Caregiver's Response to the Victim

There are several things to keep in mind when counseling victims. First of all, when someone comes to you who is being abused in the home you will find that it often takes awhile for them to tell you the truth. They will present other problems and not reveal what is going on in the home. Many are terrified after being victimized for so long, and many have been threatened, sometimes with weapons. Victims will often reveal the truth little by little. They will say things like, "He gets aggressive sometimes." "He pushes me a little bit." The reality is usually far worse. Victims will also usually make statements that justify the abuser's behavior. "He did not mean it." "He lost his job, had a hard day, or was upset about something." The victim buys into the abuser's self-deceptions.

When you realize that you are working with a woman who lives in an unsafe or life-threatening situation, her safety becomes paramount. You must show her respect. That means you will believe her and not ask for proof of violence. Assure her that any violence toward her is *not* her fault. You will need to develop a safety plan with her. You will want to help her answer questions such as the following:

- Does she have children? If yes, talk about the effects on them, their physical danger and psychological danger (witnessing it). Are they being abused?
- Where could she go? Any intervention could put the victim and those helping her in danger. The victim gets to say what she wants.
- If she is considering leaving, what does she need to set aside to have some basic things with her—keys, driver's license, money, children's medical information and school records, credit card, clothes? This involves helping her choose the necessary items, as well as having her pack them and leave them in a safe place, such as a friend's house.

In the US women can get cell phones for the sole purpose of getting police help. Hospitals often dispense them. I also suggest that she go to the local police and tell them there is violence in the home, even if she is not willing to press charges, simply to notify them so that if she calls, they will know to respond immediately. In the US we also have what we call "safe houses," which are shelters for abused women and their children. It is critical to understand that abuse escalates upon leaving, and many women have been tracked down and killed. Helping women and children be safe is something the church worldwide should be involved in.

The difficulty in counseling is that abused women are slow to tell the truth about their husbands and are often not willing to leave the home. These women love their husbands and they want their marriages to work. Statistically, women who eventually leave make up to twenty-five attempts before finally leaving the home. They typically leave and return quickly, over and over again. Their thinking is confused. They want their marriages, but they are afraid, so their capacity to make careful and rational decisions and stick to them is compromised.

Once she has left the home and not until then can she really begin the counseling work. Many, if not most, of these women have post-traumatic stress disorder, depression, and anxiety. It is difficult to treat PTSD while someone is still being abused. Sometimes it is necessary so we find ways to strengthen the victim, help her care for herself and her children, and think clearly.

Of course, one of the immediate questions when working with domestic abuse is, When can she return to the marriage? In my experience, the church and sometimes Christian counselors are anxious about the separation and eager for the couple to reunite. That anxiety leads to a premature return, and often the cycle begins all over again. Sometimes the physical abuse never returns, but one (or both parties) use threats to control the other. The husband threatens but never does use physical abuse again; the wife threatens to leave again if he doesn't please her. That is hardly the goal of care for this marriage. How are we to think about this difficult question?

Exposing Sin to Pursue Repentance

Paul's teaching in Ephesians 4 calls us not to let any unwholesome talk come out of our mouths and goes on to call us to be imitators of God and live as children of light. The fruit of our lives is to be goodness, righteousness, and truth. We are to have nothing to do with the deeds of darkness *but rather expose them*. It has often been my experience that when abuse in a marriage has been exposed, the church speaks out in horror not against the abuse but against the exposure. Somehow the one who has dragged the sin to the light is seen as the destroyer of the marriage rather than the one who has been repeatedly abusive.

The children of God are called to drag sin to the light—starting with their own—and when an individual in the church refuses to deal with the sin of abusing his wife, it is the work of the shepherds to bring it to the light. That is the only hope. Sin becomes visible when it is exposed by the light and only then can it can be rightly dealt with. There is no redemption for hidden sin. If such exposure causes a marriage to fall down that is surely cause for weeping. However, it is also cause for rejoicing because it is the acknowledged sin, failures, and ruins that God redeems. For example, suppose a man comes to a surgeon and he is limping. The surgeon opens his leg and finds it rotted and full of maggots. The response will be one of horror, sadness, and pain. It would never occur to anyone to blame the surgeon for the maggots or expect him to ignore them because, after all, the man only limped a little bit. He would have brought the problem to the light, weeping would result, but there would also be hope for health and healing. God grant that we be more afraid of sin than of its exposure. God grant that we may be more afraid of the maggots of sin than of complicated messes or the exposure of a corrupted relationship. Sin hidden within a God-ordained structure is hardly success.

Godliness is not evidenced by gifting or words alone but by spiritual maturity—a consistent demonstration in one's character of Christlikeness. There have been some immature leaders in the Christian world that achieved power and status because of their gifts rather than because of their maturity. When someone is particularly gifted verbally and theologically, it is easy for us to assume maturity. The ability to articulate theological truths well does not necessarily mean that one is an obedient servant of God.

Unfortunately, some use their abilities and theological knowledge to cover sin. We often assume that vocabulary reflects truth about character. I have seen this happen again and again in domestic abuse situations. I have watched churches send women home to batterers merely based on the words of the batterer who said I am sorry and shed a few tears. Repentance is not verbal only. It is always demonstrated consistently in a life over time. And true repentance is a process that requires time and more time to be made evident. When humans are caught in sin, they will say anything to make it better, including using biblical language to keep life running normally, especially when there is a lot at stake. The self-deception of the one who is exposed works overtime in an attempt to deceive his/her questioners, who also have the capacity to be deceived and sometimes in considering the potential outcomes conclude that deception is the better alternative than messy, exposed truth.

The habit of self-deception is the hidden engine behind many behaviors such as addictions, abuse, violence, etc. Someone can stop an addiction or an affair and still be injecting the narcotic of deception. When someone thinks verbal repentance and a few tears are all that is necessary for restoration to leadership or marriage, the addiction to deceit remains alive and well. One of the evidences of true repentance is an awareness of this, humility that acknowledges the inadvisability of trusting oneself, and a true, consistent desire to understand and make restitution for impact. We do a great disservice to those who have been living habitually deceived when we do not understand this. We will, in fact, fail to call them to stand in the painful but healing truth of God's assessment of a deceived heart.

Scripture says our hearts are deceived in incomprehensible ways. So often the church is naïve about deception and its workings in our lives. That leads to "I'm sorry," being a sufficient response to hideous abuse and stopping outward behavior a sure sign of repentance. Repentance means to have another mind about something. It is not merely words and tears and promises, but an intensely god-ward sorrow that results in lasting transformation exhibited repeatedly over time.

Ephesians 4:28 gives us a framework for what repentance looks like: "Let the thief no longer steal, but rather let him labor, doing honest work with his own hands, so that he may have something to share with anyone in need" (ESV). This is a specific application of a larger principle: stop the sinful behavior, close the habit in every form, and use all the energy from that toward reparation to the extent that you generously give out what you took. Let him who abused stop that habit in every form, laboring hard toward reparation and restitution, giving safety and integrity to all in need.

When true repentance occurs in any life, the focus of that life is the pursuit of Christlikeness and the death of anything not like him. The mind, the heart, and the mouth are being transformed in likeness to Jesus. When we hear justifications, excuses, blaming, selfishness, or a focus on the sins of another, we can be sure we do not have true repentance. In the case of domestic abuse (and also in the case of abuse of a child), the primary goal is not restoration of the family structure externally but rather the death of sin and growth in love and obedience to Christ.

Someone who has practiced deception *cannot* change immediately because the sin patterns are so habituated and hidden even from themselves. Anyone who engages in abusive behavior has practiced self-deception. They have practiced avoiding the truth. To think that someone can practice a sin pattern for years and simply say "I am sorry" and be all better is to fail to see sin as our God does. Abusing another does not simply mean that my words and my fists are a problem. The poison is systemic. My thinking, my judgments, my inclinations, my desires, and my volition have all been in bondage to the poison of sin. I have habituated injecting the narcotic of deception in order to call sin good or permissible. True repentance is consistent change demonstrated over time and is shown to be real when the cup is bumped again and again and something new spills out *indicating a new pattern*. It is not evidenced in an intense emotional moment when the stakes are high and we have an audience. It means being more concerned for the offended one rather than the self. It requires an understanding of the impact of our sin and a zeal for restitution. It means the exquisite pain of beginning to recognize that God himself has been assaulted by our sin. It means owning responsibility for the breakdown of trust, and knowing that much time will pass before it can be renewed.

In response to the evils of sexual violence and domestic violence we as the body of Christ are called to be on our knees before
God concerning where we do not look like Christ in our own lives.
We are also called to be on our feet speaking the truth, opening
our mouths for the dumb and for the rights of all the unfortunate.
The cross of Jesus Christ makes it eminently clear that perfect love
does not deny, pretend, or ignore the seriousness of sin. It is my
prayer that we will take any sin in the body of Christ with equal
seriousness. To tolerate it is to assault that beloved body yet again.
During this century may the church of Jesus Christ stand for truth,
holiness, and love—even behind closed doors.

CHAPTER 16

Understanding Sexual Abuse

It has been forty years since I first heard the words "My father raped me." I had just finished a Master's degree in psychology and was entering a doctoral program. Nothing in my personal life or my training had prepared me for such a statement. I did what all good students do when they hit a wall—I went to a supervisor.

The response I got in the early 1970s was that women sometimes tell these hysterical stories and our job is to not get hooked by them. They are essentially looking for attention and if you give it to them you will contribute to their pathology. As time passed I began to hear other stories of sexual abuse, and I made the decision to listen and told my clients I knew nothing about such things, nor did I know anyone to ask. I wanted to help and was willing to learn if they would teach me what they knew while I struggled to figure out what would help them. Probably out of desperation they agreed, and that began an aspect of my professional life that has changed me, challenged me, and continues to teach me.

Humans, as you know, commit atrocious acts against other humans. One atrocious thing humans do is sexually abuse children. A child is by definition developing or in process. Whenever you intrude on a developing process, you alter the outcome. The sexual abuse of a child shatters and violates every aspect of their being—their world, their self, their faith, and their future. Such violation forces the child to adapt in ways that are often maladaptive in the larger world. Such violation causes the child to develop a view of himself and his world that is based on repeated lies, evil, and destruction. Obviously an understanding of this must inform our response or we will be ineffective at best, and harmful at worst.

Sexual assault is said to be our nation's most rapidly growing crime. However, almost all information about the scope of sexual abuse and rape depends on information volunteered by victim's themselves. Obviously then, the true extent of the abuse is unknown because many compelling forces favor nondisclosure. This is as true in the church as it is in our culture, sometimes even more so.

According to the American Medical Association about seven hundred thousand women are sexually assaulted each year. That is more than one woman per minute. Childhood sexual abuse occurs in the lives of one in four women and one in six men before the age of eighteen. One in four women has been raped. There is a great deal of abuse and rape of men and boys that is still hidden. Think about the numbers in the context of the number of people in your church and you can begin to grasp something of the frequency of these crimes. Given the impact of sexual violence on an individual and on society, and given the frequency of its occurrence, it is absolutely crucial that we not be silent. God calls us not to be silent, but to be a refuge and a place for hope and healing.

When someone comes to you for help who has a history of sexual abuse or rape, they are usually there because that which is past is damaging that which is present and/or future. Even if they are not seeking help for dealing with the abuse, the symptoms that drove them to need care (anxiety, depression, suicidal ideation, homelessness, substance abuse) are sometimes the manifestation of an unresolved history of abuse. Your task will be to help them face what they most want to forget and learn to bear what they find unbearable. The result will hopefully be an increasing freedom from the tentacles of the past so that the present and future can be lived out creatively and productively.

Child Sexual Abuse

Sexual abuse can be defined as: "any sexual activity—verbal, visual, or physical—engaged in without consent." A child is considered unable to consent due to developmental immaturity and an inability to understand sexual behavior. There are different categories of sexual abuse. Verbal sexual abuse includes sexual threats, sexual comments about a child's body, lewd remarks, harassment, or sexually suggestive comments.

Visual abuse would include viewing pornographic material, exhibitionism and voyeurism. Physical sexual abuse includes oral sex, sodomy, digital penetration, penetration with an object, fondling, intercourse, and masturbation in front of the child or of the adult by the child.

A family member or someone known to the child perpetrates most abuse—though for older boys the perpetrator is sometimes a stranger. It is important to note that most abuse occurs within a context of a relationship with an adult from whom the child has every reason to expect protection, warmth, and care.

The majority of abusers of both male and female children are male (3 to 7 percent female)—most considerably older, though there has been an increase in younger perpetrators. Law enforcement officials said that in 1995, 33 percent of all those arrested for sex crimes nationwide were younger than eighteen.[1] This issue of minor perpetrators has become a huge problem with regard to how to respond, particularly if it is a first offense.

Rape

What do we mean when we speak about rape or sexual assault? In contemporary legal usage, rape is defined as nonconsensual sexual penetration obtained by physical force, by threat of bodily harm, or at a time when the victim is incapable of giving consent due to mental illness, mental retardation, or intoxication. In the US at least 20 percent of adult women and 12 percent of adolescent women have experienced sexual assault during their lifetimes. Prior to 2013 the FBI in their annual Uniform Crime Report defined rape as only forcible penetration of a female.[2] By that definition no males are raped in the United States. As of 2013 that definition has been significantly changed, however the numbers are still considered low, particularly as the rapes occurring in prisons are often never reported. Rape and sexual abuse organizations have reported an increase in men seeking help since the conclusion of the Jerry Sandusky case.[3]

There has been little research about boys who are vulnerable to abuse, though that is beginning to change. It is believed that boys raised without a biological father in the home are more likely to use drugs, be victims of physical and sexual abuse, and end up with mental illness or in prison. In the sixth grade, the rate of using alcohol, cocaine, marijuana, and IV drugs is twenty-five to fifty times higher for boys who have been sexually abused. Abused boys have twelve times the normal suicide rate and go on to have higher rates of mental illness. Among men with mental illness, 40 percent report childhood sexual abuse.[4] Recent research regarding men who are in and out of homeless shelters suggests a 40 percent rate of child abuse of some kind.[5] Such research indicates a great need for us to understand the vulnerabilities these men experienced in the early years so interventions can occur. The lack of discussion surrounding abuse of males has left an untold number to suffer in silence.

It is important to understand the factors that contribute to a severe impact of child sexual abuse. Not all sexual abuse is traumatic or has long-term impact. When the abuse is more frequent or reoccurs in the child's life over a long period of time, the effects are more severe. Impact is greater the more closely related the perpetrator and the victim, as well as when the age difference is greater. That is why father-child incest has profound impact in the child's life. Abuse by males is usually more harmful than by females, and penetration of any kind causes greater harm. Obviously, abuse that is violent and/or sadistic does great damage. If the child has attempted in some way to tell an adult what is happening and receives disbelief or denial and no help, the effect of the abuse is significantly exacerbated. Adults who look back on their abuse and see themselves as passive ("Why didn't I try to get away?") tend to carry a lot of self-blame. They often judge the child through an adult lens, forgetting that a five-year-old cannot easily escape a two-hundred-pound male. When children's bodies respond to sexual stimulation, they often assume or are told by the perpetrator that means they "wanted" the abuse or "liked" it. That burden of false guilt can be crushing.

Sex Offenders

Research done by Dr. Gene Abel in the 1980s asked voluntary sex offender clients how many total offenses they had committed. Confidentiality was guaranteed. The results stunned the professional community. Two hundred thirty- two child molesters reported fifty-five thousand attempted incidents, claimed success in thirty-eight thousand cases with seventeen thousand total victims. Male offenders who molested out-of-home female victims averaged twenty victims each, and male offenders who molested out-of-home males averaged fifteen each. In his research Dr. Abel computed the chances of being caught. It was 3 percent. Sadly these figures go with the statistics we have of victims in this country.[6] Diana Russell's study found 28 percent of females under age fourteen were molested and the number increased to 38 percent if ages 14–17 were thrown in. Only 5 percent had been reported.[7]

Dr. Anna Salter, author of *Predators,* says such things exist because of the problem of deception. Decades of research shows that people cannot reliably tell who is lying and who is not, yet most people believe they can. It is threatening to think that we cannot really know whether or not someone is trustworthy.

Sex offenders set up a double life. One man who was in his twenties and the youngest deacon in his church said the following:

> I lived a double life . . . I would do kind and generous things for people. I would give families money that did not have any money that was not from the church treasury; it was from my own bank accounts. I would support them in all the ways that I could. Talk to them, encourage them. I would go to nursing homes. Talk with the elderly. Pray with the elderly. I would do community service projects. Pick up litter off the side of the road. I would mow the lawns for elderly and handicapped people. Go grocery shopping for them.[8]

Listen to some quotes from child molesters about how they choose their victims and think about children in your area: "I would probably pick the one who appeared more needy, the child hanging back from others or feeling picked on by brothers and sisters." "I would find a child who doesn't have a happy home life, because it would be easier for me to gain their friendship." "Look for a kid who is easy to manipulate. They will go along with anything you say." "Choose children who have been unloved. Try to be nice to them until they trust you very much and they give you the impression that they will participate willingly. Use love as bait."[9]

It is important and tragic to add that researchers, investigators, and therapists are seeing more prepubescent abusers. It is estimated that 5 percent of sex crimes are committed by children younger than twelve. The average age of their victims is six. There are currently more than two thousand programs in the United States for sex offenders; four hundred are for treating minor offenders.[10]

Keep in mind that it is extremely rare for an alleged victim to lie about child sexual abuse. It is a fair assessment of the body of research on lying to say that most people lie on a regular basis. However, numerous studies have documented that it is rare for children or adults to lie about abuse. When victims do lie, they tend to lie to protect their offender, not to get him or her into trouble. Indeed, given the significant consequences of the allegation to both the alleged victim and the alleged offender, a child or adult would almost have to be pathological to make up a believable, detailed history of child sexual abuse.

Characteristics of Children

It is crucial when talking about an adult survivor of childhood sexual abuse to remember that the abuse was processed and "understood" by a child mind, not an adult mind. What do we know about children? They are vulnerable, dependent, and easily influenced. Children think egocentrically; they think the world revolves around them. Hence, children process abuse with thoughts such as, "If I were not such a bad boy or girl this would not be happening. I make people do bad things." These thoughts give them a sense of hope because if this is happening because I am bad, then if I can be good, it will stop. Such thinking also allows a child to continue to depend on his/her parents (which he must do to survive) because "the bad" is located in him, not in the parent.

Children are learning. They do not know much of anything. They are learning how relationships work, what is good, what is bad, what it means to be male or female. Part of what parents do for children is name the world (tree, boat, house). This includes intangible and abstract things such as good, bad, love, and trust. In the context of abuse, children learn that relationships are for using others, good is evil and evil is good, pretense is necessary, and they are trash. Such profound lessons do not simply get dropped when they reach adulthood. Rather, such lessons become the control beliefs for the adult.

Symptoms and Aftereffects

As we consider some of the results or symptoms of childhood sexual abuse, it is extremely important that we understand that these are *indicators* not proof. An individual can manifest all of these symptoms and yet never have experienced childhood sexual abuse. These are possible indicators of a history of sexual abuse. Again, please do *not* confuse indicators with symptoms. These indicators clearly suggest a painful and damaging history, but are not conclusive regarding the exact nature of that history. Ask the question about sexual abuse of course—but accept the answer given. It is *never* ethical to *tell* someone they have been abused when they say they were not or they do not know.

1. Body—Many survivors hate their bodies and cope with life self-destructively as a result. Addictions to food, alcohol, sex, and drugs are possible outcomes. Suicidal thoughts and self-mutilation can occur. Eating disorders and sleep disorders are not uncommon. Feelings of shame about the body are often strong. Promiscuity may be present. Listen to one survivor: "Does anyone know what it is like to be wanted only for your body parts? Your mind, your heart, your abilities, and your interests, are all irrelevant. Even your body as a whole is unimportant. Only specific parts matter. That is who you are and what you are good for." Somatic complaints, migraines, TMJ, GI problems, anxious scratching, sexual dysfunction can occur.

2. Emotional aftereffects can include anger, fear, and overwhelming grief and guilt. Another possibility is emotional numbness. Repeated abuse causes a survivor to learn how to turn off emotions. It is a way of getting relief when feelings are intolerable and the situation inescapable. Many use drugs or alcohol to enable them to go numb. Listen to a couple of survivors: "It is the fear that is unbearable. I cover it relatively well I think, but it never goes away. I am afraid of men, women, and the dark, of small spaces, of sleep, and of touch. I never relax. I never feel safe." This one speaks of her grief: "How can such things be? Do you

know the grief of being raped at age four? The grief that comes from never feeling safe as a child? The grief of never being parented? Some days I think it will crush me."

3. Abuse damages a survivor's thinking, for it has been shaped throughout childhood by lies and deceit. Such beliefs as "I am worthless"; "God is not good"; "love does not exist" are strong. The work of discerning truth from repeated lies is a tremendous job. The confusion is awful, especially if the abuser was a "very fine person." Listen to a survivor:

> Everybody loved my daddy. He told jokes and entertained people and provided a good living for "his girls" (Mom, me, and my two sisters). He made us go to church. No one knew that at home he would drink and come after my two sisters and me. We used to try and hide under the bed or in the closet. He always found us. Mother just kept on cooking.

Some children may engage in what we call doublethink. Judith Herman talks about the overwhelming developmental task faced by a child who lives with ongoing incest. That child must find a way to form an attachment to caretakers who are dangerous to her. She needs to develop trust with the untrustworthy; a sense of self with those who are uncaring or cruel; a capacity for self-regulation in a chaotic and unpredictable environment; and a capacity for self-soothing in an environment devoid of comfort. Her existential task is also formidable for she must find hope and meaning while abandoned to a merciless power. To preserve faith in her parents, she must reject the conclusion that they are unsafe or that something is wrong with them. The only other alternative is to assume that she is the problem. If she is bad, she can try to be good. If she has caused the incest, then perhaps she has the power to stop it. The child often thinks if he/she has been good such things could have been prevented. By the time adulthood is reached it is a formidable task to alter this thinking.

4. Problems stemming from the abuse can also reverberate throughout a survivor's relationships. Childhood sexual abuse involved betrayal, rejection, humiliation, abandonment, and deceit. Trust seems impossible or foolhardy. Relationships are invaded by fear. Control is paramount. From a survivor: "Trust is a really scary word. It strikes me as a very stupid thing to do. All of the adults in my life either hurt me or ignored the ones who did. I guess I do trust, don't I? I trust that people will hurt me."

5. Spiritually the effects of abuse are profound as well. A distorted image of God, coupled with a distorted image of the self, create many barriers to experiencing God's love and grace. God is seen as punitive, capricious, indifferent, or dead. The survivor struggles to bring together two irreconcilable realities—God and sexual abuse. Either one without the other can be understood, but how is one to reconcile God *and* sexual abuse? The tentacles of childhood sexual abuse reach into the adult life of a survivor, often infecting every aspect of his or her life. The abused child's psychological adaptations help to survive the trauma, but eventually become the very things that damage adult life and obstruct growth. Though the severity of those aftereffects varies from one individual to another, these things we have mentioned are part of the possible impact of abuse.

Post-traumatic Stress Disorder

Not all abuse is traumatic in nature. Whether or not childhood abuse was traumatic is determined by the presence of PTSD. One of the mistakes that is often made is to assume all abuse has the same meaning and impact. Such things must always be understood on an individual basis. To not do so is to fail to listen, which in essence, repeats a dynamic of abuse.

If we find the presence of PTSD then we need to understand trauma and its effects. Parenthetically, according to research, repeated episodes of homelessness in a life usually mean there was some kind of child abuse in the history. Shelters have typically focused on life and job skills, addictions, etc. and it is being learned that there is a high incidence of trauma in the homeless population. Homelessness itself can be traumatic. It makes people vulnerable to being traumatized, and there is often a history of sexual abuse, domestic violence, or street violence as well as a high number of combat vets—all of which can be traumatizing. So it is crucial to have some understanding of PTSD.

To experience an atrocity is to live the unspeakable. To heal from an atrocity, one must learn to speak the unspeakable. Our task becomes that of helping the person find a way to both speak and bear the unbearable. Trauma silences, isolates, and renders powerless. To heal from trauma one must speak within the context of relationship and have impact.

What is trauma? It involves intense fear, helplessness, loss of control, and the threat of annihilation. As Judith Herman states, "Traumatic events are extraordinary, not because they occur rarely, but rather because they overwhelm the ordinary human adaptations to life."[11] Normal responses involve things like calling for help or finding comfort in relationships, as well as the fight-or-flight reflex. Trauma occurs when these normal responses do not work. That is part of the terror of traumatic events. When you cannot fight against the trauma and you physically cannot escape it, that is when other coping mechanisms must be found. Nothing you do works to stop what is happening.

The ordinary human response to danger is complex and involves both body and mind. The changes that occur are normal and adaptive and ready the person for fight or flight. Traumatic reactions occur in individuals when action is seen to be of no avail.

This reaction could occur in those who believed they could not protect themselves, those who could not protect another, or in those who knew they could do nothing to stop the events from occurring. When action seems pointless, the human system of self-defense becomes overwhelmed and disorganized. Those things we do in response to danger seem useless and often persist in an exaggerated way long after the danger is over. Trauma produces lasting changes in physiological arousal, emotion, cognition, and memory. Sometimes traumatic events separate these normally integrated functions from one another so that what usually functions as a unit becomes disjointed. For example, a traumatized person may demonstrate strong feeling with no clear memory of the events or clear memory without emotion. Trauma often results in disrupted cognitive and emotional processes.

After an experience of overwhelming danger, two contradictory responses often occur or two opposing psychological states: intrusion and constriction. The victim is caught between amnesia and reliving the trauma, intense overwhelming emotion and numbness, impulsivity and inhibition or passivity.

Keeping in mind that the core of trauma is fear, it is easy to understand the drive to avoid the memory (child sexual abuse [CSA], rape, domestic violence, street violence, combat). When we are afraid, we want to get away. Traumatized people are driven to avoid remembering, feeling, processing, or thinking about the trauma. At the same time, the trauma itself stays alive within, buried but not gone, and its tentacles can immediately throw the survivor back into the noises, feelings, smells, and panic of the traumatic experience. These alternating states of avoidance and intrusion continue the feelings of chaos and unpredictability that the trauma caused, making it seem as if the trauma is continuing. So often, people continue functioning as if it had just happened. Flashbacks, recurrent nightmares, and intrusive memories keep the feelings of unpredictability and chaos ever-present. People cannot get better because it is still happening in the mind. They fear being triggered by the memories and often constrict their lives more and more until some vets are reduced to sitting in one chair in a room, afraid to go out because something will trigger the traumatic memory and throw them backward again.

Initially, the victim has ongoing, intrusive recollections of the event both as flashbacks and nightmares. The victim stays highly agitated and on alert for new danger. When there is a single incident trauma, the intrusive symptoms often decrease after three to six months, though if the threat of recurrence were still present obviously the symptoms would continue for a longer period.

Again, when trauma is recurring, long term, symptoms are incorporated into the personality and being traumatized becomes a way of life. If intrusive symptoms (domestic violence) decrease over time, numbing and constrictive symptoms remain. This is very important. Unfortunately because the person *seems* to have resumed their former life, to a great extent many people think they have recovered from the trauma. Sadly, the person functions but feels dead inside and disconnected from life and relationships. Many people who have been traumatized by something like childhood sexual abuse live the majority of their lives in this constrictive state. We want to respond to trauma to help people deal with their memories, emotions, and reactions in ways that return them to a place of care, connection, and meaning.

Traumatic Reenactments

Many adult survivors of CSA engage in what we call traumatic reenactments. It is in part a way of trying to gain mastery over events of powerlessness. It is an internalizing of the offender and a way of punishing the self for getting abused. It is also used as a way to quiet down high anxiety and agitation. These episodes can be severe and anxiety provoking for both the client and the caregiver/therapist.

CSA involves chronic overstimulation, affective flooding, and the fusion of sexuality, anger, aggression, touch, control, and sadism. Such experiences result in an intolerable affective state and a debased sense of self. Adults who have been chronically abused do not experience the normal regulation of emotional states, are full of self-loathing, and have little sense of ownership of their own bodies.

When a child is repeatedly victimized, his or her body and mind are exploited and adult impulses such as anger and sexual tension are vented on the child. It is not really surprising that children who have been exploited in this fashion would then use their bodies to relieve tensions and act out impulses through self-injurious behavior. This is combined with the fact that while most humans seek care and comfort in relationship when they have been hurt, the abused child cannot do so, for relationships are what bring pain. Ongoing abuse extinguishes the normal human search for connection, and the victim is left to rely on his/her own resources.

Because they are unable to rely on others for care and support when distressed, many victims find relief in self-destructive behaviors. Cutting and burning are the most common types since physical pain releases endorphins, which are essentially the body's morphine. Endorphins have a tranquilizing and anti-depressant quality that can be soothing. These self-destructive behaviors replicate the abuse cycle: fear, agitation, pain, then quiet. Many survivors are drug- or alcohol-addicted or involved in sex/pornography addictions, all of which are used to quiet an over-agitated system they cannot otherwise control.

Such behaviors are seen by the victim as a solution and by the caregiver as a problem. This will obviously produce tension in the relationship. The most effective response is education, guidance, and empathy. It must be clear that adults are primarily responsible for their own behaviors and must have the primary motivation to change them. Otherwise the relationship will be an ongoing tug-of-war based on the caregiver's discomfort and motivation to see change. Bearing witness to another's struggle and choices is instructive because we experience knowing about abuse in someone we care about and being powerless to stop it—a replica of the victim's experience as a child. We will find ourselves wanting to over-control and getting agitated and upset, all similar to the state the survivor keeps experiencing.

Response to an Adult with an Abuse History

A healing response to abuse responds in a way that reverses the dynamics of that abuse. In abuse, the thoughts, feelings, and pain of the victim do not matter. In a healing response, the victim is given room to speak (however slowly), a quick ear, an empathic response, or a voice as it were. In abuse, relationship is violated. It involves deception, betrayal, abuse of power, destruction of trust and safety, violation, shame, and humiliation. In a healing response, the victim is safe, power is never abused, respect is given, truth is always told, and honor is shown. In abuse, power is robbed, dignity stolen, and shaming helplessness occurs. In a healing response, power is restored ("What do you think, what do you choose, what are your goals?"), and the power held by the caregiver is ever and always used for the good of the survivor, not for the self.

When working with an adult with an abuse history, the first phase of that work is focused on establishing a safe and trustworthy relationship and, as much as possible, helping the survivor develop safety and stabilization in their own life. Do they live in a safe place? How is their self-care? Are they ingesting dangerous substances or engaging in risky behaviors? Is there some level of stable functioning? If not, then these things must slowly be built up as a first priority.

To respond to a survivor by first plunging into their abuse history without safety and stabilization is to set them up for failure and to most likely exacerbate the destructive coping mechanisms they are already using to cope with their history. The order of care is this: safety and stabilization first; then the telling of the story and the understanding of its impact; and finally, beginning to move into the future. It will be likely during the course of this response that a return to safety and stabilization will be repeatedly necessary as the story will raise fears and agitation that will need empathy, care, and stabilization before returning to the story again.

I have been to Rwanda many times to do trainings and have learned a great deal from the Rwandans. A wonderful and godly man who survived the genocide recently said to me, "We thought we were dead; just animals. They called us cockroaches, you know. But you came; you sat with us; you listened; *you saw us* . . . and we remembered we are human." You saw us. That is what must ever and always underlie the care for those who have suffered child sexual abuse or trauma of any kind. Always; no exceptions. You see them . . . not where you think they should be by now or where you want them to go, no matter how good that goal is. *You see them and who they are, but you must also always see who they were.* Who they were still is. The Rwandans were human. I knew that, but they did not, and I needed to sit with those who thought they were not human. Telling them otherwise would have been meaningless.

Dignity is restored through sitting and bearing witness at the pace of the wounded person before you. And every time you move in to touch the source of the pain—which you must do—it will hurt. Pain from the lightest touch will immediately activate the old coping mechanisms, which will prevent them from moving forward. It can be quite a dilemma if not understood. They want to get better. You share that goal and might even be able to see the pathway. Often when you move forward with them, they go back to their familiar patterns; they panic, resist, or get overwhelmed. The tendency is to not understand this back and forth and to push or wrongly urge forward.

If you are reading this, I assume it is because you want to effectively walk alongside those who have experienced abuse. Remember these things and *see them*—who they are and were—so you can respond with understanding rather than out of your own needs, or tiredness that day, or your goals they are nowhere near ready for.

Good intentions are not enough. Knowledge is not enough. Good counseling, ethical care as opposed to malevolent "helping," consists of responses that do not in any way repeat the dynamics of abuse. Such care is good for the victim always; it is chosen by them and never forced; it is truthfully informative; they are treated with dignity and partnered with in decisions, timing, and goals. Kindness, patience, truth, understanding, and faithfulness rule the process.

Finally, I hope you see the utterly incarnational nature of this work or ministry. "The Word became flesh, and dwelt among us" (John 1:14). He saw us; he bore witness to our devastation; he sat with us, walked with us, and heard us. You are following him. You are called to flesh out the Word; to see and know and understand so that you can meet the person where they are—as Christ did for us, entering into that place with them and, by your Christlikeness and faithful endurance, woo them out of their sorrow and night into the freedom-producing truth of God and his great love for them.

CHAPTER 17

Narcissism
and the System It Breeds

Long before the birth of modern psychology and the Diagnostic and Statistical Manual of Mental Health Disorders, there was an understanding of narcissism. According to Greek myth, Narcissus was a handsome youth with a heart inaccessible to love. One of his rejected lovers prayed to Nemesis (the goddess who dealt out retribution for those who succumbed to arrogance) and asked that she would punish him for his unfeeling heart—or as we would say, his lack of empathy. Nemesis caused him to see his reflection in the water and fall in love with himself. That reflection was of course inaccessible (as he had been to others), and he died of unrequited love. His name in the Greek is *Narkissos* from the word *narke*, which means "stupor or numbness."

It is obviously the origin of such words in English as *narcotic* and *narcolepsy*. The combined elements from the story are quite fascinating: self-love and unfeelingness toward others leading to numbness and death. And of course the conclusion of the tale is that his death resulted in the flowering of the beautiful and fragrant narcissus. The takeaway is that beauty resulted from the death of obsessive and excessive self-love. The death of his dead heart yielded life and beauty.

Many of you reading this chapter have encountered those we call narcissists. Some of you have worked with them in your counseling offices and found them a challenge. Others have encountered them in your families, in your pulpits, or in leadership of ministry organizations or work sites. They may initially seem alluring because they are often bright, charismatic, articulate, capable, and seemingly full of promise. They are often the ones we hope will make it better or take it to a new level (whether "it" is us, our future, our church, or our organization).

In this chapter I want to differentiate between narcissism and narcissistic personality disorder, with the bulk of our time being spent on the latter. Following an understanding of the disorder, I want to look closely at the relationship a narcissist has with a system, particularly when he is a leader of that system. We will also consider the characteristics of systems drawn to narcissists, and hence how those in leadership often fail to see what they are welcoming into their midst. Finally, I want to consider all of this through the lens of the Scripture, doing an exposé, as it were, of both narcissism and systems (or individuals) drawn to them based on the Word of God. We will finish with a few suggested safeguards.

Though hopefully this chapter will give you a greater understanding of the diagnosis of Narcissistic Personality Disorder (NPD), this is not a treatise in how to diagnostically determine whether or not someone fits that category. This is also not a course in the treatment of that disorder. The focus is primarily an understanding of the disorder and how it relates to the systems we live and serve in. The focus of the chapter derives from my work over the years with clergy and ministry leaders, as well as with church bodies and Christian organizations. I have seen and worked with groups—families, churches, and ministry organizations—devastated and shattered by narcissists some who have been grossly immoral and corrupt. I have seen groups that have had serial narcissists brought into leadership positions with no grasp of why they keep repeating the pattern. And I have worked with churches and other groups that have been wounded and rocked over the long term simply from the impact of a narcissist at the helm, though no sexual immorality, embezzlement, or glaring lies have been told.

Understanding Narcissism

Narcissism at its heart is self-absorption, a preoccupation with image, acting entitled, demanding, and generally uninterested in the feelings of others. All of you who have parented or treated adolescents will hear a familiar ring to these characteristics, which is why I want us to differentiate it from narcissism as the result of immaturity due to age or developmental stage or even something like trauma. Such narcissism has elasticity, is malleable, can be worked with, and is laid aside as maturity comes. For those of you who have raised kids or treated teens, I am sure you have seen that process—where a self-absorbed, demanding teen turns into a gracious, thoughtful adult as time goes on. You also know the experience of interacting with a demanding, seemingly selfish teen who then turns around and is utterly winsome with you or totally unselfish with a peer. Narcissism, like most things we deal with, is on a continuum, and so we encounter flavors of it, strong doses of it, patterns of it over a lifetime, and we also see the more rigid, enduring, shaping-all-aspects-of-life characteristics of a personality disorder. So basically the continuum goes from an intermittent flavor of narcissism all the way across to Narcissistic Personality Disorder, that rigid pattern that presents in all contexts. It is important to recognize nuances or we inappropriately label people, often as a result of our own frustration and annoyance with them, rather than a careful, clinical study and understanding of what we are dealing with.

At the same time it is important to note that several studies have shown an increase in narcissism in the US. Some studies suggest that sub-clinical levels of narcissism have risen among college students since the 1970s. Many point to cultural trends that nurture characteristics like entitlement, materialism, and an expectation of being free from suffering, which would seem to breed narcissism in our youth. Such studies are controversial, and others show conflicting data. It is at the least something worth watching in the literature.

Narcissistic Personality Disorder

A study conducted at the National Institute of Health suggested that 6.2 percent of Americans suffered from Narcissistic Personality Disorder.[1] Other estimates across studies range from 2 to 15 percent in clinical samples or less than 1 percent in the general population. Most experts agree that males dominate the arena, with estimates of 50 to 80 percent. However, women can certainly have the disorder, and I have encountered them in my practice—though in keeping with the data, at a far lesser rate.

The core characteristics of this disorder are grandiosity, lack of empathy, and an insatiable need for admiration and approval. To put this less clinically, the disorder involves these enduring attitudes: "I am bigger, better, and far more superior to you or anyone else; I have no understanding of or interest in grasping my impact on you *except* insofar as you can feed my ego or support the beliefs I have in myself." The DSM-IV says this pattern is evidenced by early adulthood and is apparent *across contexts*—a quality of all personality disorders. Just to be certain we all know what this disorder entails, let's run down the diagnostic criteria as listed in the DSM:

1. Has a grandiose sense of self often seen in an exaggeration of achievements and abilities
2. Is preoccupied with fantasies of unlimited success, power, brilliance, and love

3. Believes he is special and can only be understood by others who are special (an important point as we consider systems)
4. Demands excessive admiration
5. Feels entitled and expects favors and compliance; allows no disagreement and demands "submission" (note the biblical word)
6. Is interpersonally exploitive; uses others to achieve his ends; feeds off others
7. Lacks empathy; cannot identify with others' feelings
8. Is envious of others or believes they are envious of him because of his superiority or specialness
9. Is arrogant, haughty, proud in behavior and attitudes[2]

In order to qualify, a person must meet at least five of the above listed nine criteria. In brief, the mantra for NPD is, "It *is* all about me and don't you dare forget it." Let's consider the disorder a bit more deeply. Note that someone with this disorder takes his bearings from the externals. Look at the list: achievements, accomplishments, success, power over others, adoration, affirmation, and approval. The narcissist presents his grandiose self, not his real self, to others, so as to gain those things because they are his food and drink, his oxygen. Indeed, he believes they are necessary to his existence, they are owed to him, they are his right, and if they are denied, rage follows.

Narcissism at its core is the preservation of the self *as both good and grand*. He uses all that he has—his abilities, his brains, his charisma, his power, his success, his reputation, and whatever else is in his arsenal—toward such preservation. He will also use others. He will use you. He will exploit anything you have in the service of his ends—your abilities, brains, love, success, beauty, reputation, connections, your submissiveness—in order to preserve his self as good and grand. He will suck you dry if he can, and once drained, you will be tossed aside. He has many gifts, except the gift of humility before God that harnesses all other abilities and allows them to be governed by the Spirit of God alone. How easy it is for all of us to deify the gifts God has given rather than the God who gave them! When the church deifies gifts, she becomes extremely vulnerable to the Narcissistic Personality Disordered leader.

In the novel *The Unthinkable Thoughts of Jacob Green* by Joshua Braff, the wife of a man with NPD hosts a social gathering in their home and gives a little speech about her husband. After pointing out how exciting he is to be around and how many friends he has, she explains what it is like to live with a man obsessed with his own importance and on a constant quest to maintain it. Listen to her describe her life:

> Such is the narcissist who must mask his fears of inadequacy by ensuring that he is perceived to be a unique and brilliant stone. In his offspring he finds the grave limits he cannot admit in himself. And he will stop at nothing to make certain that his child continually tries to correct these flaws. In actuality, the child may be exceedingly intelligent, but has so fully developed feelings of ineptitude that he is incapable of believing in his own possibilities. The child's innate sense of self is in great jeopardy when this level of false labeling is accepted. In the end the narcissist must *compensate for this core vulnerability* he carries and as a result an overestimation of his own importance arises. So it feeds itself, cyclically. And, when in the course of life they realize that their views are not shared or their expectations are not met, the most common reaction is to become enraged. The rage covers the fear associated with the vulnerable self, but it is nearly impossible for others to see this, and as a result, the very recognition they so crave is most often out of reach. It's been eighteen years that I've lived in service to this mindset. And it's been devastating

for me to realize that my efforts to rise to these standards and demands and preposterous requests for perfection have ultimately done nothing but disappoint my husband.[3]

She captures it, doesn't she? The grandiosity, the "specialness," the demand for admiration and approval and agreement, the rage when such things are not given, as well as the shame and humiliation that must be repaired by others at any cost, the entitlement, the exploitation of others (even his own children) to buttress his view of himself as quite grand and oh so good, his lack of empathy even for his kids, and his constant feeding off others to support the self. "Feed me love, feed me adoration, feed me approval, feed me agreement, and whatever else you do, reflect back to me the image of myself as being all that I say I am and want to be. And God help you if you fail."

Years ago when my father was in a nursing home, we used to visit him with our then-young sons. One day as we were walking down the hallway lined with residents in wheelchairs, our sons ran ahead and soon the youngest came running back sobbing, "Mommy, Mommy, why won't they feed that lady?" I walked with him to see what the problem was. There was an old woman with severe dementia sitting in the hall, holding out her arms and saying to all who passed by, "Feed me; feed me; I am starving to death!" Her mantra often comes to mind when I am working with the narcissist. All who come by are prey, and there is no memory of having just eaten.

Think what an utterly weary task it must be for an NPD to wear the shepherd's dress as it were and to have to borrow the shepherd's voice, his attitudes, and his ways without truly having a shepherd's heart. What a burdensome charade! Leaders can call themselves Christian; they can say they are shepherds, pastors, or disciples and learn to speak in ecclesiastical words and moving tones and yet be impostors. As strangers to God's pastures, how can they direct or feed his sheep? With no spiritual eye to truly see him and discern his truths, how can they unlock such things for his flock? They grind at the mill, trying to create bread for others, yet all the while they sit in darkness and are starving, eventually feeding on those for whom they say they care. All he can do is keep conjuring up some illusive mirage in the desert, giving them a stone for bread. Such a leader is self-installed, not God-ordained, and we are easily seduced by his trappings, his deified gifts, fed by our own hunger and longings. In fact, he is a hireling, more concerned for his ego and his own starving self and skillful at shearing but not at feeding.

Narcissists and Systems

When you really hear and absorb the characteristics listed above, you wonder how in the world an individual, a church, an organization, or an entire nation can get drawn into a relationship with such a person—and go into it thinking it is simply going to be wonderful! Just think about the first characteristic listed: grandiosity. Who wants to be around that? It is puffed up and arrogant, full of itself, right? That is not attractive to most of us at all. What pulls us in?

Someone with Narcissistic Personality Disorder is an illusionist. He is an expert in masquerade, a Pied Piper. *The Seduction of Eva Volk* by C. D. Baker is a fascinating novel about a Christian family in Germany pre-World War II. They are desperately seeking hope and healing along with their surrounding culture after the first war, and they are seduced into viewing Hitler as the savior of Germany. *He* will return honor to Germans who felt shamed by the loss of WWI. *He* will feed the hungry and assist the poor. *He* will lift the despair. And indeed he did for some time. He put bread back on the shelves, money in their pockets, and pride in nationality in their hearts. Their seduction and blindness cost them dearly.

The author writes, "Eva's world was broken and fearful and so was she. Then a savior came as an angel of light. So Eva and her world closed their eyes and let him have his way." The book's subtitle is "A Novel of Hitler's Christians." Clearly the term "Hitler's Christians" is an oxymoron. So how exactly does such a thing happen?

Let's back up and get the bigger picture and then move in closer in order to understand better how it is that God's people get seduced into being led by those we would call narcissists. First, a few words about the surrounding culture in this country. I fear we have long been breathing the cultural air and it appears to have put us to sleep (there is that *narcotic* word again), so we can then be oblivious to the toxins we imbibe on a regular basis.

Consider some of the characteristics of our culture. Surely narcissism and its accompanying entitlement are one. Look at the financial world—its greed and its downfall. Look at what happens when someone thinks you are in their way. Look at the growing list of those in power who are using females for their own gratification. From big to little issues, it appears to be my right to get what I want and if you are in my way or I need to "adapt" the rules, so be it. We value materialism, affluence, pleasure, and accomplishment. We have bought houses we cannot afford, goods we cannot afford, and pursue sex without concern for parameters or impact. We expect life to protect us from suffering and if it does not, we sue someone. We expect to get what we want, avoid what we don't, and have the right to live pain-free existences. Busyness is seen as equal to productivity and productivity and success trump real relationship. We are a nation full of self-absorbed, anxious, and angry souls. And it is clearly not turning out as we expected, hoped, or demanded, which means we are starting to feel desperate—not unlike post-WWI Germans.

Like Israel of old, much of the church today has been captivated by the surrounding culture. There are precious and wonderful exceptions to this, but it has infected us for sure. We get intoxicated by personalities, large ministries, charisma, success, large followings, brilliance, and moving oratory. Surely that would make us as the church as vulnerable as the Christians in Hitler's time to succumb to one who promises us bigger and better and says it is all for God.

The same gifts and abilities that can make a man an effective preacher and powerful leader can hide narcissism. When natural virtues or gifts are used to determine qualification for leadership rather than spiritual virtues demonstrated in character, when visible means of growth and change are used rather than invisible, and when the promise of great and grand rather than the becoming small lures us into thinking we will be accomplishing great things for God, we are easily swayed into believing the illusion and falling into line behind the bigger, brighter, more articulate leader. We adopt the grandiosity of thought as it makes us feel good: we will build, we will grow, we will draw them in. We will care for the poor, we will develop ministries, we will raise money, we will make a difference, and we are seduced into believing the illusion and thinking we are doing it all for God. Along with the narcissist we set ourselves and our system in the center. Christ is on the circumference, as if he were some satellite of a moon, shining brightly for our special group alone. What is hidden from view is that those being brought along into this grand vision do not see that ultimately the grand vision is simply the self of the narcissist and not God at all, and those accompanying him are merely supporting actors in his play of self- magnification.

Let's consider a couple of possible scenarios. Church A has been through some difficult things. They lost a beloved pastor to death, which resulted in a significant attrition of membership. They hired a new pastor that did not work out. He did not seem to be able to stir the church and increase the membership, so they parted ways. The system is depressed and many remember years ago when the church was alive and flourishing. They long for that again. They have interviewed pastoral candidates and have not found anyone they think can help them get back to that—until recently, that is. They just interviewed a young man in his early forties who is brilliant and very articulate. His preaching has a bit of a soaring quality to it. He has given the congregation hope—hope that they can be a vibrant, growing church again—one that can bring change to the community and that will bring people to God. The candidate told them a great deal about his hopes for them and what he can do to renew the church. He knows the right way to do this—to help them grow and discover all they are meant to be.

Initially, when the narcissist joins up with a system, it is energized. The illusion is bought. We will be bigger and better. We have a brilliant preacher, and his charisma and mastery of words weave together to paint a rosy future full of hope. Of course, none of these words are used. The picture of promise is painted with spiritual language laced with words like *deeper, fuller, more*, with scriptural phrases tacked on. And vulnerable, hungry sheep follow behind, believing and hoping in the illusion, thinking it is of God. Grand growth and success are anticipated by all—for the glory of God, of course. Indeed, many of the sheep think that is actually true.

A depressed, struggling, hungry system—be it a family, a nation, a church, or an organization—is easy prey for a narcissist. He believes he can deliver the moon, or perhaps believes he *is* the moon. He seems to bring hope, promise, life, and growth. The faith of the struggling system is placed in him—subtly, not seeing that it is a misplaced hope. Rescue is on the way. A champion has appeared on the horizon. He is a master of words and stirs hearts. The pied piper is playing his tune, and unwittingly the people follow like sheep without a shepherd. Thinking he is coming to feed them, they do not see that they are going to be food for him. Thinking he is coming to bring hope and change and growth to them, they fail to see that if they do not deliver such goods to him, he will be enraged and lay the blame at their feet—accusing them of not wanting to do right, not being submissive to God, not having enough understanding—and so they have become the obstacle to all the greatness or good he could have brought.

A second possible scenario can be found when a group is not depressed and hungry but rather already considers itself superior—more knowledgeable, more spiritual, and as holders of a special or unique mission. Church plants, new organizations, spin-off churches, and older traditional organizations that have a sort of spiritual blue-blood mentality can be vulnerable to this group. When you are part of the "we know how to do it better" group, then a leader must by definition be grander and greater than the ordinary. A special group demands a special leader, and vice versa. Extraordinary requires extraordinary leadership so you can easily end up with a narcissistic orgy. Initially group and leader adore the reflection of the self seen in the other. Your superiority is proof of mine. We are an elite system. We picked an extraordinary leader, and we will do exceptional things for God.

Such a group eventually becomes cannibalistic and ends in death as both the group and the leader feed off each other, never finding satisfaction and killing each other seeking it. Such a scenario can be cyclical—I have seen it. At the end, the group is wounded and broken by the perceived and real failures of the leader, and the group deals with that wounding by seeking out another special leader who will really get it and do it right this time. It can actually lead to serial narcissists in leadership in the same system.

It is not a stretch at all in these two scenarios to see how embezzlement of money or clergy sexual abuse can flourish. Narcissists feed on the externals. They are gluttons for affirmation, approval, love, success, and power. They lack empathy and are interpersonally exploitive. It is certain that they will be disappointed and wounded. Whether they ride in as champion on a white horse for a depressed group or arrive to great fanfare and mutual admiration to a "special" group, it is inevitable that the group will fail them. Whatever they get will fall short of their felt need or will be less than they deserve. That means the narcissist will feel threatened and hungry.

It is an easy jump from that letdown to feeding more overtly on a congregation by funneling money to feed importance or by preying on others for sex. He will use all the natural abilities that put him in leadership as he continues to feed—manipulating words, emotions, and power to get what he wants and to keep it hidden. Such shepherds are described in Ezekiel 34, shepherds that feed themselves rather than feeding the flock. When caught, their horror is about the damage it will do *to them* to be so accused and the fact that others are failing them by getting in the way of their ability to live out their specialness.

Sometimes the system itself protects them, colluding with them regarding their specialness. For example, in response to a pedophile, church leadership might say, "He is so gifted in ministry; surely you would not want to destroy such potential." The profound lack of empathy (in the narcissist or the system), let alone repentance, is unsettling, frightening. It renders others and the impact on them invisible, erased, which is a form of death. When the system itself has caught the disease, it is inclined to cover up such things as clergy sexual abuse or pedophilia because it will "damage" the church or organization to expose it.

Two caveats before we continue. One, a reminder that I said initially that narcissism is on a continuum. There are many human beings both in leadership and out with flavors of narcissism. Be cautious with the diagnosis. Two, clergy sexual abuse is a horrible thing under any circumstances. However, not all those who commit such abuse qualify for the diagnosis of Narcissistic Personality Disorder. There is more than one road to that serious assault on the sheep of God.

Scriptural Perspective

Clearly, we need to shine a light on this issue. None of us wants to be entangled in such relationships, nor do we want any part of the precious body of our Lord to be damaged and destroyed by leaders who look good and promise great things. So let us look at this for a bit through the lens of the Scripture after at first confronting something of the current Christian culture. Note also before I proceed that I am well aware that there are wonderful exceptions in the Christian world to what I am about to suggest. I am certainly not sweeping all our churches and organizations into the same pile.

Culture is a major shaping influence in all of our lives. It is also far more pervasive and complicated than simply what we term popular culture. We live in a world of global corporations, instant contact with distant people, pretty much constant noise, high-speed travel, mountains of information, and a wealth of material goods. The world values bigger, grander, faster, and more of just about everything. It is easy to be caught up in such things and apply them unthinkingly to the work of God. Surely, bigger is better for him. Surely, success means more people can be reached. Surely, faster is proof of his blessing. And that means smaller, struggling, and slow is judgment of some kind, failure in some way. To have such qualities is to feel bad, and to feel bad is to long for relief or rescue. To long for relief and rescue is to be vulnerable, which of course describes every frail, finite, fallen human being.

We are full of longings, you and I. We were created for God, which means we were created to live with his greatness, his infinity, his glory. We were meant to know him and walk with him and converse with the sovereign Lord of all things, seen and unseen. And here we are broken, dying, and scrambling around in the dirt still looking for glory. And you know how we got here? We got here because something material and finite looked good and we

298 SUFFERING AND THE HEART OF GOD

believed the lie that it would make us like God. Not much has changed, has it? Do you think there was a bit of grandiosity in that original reach?

Keep in mind what I have said: there is a difference between narcissism and Narcissistic Personality Disorder. However, holding that thought, we must recognize that the seed of such things is in all of us. Not recognizing that is part of what makes us vulnerable to narcissistic leaders. We have longings for greatness that are ultimately not longings for our own greatness—though we are easily seduced to that end. They are at bottom meant to be longings for the great God who created us and loved us. We sadly try to fulfill such longings with finite things, thinking somehow they will make us great, which is to say, like God. In the context of our discussion, those longings get twisted until we believe that the leader with NPD *is* the messiah who will make it better and that somehow the system aligned with such a person is grander as a result. It is a form of what we might call *vicarious narcissism*.

Remember in high school when we used to think that if we could not *be* the most popular person in the room, at least if we could be *with them* and appear to be their friend, then their bigness, their grandness would somehow rub off and make us special too? It is also not unlike what many of you have seen in your offices when you encounter a marriage between a borderline and a narcissist, a clinically challenging duo. The borderline is struggling with feeling like she has no self and she is mighty hungry, and the narcissist rides into town with seemingly enough for both of them. He promises he can fill her up, make her better—all an illusion. His real message is, "You get grander and better by my hand, which will feed me, feed me, because I am starving to death."

That is a small picture of the dynamic with a system—a family, church, or ministry—and a leader with NPD. Such a leader will seemingly fulfill the alluring promise of making it all better, bigger, and grander. "And you will be like God too—bigger and grander as well. I too can be bigger, brighter, and more beautiful because the other is and I am near."

We need to beware the promise of the words. Such words were crafted by the Enemy of our souls to touch human longings, and we were seduced away from the greatest Glory of all. The Enemy was crafty, we are told. He took truth and injected a lie into it. He was a word master. If you talk with those who have been in a system with someone with NPD at the helm, they will often talk about his use of words—a brilliant, articulate, powerful word user, especially spiritual words—but the words are crafty and their purpose is to seduce, exploit, and manipulate others to feed his grandiosity.

There is a fascinating segment in *Through the Looking Glass* where Alice is speaking with Humpty Dumpty and he says,

> "There's glory for you!"
>
> "I don't know what you mean by glory," Alice said.
>
> Humpty Dumpty smiled contemptuously. "Of course you don't—*till I tell you*. I meant 'there's a nice knock-down argument for you'!"
>
> "But glory doesn't mean a 'nice knock-down argument,'" Alice objected.
>
> "When I use a word," Humpty Dumpty said in a rather scornful tone, "it means just what I choose it to mean."
>
> "The question is," said Alice, "whether you *can* make words mean so many different things."
>
> "The question is," said Humpty Dumpty, "which is to be master, that's all."[4]

Humpty Dumpty here makes a really good NPD study. He uses words to accomplish his purposes. He is above the rules that govern their use or meaning and is scornful of Alice, who thinks words should be used according to their correct meaning.

Quoting Hitler again: "By the skillful use of propaganda [which is, of course, largely words], one can make a people see even heaven as hell or an extremely wretched life as paradise."[5] Leaders with NPD have convinced followers of all kinds of things, essentially calling evil good and being believed. Emotional, spiritual, and verbal power is used to manipulate and control others into feeding the narcissist. Having sex with parishioners is love and care that they can never find anywhere else. Draining money from others is good and great because it is for the cause of God. Drinking the Kool-Aid, abandoning all other connections with others, submission in service of the leader who knows best and is only trying to do what is right for you is all called good and godly and will be misunderstood by others who are lesser sorts of creatures and not part of the inner circle.

Consider with me the stunning contrast all of this is to leadership in the manner in which Jesus led. We cannot do an in-depth study of this and I have spoken on it before, but briefly reflect with me.

1.   Divine leadership as seen in Jesus Christ follows the opposite course to typical human leadership. Leadership that bears likeness to Christ descends from heaven to earth; it goes from up to down; from expansive to limited, from broad to narrow; from glory to dirt. It descends in love and humility in order to feed and nurture the other (John 13; Philippians 2).

2.   God measures leadership, not by its sphere, not by its size, not by its approval ratings, but by its heart. The kingdom to be conquered is that of the heart. A leader is a man or woman who sees life from God's perspective and is focused on the kingdom of the heart. If you want to lead as your Lord led, then he must rule your heart. He must rule your heart no matter the temptation to feed yourself, or to do great things for others, or to use power for what you call good, or to raise yourself up. His rule of the kingdom of your heart is his foremost concern. If he has governance

of your heart, then whatever else you do will be done in a way that manifests the character of Christ and honors him. Evidence of God's rule in the kingdom of the heart always results in love and obedience to him (Matthew 5).

3. The third characteristic is that such leadership—divine leadership— requires a crucifixion. The way of the cross is a life of voluntary sacrifice governed by love—love of God. God longs to make us into a priestly kingdom. Priests presented the sacrifices. Sacrifices involved death. As we rise to ascend in the kingdom of God, we will find that crucifixion is required—the crucifixion in us of all that is not like Christ. Such death in the leader leads to life in the followers. Divine leadership is unlike leadership that feeds on the followers, sucking them dry, or treating them as invisible such as we have described (Galatians 2:20).

4. Leadership in the name of Jesus is a regressive leadership—a leadership that goes back. That sounds strange, doesn't it? When we think of leadership, we think of being in front, leading the way forward, heading the charge. Anything backward seems the opposite of leading. Think about it. He who is rich beyond measure goes back for the poor. He who is whole goes back for the broken. He who is freedom itself returns for the captive. He who is the Light goes back for the blind, and he who is strength returns for the bruised. He goes back to get those who are utterly unlike himself! How stunningly different from the focus on the grand and great leader and the concept of vicarious narcissism (Isaiah 61:1–3).

5. Leadership that bears the fragrance of Christ feeds on him so that his truth and grace can be poured into hungry souls. Such leaders are diligent to ensure that they feed continually on him and his Word, allowing it to transform their hearts and characters so the food they give to the sheep bears his stamp (John 1:14; 1 John 4:17).

Leadership without the above characteristics is not Christlike leadership no matter what a word master says. Christ has shown us the way; he has exemplified such leadership in the flesh for us so we do not have to be seduced. We are complicit with ungodliness when we turn a blind eye, support and protect existing perversions, or are compliant with narcissistic leadership in the name of success or anything else. Such leadership is described by Jesus in John 17:19: "For their sakes I sanctify Myself, that they themselves also may be sanctified in truth." In other words, "I am made holy; I am obedient to God *so that* the sheep that follow me may also come to bear his likeness."

Safeguards

1. We must guard our hearts. They are to be ruled by him alone. No longing, no goal, no human promise is to own us. Examine your longings; know what they are because they make you vulnerable to fulfillment in illicit places. Examine the longings of the systems you belong to for the same reason. Systemic desires are powerful because there is added power in a group. How are you handling them? Do you know your vulnerabilities or those of the systems you are part of? We are to love and obey God above all else, even when our hearts are broken and hungry, and oh how we want to reach for the fruit that will make us like God at such times! Dietrich Bonhoeffer lived in stark contrast to "Hitler's Christians" and would not fill himself at the well of Hitler's seemingly good and grand promises.

2. As the people of God we need to be immersed in Scripture. How will we recognize falsehood and subtle lies if we do not thoroughly know the truth? We are not to be dumb sheep standing around waiting to be fed. The green pastures are there for all of us and we need to eat. Discernment,

acute spiritual vision, and a deep understanding of God's truths will help us mightily when those who appear as shepherds come into our lives for the real purpose of feeding themselves.

3. Christlikeness is visible in character, not merely words. Words can make glory into anything—remember Humpty Dumpty. Glory is defined by God and his Word, and he himself is its essence. That which does not look like him is not glorious, no matter how big the crowd or how great the applause or good the feelings. We are so easily seduced by words and passion.

4. Beware of those who promise great ends. This is a fallen world and will be so until God makes all things new. The Enemy of our souls had great goals. He wanted to raise his throne above the stars of God and ascend above the heights. He promised Adam and Eve something similar. Apparently we are vulnerable to such promises. God's purpose is ever and always love and obedience to himself, evidenced by a growing likeness to the character of Jesus Christ. That is the great end, and we do not get there on stages, with big audiences, bright lights, and approval. We get there slowly and quietly in the kingdom of the heart.

It is my prayer that we will be wise as serpents in this day, vigilant and ever discerning what is both around us and in us. I pray we will recognize those who seem to look like shepherds but are either broken sheep that will devour other sheep or wolves masquerading. I pray we will be harmless as doves, not full of toxins ourselves.

Seeing devastating harm done to the body of Christ can easily lead to anger and bitterness and other things that poison the heart. We need to be wise and discerning, but not poisonous; we need to be harmless, not damaging the body of Christ, but not helpless. I also pray that our longings, individually and collectively, will be placed in the only safe place there is for human vulnerability and hunger—and that is at the throne of our God. No human leader, no matter how gifted, no matter how silver-tongued, can satisfy those longings, and if he thinks or says he can, consider it diagnostic.

CARE FOR THE COUNSELOR

CHAPTER 18

Ten Lessons
for Counseling Students

I pursued the field of psychology and in the early 1970s earned my doctorate. Sometime during those years I sat with a woman in her twenties and for the first time heard the words, "My father used to do weird things to me."

I did not know what she meant. Those were the years before public or professional discussion of childhood sexual abuse. There were no books, no seminars, and no courses on the topic. Incest was something Freud mentioned that he had heard about from female patients, but, he purported, it was clearly fantasy-based. A supervisor of mine held a similar belief and, as I mentioned in a previous chapter, told me not to get hooked by these stories or I would contribute to their pathology. Other women mentioned similar things to me, and ultimately I chose to believe the women rather than the supervisor.

Mentored by a leading feminist in Philadelphia, I began hearing about rape and domestic violence. I also worked with Vietnam veterans and immersed myself in PTSD. I began reading literature that came out of the Holocaust in Nazi Germany in an effort to understand trauma (which was then unnamed) and the impact of evil on humans. I began to understand sexual abuse as a form of violence, an abuse of power, a trauma, and a kind of oppression.

I heard about evil and suffering unlike anything I had ever imagined. I saw women who had suffered from chronic, sadistic abuse at the hands of fathers, grandfathers, uncles, and teachers. A coed I had helped through depression was murdered with her hair drier cord. The father of an adolescent girl I was seeing was escorted from my office in handcuffs because he had been sexually abusing my client. I discovered a nine-year-old foster child who had been sexually molested, removed from her home, and placed with a "Christian" family had been abused there as well. I found myself plunged into unspeakable sufferings before I had turned thirty years old.

These events were profoundly shaping. God used desperate people to teach me to swim against the current. He was teaching me to heed his voice no matter what others said. Many at that time said such abuse could not be happening, women were looking for attention, I was been sucked in, and psychology was evil.

I began to learn how to pull away from the noise and voices surrounding me and seek to hear the voice of God and know his thoughts and his heart. I began to learn from Vietnam vets and from the Holocaust literature ways of responding to trauma. I saw that violence silences the voice of humans, shatters relationship, and abuses power. I began to understand that oppression is soul-damaging and produces despair. Relentless injustice mars the image of God in humans and makes them far less than who God has called them to be. In fact, relentless oppression can make oppressors out of victims.

God spent years teaching me about what it means to be human, what suffering does to humanity, and some things about relieving suffering and helping others heal. He took me to school among people. It was as if he had said to me, "Come child, and let me show you something of suffering humanity." He began that lesson with my childhood friends. He taught me through the life of my father. Those lessons continue today and there is still much to learn, but I can tell you that I have learned something about what is happening to people. They are suffering, many in unspeakable ways. They are being violated, trampled, abused, oppressed, trafficked, and silenced. The image of God, already marred due to the fall, has been so shattered in some as to be almost unrecognizable.

Then somewhere, many years back, God added a second track to my educational experience in his school. At some point he came again and said to me, "Come child, and let me show you my church." He brought me pastors—pastors and their children, pastors and their wives. He brought me pastors who were weary and burned-out and who struggled with the clash between ministry and marriage. He brought me many who had been chewed up and spit out by their churches. He brought me missionaries who crawled home on all fours after too much work and too little support, divisions on the field, histories they had never dealt with and trauma, such as rape or kidnapping by terrorists. I was tending to victims and to shepherds, and sometimes shepherds who were victims. I was saddened by what I saw among the shepherds. Many were weary and used up and often tossed aside by the people of God.

And then one day, God allowed the worlds to collide. I entered the murky waters of shepherds who made victims out of sheep. There were missionaries who raped the nationals they had gone to serve and pastors who abused their power to feed off the women in their pews or counseling offices. I encountered churches that closed ranks to protect the abuser, rather than the victim. I saw sin hidden and ignored, rather than exposed to the light of God. Shepherds and churches became the predators. Institutions and organizations were protected rather than sheep.

I sat with a "Christian" leader who battered his wife black and blue, who repeatedly twisted the truth and told me I was young and did not yet understand that sometimes a little force was necessary to accomplish God's will in the home. I made a phone call to a pastor about a woman in his church whose life was in danger. But he sent her home because that is, after all, where women belong.

I worked with a young girl who was sexually abused by her youth pastor. The church leadership helped him move away so he could continue his "dynamic" ministry elsewhere. "We wouldn't want a little mistake to destroy such a gifted man, would we?" I worked with pastors and missionaries addicted to pornography, who had sex with the women they were called to shepherd, who solicited prostitutes, and some who preferred little boys.

I struggled. I struggled with disbelief, anger, cynicism, and judgment. I wanted to make whips and turn tables over. A subtle arrogance crept in. Arrogance assumes superiority. Cynicism expects the worst of people. And I, who judged others in the body of Christ for being whitewashed tombs full of abuse and immorality, had myself become a whitewashed tomb full of pride and bitterness. I had become that for which I had disdain—a whitewashed tomb tending other whitewashed tombs.

A change in me began the day I knew I could no longer do the work that was in front of me. I was at the end of me—my skills, my stamina, my endurance, and my willingness. I did not see how I could go into one more dark and poisonous place. I was catching the disease I was working with. I got down on my face before God, told him I was finished, and asked him what to do.

And he began to teach me. He taught me that this is not my work but his. I am merely invited to participate in what he is doing in this world. It is not my burden. It is his. I am invited to be his yokefellow and walk with him in this world. And over time I learned from the One who was so carefully teaching me that he did not simply want me to see humanity or to understand suffering or to see his church, but he also wanted me to grasp his heart for them. His heart for victims—whether they be victims of sexual abuse or troubled churches or the stress of ministry—was a little easier to grasp. His heart for shepherds who make victims out of sheep was more difficult. But he has gently insisted that part of his teaching is the giving of his heart for he what reveals. Without that such information would corrupt and disfigure the one who held it.

You see, there is a terrible poison in this world. You cannot touch or work closely with that poison, in your own life or the lives of others, without being contaminated and marred unless you are saturated with the thoughts and heart of God.

Now he has given me his heart for his suffering people and for his church, she who is still blemished and spotted; she whom he died to redeem and purify. He has said that loving him means loving his body. One cannot love the Head and despise the body, for they are one. He has said that if I love him then I will love his people. Failure to love his people, even his predatory shepherds, is a failure in my love for him. He has taught me also that loving as he does includes a call to truth and light. To ignore, hide, or excuse sin in the body of Christ is to work against him because he came to bring about the death of sin. Any pretense that sin is somehow tolerable is a choice to infect and poison the body of my Lord.

So you see, his invitations to me of "Come child, let me show you suffering humanity" and "Come child, let me show you my church," were really invitations into the heart of the Great World-Lover. I did not initially recognize them as such. I do now. In the context of those experiences, I want to give you some things I have learned that you will perhaps not be told in graduate school.

1.   Counseling is not nice. We think it has to do with caring, compassion, perseverance, and wisdom. Those are all nice things. And indeed it does have to do with those things. However, counseling also has to do with indescribable suffering, inarticulate moaning, impenetrable darkness, inconceivable deception, cruelty, brutality, and evil. To enter this field is to invite garbage into your life.

     People come during alarm moments, times of emotional noise, chaos, and intolerable pain. They want it stopped now. They're afraid—they want help, want the noise to stop, want the fear to subside, want to feel safe. They'll bring you their anger, rage, violence, sobbing, ranting, fear, panic, and grief. You will face indescribable suffering and deep, habituated sin. You will sit with raped children, battered wives, and grieving parents. You will hear about things done to humans that you cannot comprehend. You will listen to abuse, violence, rage, humiliation, betrayal, loss, and staggering neglect. No matter how articulate you are, you will be greeted with suffering for which you have no words. You will face sin. Some of it we are familiar with: infidelity, abuse of power, oppression, and violation. You will also face sin that is decades old and so habituated that the person in front of you seems to have become the sin itself. You will sit with evil, sometimes evil so pronounced the hair will stand up on the back of your neck.

2. You will be exposed. We go into counseling because we think, or others have told us, that we are kind, caring, a good listener, or compassionate. Perhaps we see ourselves as patient, giving, or intuitive. Whether or not such things are true about us will be exposed in this work. And even if they are true, someone somewhere will try you and take you to the limits of your good qualities. You cannot sit with unrelenting addiction or battering or spewed abuse when someone has projected something onto you that really does not belong to you without coming to the end of your patience or even rationality! When you do counseling, people line up to bring you the worst of themselves. As I am sure you know from your own personal relationships, the worst of someone tends to bring out the worst in us. If you think that is not true, then pay attention to yourself in traffic when you are surrounded by bad drivers!

When you are exposed, remember that the client is not the enemy or someone you have to manage so you will no longer be exposed. Consider the exposure something orchestrated by the Spirit of God, and ask him to show you yourself, to search you out, and to give you more of Christ so that when that space in you is rudely bumped into again, the likeness of Christ will spill out.

3. Learn to sit with pain without immediately injecting a narcotic—into your client or yourself. Do not fear pain. When you sit with overwhelming pain it will frighten you, and you will want to alleviate it quickly so both people in the room can feel better. Be careful. Pain is the only protest in the human constitution that something is wrong. It is the only thing that raises its voice against existing abuses. If you jump to silence pain, you will fail to find the wound. Pain is a signal; it indicates danger. Pain is the Martin Luther of the human framework; it plasters the wall of the city with the announcement that something is wrong. When pain exists physically, we call it disease. The absence of pain (as in leprosy) will lead to destruction of that which is diseased. When pain exists emotionally, we call it suffering. The absence of emotional pain is numbness, deadness. It is also the incapacity to feel joy. You cannot do away with one side of the emotional continuum without eliminating the other. When pain exists in the moral realm, we call it conscience. The absence of moral pain is sociopathy or deadness. Yes, work to alleviate suffering, but do so carefully. Listen to pain, study it, and hear its story. It is one of the ways that you will learn what is wrong or diseased in the person you counsel.

4. You will be doing *God's* work *with* him. Caring for broken people is *not* our work. It is a piece of the work of God in this world, and we have been called to share in it. If you are gifted to bear the burdens of others, then it is *his* work you have been gifted to do. We think it is our work and we ask God to help us with it. This is backwards. It is his work, the people are his people, and you are not your own. Most of us who go into this work carry at least a

slender messianic strain. We think we can help! We think we can help sin and suffering! Yet we cannot even manage our own! There is one Redeemer, and I am not he. I am his servant. I need to live in my life and in this work as *his* servant. "My food is to do the will of Him who sent Me and to accomplish His work" (John 4:34). Do we really entertain the thought that we can do God's work in this world without utter dependence on his Spirit and obedience to his Word in our personal lives?

5. You will be doing *God's* work *for* him—not working for clients or for ourselves. It is easy to think it is for the sufferers—their burdens, their suffering. But if the work is done for them, then it is also governed by them. Whether they are pleased, less afraid, happy, etc. determines success. But some pain cannot be gotten rid of, some people have wrong goals, and some will not be pleased no matter what. If you work for them, you will be in bondage to their whims. It is also easy to work for yourself. Counseling can lead to feeling important, wise, or needed. It can also allow you to run into the pain of others to avoid your own. If we engage for ourselves, it can easily lead us to feed on the sheep and use them to make ourselves feel better. It is God's work, and our offering is to him who is pleased by obedience, not success or importance.

6. You can only do God's work through him, as he does his work in you. We cannot do the work of the Redeemer unless he first does his redemptive work in us. Let the work expose you to yourself. And allow that exposure to take you to the cross with a heart that pleads for God's redemptive work in you. Counseling is difficult work. The work of God is a work that moves into the lives of the afflicted, brokenhearted, mourning, and captive. We prefer moving into health, wholeness, joy, and freedom. We must bow to the work of redemption in us, for it is only as he makes us like

his Son that we will be willing and fit to move into those places we most want to avoid. I have had to learn to bow and seek him to do his work in me so his work through me might be accomplished. How else will we speak the truth of God or bring the love of God to bear unless we have faced that truth and known that love in our own lives?

7. The "stuff" of therapy is contagious. We were created to be image bearers and meant to bear the image of God in our person. Partly that means humans are capable of bearing an image. We are malleable. We can be shaped into the image of something. No matter our status or level of education, we are still dumb sheep. When we sit with something long enough, we bear its image in our person. Older married couples tend to gain likeness to each other—each has impacted and altered the other. You cannot sit with depression, abuse, strife, fear, etc. and not be shaped by it. We will catch the soul diseases of others. We read more and more in literature about secondary traumatic stress disorder. It is the nature of human beings to be impacted by what they sit with. If I habitually reflect trauma or sit with trauma, I will bear the image of trauma in my person. We see this even in the person of Jesus, who though he was perfect, bears in his person the image of our sin and suffering. If it was true of him, how much more so for us who are sinners ourselves!

8. Be a perennial student—of people and of God. Relentlessly seek the mind and heart of God. First, know about people. Know about suffering. Understand what suffering does to human beings. And yet, in knowing, never assume you know. No matter how many people you see, each is unique. If we do not understand such things, we will make wrong judgments. We will prematurely expect change. We will give wrong answers. We will fail to hear because we think we know. Listen acutely. Study avidly.

Secondly, know God. Know his Word. Be an avid student of that Word. If we are going to serve as his representative to others, we need to know him well. We are often so presumptuous that we speak for him where we do not really know him. We need to be so permeated by his Word that we learn to think his thoughts. May we never forget that to know his Word, according to him, means it is woven into our lives and we are obedient to it. We are to bear the image of the Word in our flesh.

9. The gift of the work is the cross.

> Thus says the LORD . . . "I will go before you and make the rough places smooth; I will shatter the doors of bronze and cut through their iron bars. I will give you the treasures of darkness and hidden wealth of secret places, so that you may know that it is I, the LORD, the God of Israel, who calls you by your name." (Isaiah 45:1–3)

As you walk the rough places and bang up against the doors of bronze and iron bars in the lives of people, know this: it will stamp out any idealism or hope you have for human nature; it will bring you to the end of yourself; you will want to give up or lose yourself in despair or cynicism—and then, then you will see the cross, high and lifted up. Your Lord is there, bearing everything you encounter—the abuse, the rage, the addictions, the black depressions, the battering, the trafficking, the racism, the suicides, the slow deaths to cancer, and anything else you can think of. All of those awful things—those things that repel you and make you want to run—will lead you to him, crucified.

He is also there bearing everything you are—your anger, your fears, your impatience, your weakness, your arrogance, your stupidity, your own sinful struggles, and your inadequacies. All of those will also lead you to him, crucified. You see, counseling is not a nice place; it is a place of darkness. But he is the treasure in that darkness. And finding him there, crucified, you will find hope in the despair, light in the darkness, joy in the suffering, and resurrection in the death. Finding him crucified means you will be transformed, people will be transformed, and you will endure until you see him face to face and hear his blessed "Well done."

10. We must always do this work in utter dependence on the Spirit of God. Another way to say that is that we must be cloaked in humility. Do we really think we have what it takes to truly understand the complex, deceptive humans who sit across from us? We rarely understand ourselves! Where else will we find wisdom? How will we know when to speak and when to be silent? How else will we love when we are tired or be patient when we are weary? How will we know the mind of God apart from the Spirit of God? How can we walk the long road of healing and transformation apart from the work of the Spirit in our lives? And how can we think that the life-giving power of Christ crucified will be released into others' lives unless we have allowed that cross to do its work in us? To walk with suffering sinners is to confront lies, darkness, and evil. Sometimes the suffering is unspeakable and runs unbearably deep. Try sitting across from a woman trafficked since she was five; try sitting with a genocide survivor from Rwanda. Apart from the work and Word of God in my life and through my life, what have I to offer such people? We cannot fight the litter of hell in a life unless we are dependent on the Spirit of God. And if the suffering were not overwhelming enough, what about years and layers of deception and lies and sin found in the life of someone who has been a sex offender since age twelve? We cannot bring life to dead places or light to darkness apart from the Spirit of God.

For me, the practice of Christian counseling is being a servant of God, steeped in the Word of God, loving and obeying God in public and in private, sitting across from a suffering sinner at a vulnerable crossroad in his/her life, and bringing all of the knowledge and wisdom and truth and love available to that person while remaining dependent on the Spirit of God hour by hour. *That* work, no matter what you call it, will be used by God to change us into his likeness; *that* work will result in his redemptive work in the life sitting before us; *that* work will bring glory to his great Name.

CHAPTER 19

Secondary Trauma

There are generally three basic responses to stress: burnout, secondary traumatization, and post-traumatic stress disorder. We will consider these three responses according to their level of difficulty. The first and mildest response is burnout—a state of physical, emotional, and mental exhaustion caused by long-term involvement in an emotionally draining situation. It is a gradual process and the symptoms include irritability, pessimism, sleep problems, inability to concentrate, and feelings of apathy. Burnout is a common occurrence among caregivers of any kind. You cannot deal with an endless line of needy, broken people and not at least struggle intermittently with burnout.

Stop and think through some stressors in your life and work. Some of you have stress in your private lives, but there may also be stressors in your physical environment. Lastly, there can be organizational stress: conflict with colleagues, hostility toward your work, or isolation.

The second possible response to stressors is called secondary traumatization (ST)—the transformation of a person's inner experience resulting from empathic engagement (caring connection) with another's trauma ("it gets in"). It was previously referred to as "vicarious trauma" meaning that we can be impacted or bear the image of another's trauma in ourselves. Secondary trauma can appear suddenly and include symptoms such as overwhelming feelings (tears, rage), emotional shutdown, feeling disconnected from others (even loved ones), a sense of helplessness, and a lowering of morale.

Stop and think about the many people you work with who experience trauma: sexual abuse or rape victims, domestic violence victims, combat vets. Some of you work around the globe in war-torn countries, refugee camps, and poverty-stricken areas. You work with them, you have concern for them, you care about them, or you may love them. They are dealing with horrific things, and the care and concern you have (and should have) creates a door to the inside of you through which you can easily find yourself overwhelmed and shutdown. I have worked with trauma and abuse survivors for many years and have often experienced ST. It can result from the relentless nature of the work, or it can happen suddenly through hearing or seeing something about someone you are caring for. I have sometimes heard stories of abuse or trauma and then gone to bed and been awakened by nightmares about the story, or my husband wakes me because I am crying in my sleep. I myself have not experienced the trauma, but having borne witness to it; I am then vicariously traumatized.

The third and final response on our continuum is Post-traumatic Stress Disorder, which is a group of pervasive symptoms following witnessing, experiencing, or being confronted with an extreme traumatic stressor (death of another, threatened death or serious injury to self or another, threat to physical integrity or self or another), and a response of intense fear, helplessness, or horror. The symptoms include hyper-arousal (adrenal response), avoidance of anything associated with the trauma, and a numbing of feelings. Other symptoms that may appear are being "on guard" constantly, flashbacks (like a daytime nightmare), sensitivity to light and sound, exaggerated startle response, night terrors, mood swings (rage, temper tantrums, shame, tears), difficulty sleeping, and difficulty concentrating.

As we said, Judith Herman has told us we can catch the disease we are working with. You cannot do the work that you do under the circumstances in which you live and not at least sometimes get emotionally overwhelmed. Repeated exposure to human evil and cruelty inevitably challenges your faith. It also heightens your sense of vulnerability. You can easily feel helpless and incompetent in the face of trauma histories. You feel grief for those who never got to be children. You may feel as if you are in mourning. The work you do will constantly challenge your emotional balance. You will struggle with wanting to withdraw. Examples of withdrawal are doubt or denial of the realities you see around you, numbing of your emotions, distancing from the work, or abandoning people you were helping. Or we can swing the other way and begin to act impulsively by trying to rescue others in unrealistic ways or trying to control others. I suspect that to some degree these reactions are inevitable. We are hardly infallible, and we will all lose our balance from time to time. The key is to have things in place to protect us so that momentary imbalance does not become a way of life.

Secondary Traumatization and Care of the Therapist

Judith Herman, in *Trauma and Recovery*, says,

> Trauma is contagious. In the role of witness . . . the therapist at times is emotionally overwhelmed. She/he experiences, to a lesser degree, the same terror, rage and despair as the patient. . . . This phenomenon is known as . . . Vicarious traumatization . . . In addition to suffering vicarious symptoms of PTSD, the therapist has to struggle with the same disruptions in relationships as the patient. Repeated exposure to stories of human rapacity and cruelty inevitably will often challenge the therapist's basic faith. It also heightens her sense of vulnerability. . . . The therapist also shares the

patient's experience of helplessness. . . . It is not uncommon for experienced therapists to feel suddenly incompetent and hopeless in the face of a traumatized patient. . . . The therapist also identifies with the patient through the experience of profound grief. The therapist may feel as though she herself is in mourning. . . . Unless the therapist has adequate support to bear this grief, she will not be able to fulfill her promise to bear witness and will withdraw emotionally from the therapeutic alliance.[1]

Further down she states that counter-transference has the potential to serve as a guide to understanding the patient's experience. In other words, secondary PTSD can assist us in our grasp of our client's experience with abuse. Working with trauma constantly challenges the therapist's emotional balance. Like the client, the therapist fights overwhelming feelings by withdrawal or by impulsive, intrusive action.

One critical safeguard is a solid support system. Unfortunately, many find themselves trying to work with traumatized clients in the absence of a supportive network. Sometimes that is due to long-standing denial within the mental health fields. There has been improvement in that area in the past few decades, but we still have work to do in this regard. Denial of trauma is not something only individuals struggle with, but larger systems as well.

I read a fascinating book some years ago in preparing to travel to Rwanda called *We Wish to Inform You That Tomorrow We Will Be Killed with Our Families*. Written by Philip Gourevitch, a staff writer for the *New Yorker*, it is his report from the killing fields of Rwanda.[2] As you know, in 1994 the Hutu majority was called on to murder everyone in the Tutsi minority. The massacres were largely done with machetes, and one million people were killed in one hundred days. The title of the book comes from a letter written by pastors in the Tutsi minority to their church president, a member of the Hutu majority.

Gourevitch speaks at length about the collective denial of the international community while this atrocity was going on. The world and its governments did what we all do when faced with overwhelming trauma—they pretended it was not happening. If you have seen the movie *Hotel Rwanda*, you know what I am talking about. It is often the natural human response to simply deny what we cannot manage. Therapists who bear witness to trauma are not exempt. It is an important point because while we certainly err on the side of denial, minimization, or numbing, I fear we can also err on the side of expecting ourselves to handle trauma without any significant struggle or impact. We will be much more realistic about ourselves, and likely to take better care of ourselves, if we simply accept the inevitability of the impact of trauma.

Saakvitne and Pearlman, in their workbook, *Transforming the Pain*, define vicarious traumatization as the "transformation of the therapist's inner experience as a result of empathic engagement with another's trauma" (i.e., it gets in).[3] Secondary traumatization is an occupational hazard, an inescapable effect of trauma work. It is not viewed as something our clients do to us, but rather as a human consequence of knowing, caring, and facing the reality of trauma.

The impact of secondary trauma is determined by the unique interaction between the situation and the person of the helper. That means that the impact is variable. Obviously in an unsupportive work setting with no support network and your own personal history of trauma, the impact will be far greater than in other settings and for other people. It is absolutely necessary that we be aware of the factors in our lives that escalate the impact of the trauma we are working with.

It is not uncommon for trauma workers to be troubled by disturbing imagery from their clients' stories. These images can come during the day, during sex, or in nightmares. They may be visual, auditory, olfactory, or emotional responses to certain cues. They are often hard to talk about and frequently disturbing. Often they are related to a specific scene we have heard described. I once had an astute client ask me whether or not my brain got mixed up about whose memories were lodged in my head. The answer is yes.

One of the effects of secondary trauma can be intrusive images. Like those we care for, we can get images in our minds of the atrocities we have heard about. They may intrude while trying to sleep, while in a worship service, or while enjoying family. They feel intrusive, as if they are stealing time from us or contaminating a good thing. The following are some helpful steps to deal with such images:

1. Acknowledge the image; do not simply push it away.
2. Tell another caregiver. It then ceases to be secret and loses some of its potency.
3. Ask yourself why image stays with you. Does it connect to something personal?
4. Ask yourself what it triggers or hooks to in you. Do you have a trauma history yourself?
5. Ask yourself which needs in you are threatened by the image. Safety, control, trust, intimacy, etc. Are these already areas of struggle for you rendering you more vulnerable?
6. Determine what you can do to address and lessen your stress level. What do these strategies give you? How do they speak against the trauma (e.g., they form connection, focus on beauty, fight against other trauma)?

On the practical level, there are three areas of importance that must be tended if you are to endure. They are self-care, relationships, and faith. You cannot last the long haul and avoid damage to yourself unless you pay attention to these areas.

Self-care

Self-care includes your food, exercise, sleep, medical care, and recreation. It largely involves care for our body. When we deal with people in great need or crisis, we tend to neglect the care of our bodies (mirror the survivor). Sometimes that is unavoidable, but it cannot continue for the long haul or we will break down both physically and emotionally. We live in frail, finite bodies that require care and nurture. It is critical not to get so caught up in the needs of others that we end up destroying ourselves.

Relationships

Good, supportive relationships have a tremendous effect on an individual's resiliency and emotional health. Pain and suffering often isolate us from others. Stressful schedules and overwhelming needs keep us busy, and one of the first things to go is supportive connection with others. The sense of being cared for in the work environment is important for our endurance. If you cannot find it in your work environment then seek it out through peer supervision or consultation.

Faith

For me a living faith that brings truth, comfort, and hope is also crucial. Evil and suffering have a tremendous capacity to swallow up our faith and leave us full of despair. Work with sexual abuse, rape, trafficking, war, and genocide all carry things like evil, darkness, chaos, isolation, and despair. It is crucial that you find ways to counteract the impact of those things. It means you must deliberately seek out good, beauty, order, safety, connection, intimacy, comfort, worship, and hope. These are antidotes to the poison in the work. Without such antidotes, you will slowly die emotionally, physically, and spiritually.

Christ Has Gone Before Us

Let me give you a few final thoughts about secondary traumatization. I believe that we are image bearers, we are malleable, and it is our nature to be impacted by what we sit with. If I habitually sit with trauma, I will bear the image of trauma in my person. I have been profoundly moved through my own struggles with this work by the fact that as I walk through the trauma of my clients and live with its impact on my life, I am following the footsteps of my Savior. He who became flesh and entered into our trauma, literally taking our sin and suffering on himself, has gone before us.

Think about some of the aspects of secondary trauma. It affects our identity. His identity was eternally altered—he who was God became man. It damages connection. He who was one with God cried out, "My God, My God, why have you forsaken Me?" Trauma overwhelms us with strong feelings. My soul is sick unto death! I am deeply distressed and troubled. My soul is overwhelmed with sorrow (Matthew 26:38). Sense of safety? He was abandoned by the Father and entered hell itself.

Paul says in Colossians 1:24, "Now I rejoice in what I am suffering for you, and I fill up in my flesh what is still lacking in Christ's afflictions, for the sake of his body, which is the church" (NIV). In 2 Corinthians where he talks about his ministry to others he repeats again and again the principle, *If I endure affliction, etc., it is for your comfort.* As we sit with the trauma of others and feel it reverberate throughout our persons and our lives, let us remember that there is nothing that Christ has called us to do that he himself has not undergone, and in doing as he did we bring his comfort and healing to those whose lives are damaged by the evil of others.

About one month after 9/11, I was invited to New York to speak at a conference on trauma. During my stay there I was granted permission to go into the pit at Ground Zero to spend the night among the workers who were digging for bodies. I left the pit about 3 a.m. and got into a taxi with an iron welder. He had no idea who I was or what I did for a living. I asked him about his experiences at Ground Zero. He told me about arriving on the first day and walking around with trash bags picking up body parts. He said his father had been a Vietnam vet with Post-traumatic Stress Disorder and was a raging alcoholic. He grew up bearing his terrible rage and swore he would never do that to his own family. He said many of the workers would leave the pit and go get drunk in order to cope with the work. He refused and would spend the night letting a taxi drive him around the city before he went home. As I was getting out of the taxi in front of my hotel, he took my hand and said, "I refuse to drink away what I have seen, but tell me, ma'am, what am I to do with the memories?"

Have you ever thought about the memories of the workers we send out around the world? Or even those in our own cities and towns? Have you ever thought about the memories of hospice workers, police, or child welfare workers? What about the memories of those rescuing women and girls from brothels or street children from city dumps or those ministering in refugee camps or war zones? What about the memories of those caring for AIDS victims, Ebola victims, burying one after another?

I am sure, like me, many of you have worked with such caregivers. In them we see that trauma is contagious. We see secondary trauma. If you sit with trauma long enough, you too will be traumatized. Those whom God has called to bear witness to human suffering pay a price. In fact, those who are most effective are also the most vulnerable to the contagion effect. Why? Because the greater a person's capacity for feeling and expressing empathy, the more at risk they are for developing secondary trauma. As counselors you understand something of this. There are times when the suffering of one of your counselees gets inside you and impacts you profoundly. The process of attending to trauma is traumatic itself. You develop a sense of helplessness in the face of

great suffering, and you often have a feeling of confusion or dis-
orientation. How can you walk among the squalor of the brothels
of India and then come home and pay four dollars for a cup of
Starbucks without feeling confused? How about walking through
the squalor of memories of sexual abuse at age four?

You also feel isolated from others because of the images of
abuse and violence that you carry in your mind. What is heard and
seen becomes a violent attack on your sense of integrity, your view
of the world, and your faith. We must not neglect the workers who
desperately need our love, our ears, our time, and our care. We
must not neglect ourselves. An army that does not actively care for
its soldiers is foolish, for its ranks will soon dwindle—or end up
with soldiers that are a danger to themselves or others. We need
to care for each other. When we do not care for the workers in the
Ground Zeros of this world, they become the victims of the very
tragedies they have gone to heal. We are some of those workers.

The one being who endured the greatest trauma ever known—
our Savior—is eternally scarred. There is no suffering that we will
bear witness to that our Savior has not first borne, for he himself
bore our griefs and carried our sorrows. But in bearing such things
for us, he has been left marred for all eternity: "See my hands and
my side?" We who are far more frail and finite cannot expect to
confront the litter of hell in others' lives without consequence.

Our Savior has called us to be involved in his redemptive work
in this world. He has called us to go to the places of disease and
death and darkness. Having called us there, he does not then abandon us. He goes with and in us. He comforts us, he equips us, and
he nourishes us. He also strengthens us, he listens to us, and he
perpetually prays for us. A body that does not follow its head is
a sick body. Any servant of Jesus Christ that has gone out in his
name and then been abandoned shows that we have failed to follow our head. Sadly, churches and Christian organizations have
often seen the great needs of the world and responded to that need
by sending others to accomplish the task, not realizing that part

of God's call is to continually care for those who are sent. Many servants of Christ have suffered needlessly and dropped by the wayside because of the failure of the body to follow its head in lovingly tending those who are ministering to others. We understand this need. We need to care for ourselves wisely and for each other, and in doing so, model for the Christian world how God has called his workers to be nurtured and not neglected.

Jesus was a cross-bearer. He leads us in the way of suffering and sorrow. His final word to us when he was here in the flesh was the promise that he would never abandon his servants: "I am with you always." May we also *never* abandon his work of caring faithfully and praying perpetually for those who have been abused, oppressed, and abandoned. May we also honor his work in and through us by caring for ourselves as his instruments.

CHAPTER 20

Beauty in Garbage City

On the eastern edge of Cairo's city of fifteen million people is a place called Garbage City, where thousands of people collect, sort, and generally live with garbage. The people who inhabit this city are the trash collectors of Cairo. Garbage is their livelihood. In order to experience Garbage City you would take a taxi from Cairo and walk in from the highway, through the open-air market, through the streets, past donkey carts and people hauling garbage. More garbage towers from old pickup trucks. Spills are unimportant as it all ends up in the neighborhood's streets anyway. If you continued traveling you would come to a valley about the size of half a ball field, which is in essence a large pit or incinerator where the waste that cannot be recycled is burned.

There is no greenery, no growth in Garbage City. The streets are literally compressed garbage. If you look down as you walk, you may see an old can, a dead cat, rotted food. As you look around you will see heaps of garbage, though some of the piles are in more hidden places. The smell of the place is often pervasive and when you leave it sticks to your clothes and your hair. To go there is to be surrounded by and to wade through garbage.

There is however, a surprising aspect of this place called Garbage City. You can find beauty there as well. If you walk into the city, past the valley of incinerating garbage, you will come to a clean place with white walls and concrete floors. There you will see a room where woven handbags, rugs, and placemats are displayed. Hanging on the walls of another room are quilted wall hangings, comforters, and pillow covers. Women are there sorting rags according to color and placing them in different baskets. Others work at two looms to create beauty out of garbage.

If you continue down the steps, you will hear the sound of water in large tubs as bags of shredded paper dissolve into pulp. Women in rubber aprons spread the mush onto sieves, pull the sieves out of the vats, and stack them into the press where the new paper is drained. The paper is then dried in the sun and cards are made with gold embossing and marbled designs. More beauty created from garbage.

There is a Coptic church in the garbage community that began as a Sunday school nineteen years ago. As you walk through Garbage City and up the mountain, alongside the chirping rats that scurry about you, you will enter one of two cave churches built on this mountain. The larger cave seats ten thousand and rivals the Red Rock amphitheater in Colorado in its dramatic beauty. Thousands of people gather—people whose lives are full of garbage, people who work with garbage, people who smell of garbage—for praise and preaching service. It is beauty in the midst of garbage.

I first learned about Garbage City from a woman who stopped there briefly on a short-term mission trip. I was fascinated by the concepts embedded in the reality and spent more time listening to a young college student who had interacted with some of the women in Garbage City. She wore a ring given to her by a young woman there—a beautiful ring made from garbage. She spoke about the difficulty of looking down at her beautiful ring and remembering that it had been made from garbage. "It is hard," she said, "to hold both images simultaneously."

I have found that it is often God's way to teach me about himself and about life in the most unexpected places. Garbage City was one of those surprises. When I first heard about this place, it was in the middle of a day with challenging patients. The procession began at 8 a.m. with violent, chronic sexual abuse and continued through chronic pain, pornography addiction, bipolar disorder, chronic sexual abuse twice more, a parent with terminally ill children, and rape. The children really got to me, and I drove home weeping.

At some point I found myself banging on the steering wheel saying, "Dear God in heaven, *I* live in Garbage City." At that moment on my CD player a beautiful soprano voice began singing an anthem by George Frederic Handel based on Psalm 96:9— "O worship the Lord in the beauty of his holiness . . ." My day and that verse crashed together in my head, and I found myself asking God to teach me about his beauty in the midst of the Garbage City in which I live and work. What he has given to me I bring to you.

You know, sometimes it is hard to see that I live in Garbage City. I live in a lovely home with a loving husband and two fine, healthy sons, and I get up in the morning and go to a job that I love with colleagues who enrich my life. I am immensely grateful for all of that. I have, compared to many people on this earth, a life filled with beauty. But I know, as surely as I stand here, that the world in which I live is full of garbage. How is it that I know that I live in Garbage City?

I know I live in Garbage City because if you go to Rwanda and walk in certain places, you step on the skulls of people who were killed in the ethnic cleansing there. I know I live in Garbage City because I have watched the faces of the old women who crossed the border as they fled from Kosovo, having lost their families to ethnic cleansing. I know I live in Garbage City because kids the age of my teenage son went to high school one morning in Colorado and never came home. I know I live in Garbage City because I have listened to nurses describe in detail the horror of partial-birth abortions. I know I live in Garbage City because there are children in many countries who are forced to fight as soldiers, who are sold as sex slaves, or who are dying of AIDS.

It is worse than that, however. Garbage City is not just seen and heard on television and in newspapers. I know I live in Garbage City because garbage is spilled out in my office hour after hour. I hear the details of the sexual abuse of five-year-old girls or eight-year-old boys abused by youth pastors and camp counselors. I sit with women whose facial bones have been rearranged by a man who calls himself a "Christian" husband. I sit with women whose husbands are locked into Internet pornography or prefer prostitutes to the women they said "I do" to.

I know I live in Garbage City because I sit with pastors who are suffering terribly over split churches, betrayals, and slander. I sit with missionaries who have been kidnapped, tortured, and raped because they wanted to tell others about the person and work of Christ. I know I live in Garbage City because I also sit with pastors who have sex with the women or teens they have been called by God to shepherd. I sit with missionaries who molested those they went to serve. I sit with Bible teachers who solicit children.

It is even worse than that I'm afraid. Not only are you and I surrounded by garbage, but we create our own as well. We have been guilty, some of us, of using our clients to meet our needs, if not sexually, then at least emotionally—taking from those who come to us needy. We court money, fame, and approval at the expense of our faith and our integrity. We have undealt with pain and difficulties in our own lives and marriages. Some of us hide behind addictions to alcohol or pornography, even as we work with those who come for help in such areas. We do indeed live in Garbage City.

To live in the real Garbage City is to be impacted by the garbage. When you live with garbage and work with garbage, you start to smell like garbage. If you are there long enough, that smell permeates everything, and even if you walk away from the garbage, somehow it is still with you. There is a professional term for that in our field. It is called Secondary Traumatic Stress Disorder or "compassion fatigue." The process of attending to the garbage that is in this world and in our work can result in harmful bio-psychosocial effects not unlike those experienced by our clients. To sit with sin and suffering with any empathy at all is to become vulnerable to the emotional and spiritual effects of vicarious traumatization.

The lesson of compassion fatigue is that garbage is contagious. Judith Herman, in her book *Trauma and Recovery*, said engagement in the work of trauma "poses some risk to the therapist's own psychological health."[1] This is true even on a much milder scale. What happens when you encounter a group of people who are criticizing someone or something? The most natural thing in the world is to join in. Garbage is contagious. If that is true in the everyday social realm, how much more when we sit day after day with garbage? Do we really think we can wash our brains with stories of incest, hatred, violence, and disease without the poison of it all saturating our persons and our lives?

We sit in the midst of it, having somehow gotten the idea that it is possible to make beauty out of garbage. That is, in essence, what we are about, isn't it? We have this notion that rags can be transformed into beautiful wall hangings and trash turned into marbled paper. And so we teach, supervise, train, and counsel others toward that end. And it happens, doesn't it? Some of us have seen the fragmented minds of Dissociative Identity Disorder made whole. Or the broken lives of incest survivors transformed into lives of beauty. We have seen addicts clean, abusers made safe, marriages restored, and the fearful learn to love. We work together as researchers, teachers, counselors, and pastors day after day hoping to see beauty appear in a garbage-filled life.

It takes its toll, doesn't it? Some of you are weary. Some of you have lost sight of the beauty and feel hopeless. Some of you have private lives full of garbage and are ashamed to get help. And some of you, if given a checklist for Secondary Traumatic Stress Disorder, would fill in all the little blocks. You are burnt out.

What I encountered on my ride home that day is one of the great dangers of this field. There is the danger of seeing and sitting with so much garbage that you cannot see beauty anymore. Remember how the student that had been to Garbage City said it was hard to hold the two realities of garbage and beauty simultaneously? The garbage can be overwhelming. It often seems far more pervasive than the beauty. Another danger is that of sitting with garbage so long that you lose the ability to recognize it for what it is. You get numb. You've seen so many bad things that a little bit of bad doesn't seem bad anymore. And then you become blind to your own garbage. The hideous result is that instead of helping make beauty out of garbage, we simply mix our garbage with the garbage of others.

Making beauty out of garbage is an odd business. How is such a thing to be done? Can it really be done? And if so, how are we to assist others in making beauty out of garbage without becoming garbage ourselves? How are we going to continually draw near to disturbed minds and hearts and not become disturbed ourselves? What will enable us to do this work and what, oh what, are we to do with our own garbage?

If you recall, I said that the juxtaposition of my day and the anthem, "O worship the Lord in the beauty of his holiness," made a crash in my head. I found that the answer to my plea that day—"teach me of your beauty in the midst of the garbage"—lies in another crash—a crash far bigger than the one in my head. A cosmic crash, in fact. It is a place, an event, known as the cross. On that cross was a crash that shook the earth on its foundations, darkened the midday sky, opened graves, and rocked hell. It was the crash of the greatest and most hideous garbage ever known up against the purest, loveliest beauty ever known.

I fear that the very thing central to who we are in our identity and what we do in our lives and our work often takes a back seat. Outside of the cross there is no hope for the garbage or the people who make it. We have a lot of skills. We could probably find somebody who has expertise in almost every therapeutic intervention known to mankind—at least the mainstream ones. Skills don't make beauty out of garbage. There are a lot of theories out there, some brilliant minds. Theories and brilliant minds don't make beauty out of garbage. Now I am all for topnotch skills and brilliant theories. As a matter of fact, I believe as Christians we should outshine the secular world in these matters, for we are called to excellence by our God. However, we dare not forget that it is the cross of Jesus Christ that is the only hope of this world. Our constant danger is that we cry, "Behold this new method, Behold this new theory, Behold this new training," and forget to cry, "Behold the Lamb of God who takes away the sin, the garbage, of the world!"

Are you discouraged today? Weary with your work and the pain and suffering of others that you bear daily? Or perhaps you are weary and sick over your own garbage. It is at the cross, and only at the cross, that you will find yourself able to say with Christian in *Pilgrim's Progress*, "He has given me rest by His sorrow and life by His death."[2] In other words, in the place of greatest garbage, the cross, my garbage is exchanged for beauty.

Listen to what I have seen in my quest for how to see the beauty of God in Garbage City. You who in your work, and perhaps in your own life, often sit with the litter of hell, let me show you garbage transformed into eternal beauty. You, who see the tentacles of the underworld and touch sin in the raw, come, and I will show you glory in the midst of decay.

The cross is without question the place of greatest garbage. There we see garbage most intense, pervasive, and strong—so strong, in fact, that it appears to destroy, to obliterate, beauty. The cross is a place of death and evil; decay and wrath. It is a place of darkness, thirst, isolation, rejection, abandonment, and bondage. It is the absence of God and all that is good. It is hell itself. The cross is the personification of garbage.

And whom do we see there? The Lily of the Valley, the Rose of Sharon. We see the fairest of ten thousand, the beauty of God incarnate. We see purity, holiness, infinite love, compassion, and eternal glory. And all that beauty, which is beyond the comprehension of our finite minds, is crushed, destroyed, poisoned, stained, silenced, and murdered. Beauty, like the earthly sun, eclipsed. If beauty be eclipsed, what does that leave? Nothing but garbage. If heaven is killed, we are left with hell. The garbage has swallowed up beauty. Death has swallowed life. Quit your jobs, for what is the point? Who wants to spend a life simply rearranging garbage?

But you and I know that is not the end of the story, don't we? Or do we? Have we forgotten? Have we lost sight of what followed? Do we live functionally as if garbage is preeminent? Or do we live, both personally and professionally, as those who remember that Beauty is triumphant?

What happened there that day? I'll tell you. Decay was transformed into glory. Death was swallowed up by life. Evil was transfigured into holiness, and the wrath of men into praise. Darkness was changed to light, and hell defeated by heaven. Thirst is transformed into living water and brokenness into the bread of life. Alienation led to restored relationship and bondage led to freedom. There is indeed beauty in Garbage City. What colossal warfare must have been fought in the body of that lone figure for such a thing to be!

Herein lies hope for Garbage City—both the one within and the one without. If garbage can be transformed into beauty on such a scale as this, then surely it can happen in my small life or in the lives of my clients. And I know it can, for I have seen it occur again and again, in my life and in the lives of others. It is at the foot of the cross that we have the answer for Garbage City. It is at the cross that we have the answer to my plea—show me beauty in Garbage City. It is at the cross that we have hope for our own garbage. And it is at the cross that we have a defense against the ravages of others' garbage.

The cross, a thing of beauty? Yes, for it is at the cross that we behold all of the beauties of Christ in perfection. All of his love is drawn out there. All of his character expressed. The wounds of Jesus are far more fair than all the splendor of this world. The cross is indeed a place of beauty.

Amy Carmichael, who rescued little girls in India from marriage to the gods, which meant sexual abuse at the hands of Hindu priests, said the following: "We can only touch evil by virtue of the cleansing blood. Nothing but the white fires of God's holiness suffice for such contact. Move out from the full stream of Calvary and you know yourself not only defenseless, but stained."[3] The truth of the matter is that you and I work with sin and suffering. Unless we ourselves grasp the truths of the cross, the hope of the cross will not pass from our lives to others, for we cannot give them what we do not have. Not only that, we will be stained by their garbage in trying.

I have found again and again as I work in Garbage City that part of the call of God on my life is to deal with my own garbage. Whatever makes me think I can assist another in the transformation of garbage into beauty when my own life is littered and untouched? I have been in this field for awhile and as a result have done a decent amount of supervision. If my own life were not enough demonstration, I also know from the lives of others that we carry much garbage. I suspect there is a lot in your hearts as well. Those things we refer to as "issues" or "stuff" or with fancy words like "countertransference" are simply more palatable words for garbage. The things in my history that have twisted me, the hidden sinful attitudes of resentment, rage, and fear. The brokenness that comes from being sinned against. The anguish of painful tragedies. The addictions to work, to helping, to acclaim. The impatient responses, annoyances, and anger that spills out on resistant or stuck clients. The misuse of power or emotional intimacy. If I am not continually working with such things before God, seeking him to transform such garbage into a beauty that reflects his character, then I am a danger to those I seek to help.

And how dare I suggest that I can lead others to places where I refuse to go! What kind of guide is that? May you and I have the courage to say with the psalmist—"Let the beauty of the LORD our God be upon us . . ." (Psalm 90:17 KJV). Such a statement requires courage because it means doing whatever it takes, or more aptly, asking God to do whatever is necessary, for obviously such beauty cannot be present unless garbage is transformed.

Not only must the work of the cross be allowed to touch and transform our own garbage, it also needs to alter our discernment, our perspective on garbage. If you stay a little bit dirty long enough or hang around dirt long enough, then your perception, your judgment of dirt gets altered. A little bit dirty isn't so bad. Only really dirty qualifies as bad. A glance at pornography, rudeness with a spouse, harshness with a client, what are these compared to addiction, battering, and abuse? Seen in the light of the cross they are garbage.

Not only can we fail to discern that a bit of garbage is qualitatively just as much garbage as a truckload, we can also fail to discern what is garbage and what is not. How am I to know what is transformable and what needs to be incinerated? I do not want to hold onto that which is garbage, nor do I want to toss out what can be made beautiful. My judgment about such matters is not reliable. Who would have thought that a history of violence and sexual abuse could be made a thing of beauty? What a notion to suggest that death can be transformed into life! And how odd that success, acclaim, approval, and the praise of men are nothing but garbage. Dung is what Paul calls them. He counts them as dung.

That Scripture (Philippians 3:8) was vividly illustrated for me several years ago. I spoke at a conference in an area full of farms. A friend was with me, and we took a walk after my talk. It was quite late and we were in Amish country. There were no streetlights, and we could not see. A little way down the road we came upon a couple of ostriches behind a fence, and I decided I wanted to see them up close. Fearlessly and unseeing, of course, I walked across the grass and through the ditch surrounding the pen, only to discover that I was literally sliding in ostrich dung. It was a most unpleasant surprise. Unexpected, unseen garbage. When we returned to the motel, I put my shoes outside the room. They were a huge mess. When I got home, I threw them out—they were hopeless. And that was when the Scripture came to me—I do count them but dung, garbage, rubbish. And what is Paul referring to? Evil? Immorality? Addictions? Violence? No. Such things as these can be made into beauty. He should know because he was a murderer. Paul was referring to self- righteousness, zealousness, law-keeping, a list of grand qualifications—garbage.

We have it backward, don't we? We want to take things like evil, violence, abuse, addictions, tragedies, and anguish and throw them away like dung. They are worthless. They are in our way. The message of the cross is that the most unlikely things can be made beautiful by our God, and the things we esteem are truly garbage.

If that is so, then the cross not only speaks to your garbage and mine, but it also speaks hope to those broken sinners who stream through our doors seeking help and healing. Because in Jesus Christ garbage has been swallowed up in beauty. Death has been swallowed up in life, and you and I are called to go with hope to the garbage makers and garbage collectors of this world. The crucial task of therapy, of counseling—and this constitutes its difficulty—is to somehow make livable or acceptable the intolerable and utterly unacceptable, or to make beauty out of garbage. It is to make fruitful what is barren, bearable what is unbearable. The crucial task of therapy is to go where we do not want to go and perform what we cannot do. Who is equal to such a task? Only one who knows the power of the cross.

You see, because of that cross, you and I are now called to go where Jesus went. And where did the feet of Jesus go? They walked among the sick, the dying, the tormented, the terrified. They walked in garbage, and in that walking, garbage became beauty. "Beautiful are the feet of him who brings good news . . ."

(Isaiah 52:7 ESV). We are told that he makes the place of his feet glorious (Isaiah 60:13). But they are scarred feet, aren't they? Yours will be too in some fashion. You cannot work with the dual mysteries of iniquity and suffering and not be scarred. Secondary Traumatic Stress Disorder is a reality of life in this world. But like our beautiful Savior, even as you walk on garbage streets, picking up garbage items, smelling like burning garbage, his work in you and through you will be one of beauty. The beauty is possible because he bore the garbage. He was made garbage for us.

I do not think we can survive intact without these truths. The experts—whoever "they" are—tell us rightly that we need to get proper supervision, a balance of fun and work, good sleep and exercise if we are to protect ourselves from burning out. This is good and wise advice. It is, however, insufficient. You and I are too small for the weight of the world's garbage. You and I have garbage of our own. Apart from the ongoing work of the cross in our lives, you will never see beauty made out of garbage because such a task is beyond our ability; it is a supernatural work.

First John 5 states the dual realities in which we live—the realities the young college-aged woman had difficulty holding onto simultaneously—garbage and beauty. "We know that we are the children of God, and that the whole world is under the control of the Evil One. We also know that the Son of God has come . . ." (author paraphrase). Children of God in a world controlled by the Evil One. I fear the odds are against us. We are no match for such garbage. Our wits are too slow, our understanding finite and our strength too frail. *But*, glorious but, "we also know that the Son of God has come . . ." Eternal Beauty in Garbage City. And in his coming he walked in our garbage, he was crushed by our garbage, he transformed our garbage. And now, even as we continue in Garbage City, he has commissioned us to walk in garbage, to let it touch us. He has also called us to count the things of this age as garbage—the tinsel, the applause, the success—so that he might work through us to transform garbage into beauty, first in our lives and then in those we serve.

Do you hear the call? It is a hard call. It is a call to be relentless about the garbage in our lives. It is a call to fight and wrestle with that garbage, pleading with God to incinerate the dross and transform the ugliness into beauty. That means we relentlessly deal with our petty squabbles and divisions and criticisms. That means we willing deal with the hidden stuff—the bitterness, the addictions, the power-seeking. That means we seek the glory of the Father *without compromise*, without stealing a bit for ourselves. That means we are not governed by money or success or acclaim, but rather count such things as dung so that we might have Christ the Beauty Maker.

It also means grappling with the garbage of others. Walking with mean people, slow people, tormented people, dirty people, and resistant people. It requires the supernatural grace of God to live twenty-four hours of everyday, walking in the midst of garbage redemptively. We think we have to do exceptional things for God, but we do not. We are to be exceptional in the ordinary—to make beautiful hangings out of rags and marbled paper out of trash. It is hard, isn't it? We get weary. And I know many of you are weary now, wondering if you can continue. The battles with our own garbage last a lifetime. Add to that the battles with the garbage of others and it is easy to see why many quit.

> Do not lose heart. Though outwardly we are wasting away [easing toward death, the ultimate garbage], yet inwardly [because of the cross] we are being renewed day by day. For our light and momentary troubles are achieving for us an eternal glory [an eternal beauty] that far outweighs them all. So we fix our eyes not on what is seen, but on what is unseen. (2 Corinthians 4:16–18 NIV)

And what is it that is unseen? The ultimate beauty.

And then I saw "a new heaven and a new earth," for the first heaven and the first earth [garbage city] had passed away. . . . I saw the Holy City . . . coming down out of heaven from God, prepared as a bride beautifully dressed for her husband [garbage utterly transformed]. And I heard a loud voice from the throne saying, "Look! God's dwelling place is now among the people [the people of garbage city], and he will dwell with them and be their God. He will wipe every tear from their eyes. There will be no more death or mourning or crying or pain, for the old order of things [all garbage] has passed away. He who was seated on the throne said, "I am making everything new!" Then he said, "Write this down, for these words are trustworthy and true." (Revelation 21:1–5 NIV)

And who is he who speaks such words of hope? It is the Lord of Glory, the Lord of all Beauty, who wears the appearance of a slain Lamb as his court dress. He who for all eternity will alone bear the scars of garbage. There will be no sign of garbage on us. We will be utterly free of all remnants. But somehow, in that place of great beauty, the most Beautiful One of all will bear in his person the scars of ugliness. For you and for me, those scars will be the most beautiful sight in all heaven.

God's call to us as Christian counselors is that, like the people of Garbage City, east of Cairo, and like the One whose Name we bear, we will be people who are willing to work with the garbage of this world. Our willingness is possible only because of the work of Christ on the cross and the power of God exhibited in that place. We know because of that cross, that hideous, beautiful cross, that we can collect the garbage of this world, our own included, and be redemptive instruments used by God to transform garbage into beauty.

May you and I, like the people of Garbage City, walk amid the rats and through the trash and into the caves so that in those places might be heard praise and worship for the Lamb that was slain. May we count Him alone as worthy and all else as rubbish. May we desire one thing—to gaze upon the beauty of the Lord and to seek his beautiful face. And then may the beauty of our Lord be upon us. May he establish the work of our lives.

A Survivor's Expression of Faith

This is the work that one survivor has done as she continues to wrestle through this dilemma. This is a young woman in her twenties who was sexually abused by her father and others during all of her childhood. These were written by one who knows what it means to be raped by the man you call Daddy. They are written by someone who has struggled long and hard, and continues to do so, with why God did not stop it. "What was God thinking and feeling while my daddy raped me?" I am going to show you two small books she has written in her struggle to apply the truth of the Word of God to herself and the lies she learned as a result of the abuse. I think you will see clearly how she wrestles with both the lies she learned from her father and the truths of the Word of God. These are exceptional books. Many survivors do not struggle with these issues so articulately. They clearly demonstrate the grappling that goes on and carefully delineate between the lies and the truth (a process that is often muddy for survivors).

This woman has allowed me not only to show these here, but has also given me permission to use them with other survivors. I have found them extremely helpful with adults for two reasons. One, they respond to their thinking. Their questions and thinking are frozen in these areas. They still talk and think and reason like an abused child about God. Two, these books keep the work of Christ on the cross central. That truth, and that alone, is the only sufficient answer to the thinking, questions, and struggles that the abuse causes. It is at the cross that the two irreconcilable realities come together.

These can be powerful tools as you counsel those who have suffered from sexual abuse. A word of caution is needed however. These are not quick fixes and I have found they are effective later in the counseling process when the client has had the opportunity to experience safety in the relationship and understanding about the abuse and its impact. Once the abuse history has been grappled with spiritual questions are asked differently and the capacity to hear truth has greatly increased. Do not rush; the truth will not go in if these are used prematurely.

MISTER JESUS KNOWS ALL ABOUT THAT

"WHEN THE SOLDIERS CRUCIFIED JESUS, THEY TOOK HIS CLOTHES..."

JOHN 19:23 NIV

EMMA AND MANDY HAD A SPECIAL
FRIEND NAMED MISTER JESUS.
THEY LOVED MISTER JESUS AND
MISTER JESUS LOVED THEM.

EMMA AND MANDY TALKED TO
MISTER JESUS ABOUT LOTS
OF THINGS.

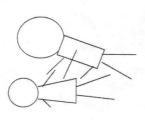

BUT THEY DIDN'T TELL HIM ABOUT
HOW THEIR DADDY HURT THEM AND
MADE THEM FEEL YUCKY INSIDE.
THEY DIDN'T TELL ANYONE ABOUT
WHAT DADDY DID TO THEM.

ONE DAY MANDY AND EMMA WERE
TALKING ABOUT HOW ALONE THEY
FELT. MANDY SAID, "MAYBE WE
COULD TELL MISTER JESUS ABOUT
WHAT DADDY DID TO US."

EMMA DIDN'T LIKE THAT IDEA. SHE
THOUGHT THAT MISTER JESUS
WOULDN'T KNOW ANYTHING ABOUT
BEING HURT LIKE THAT.

EMMA THOUGHT SHE AND MANDY
WERE THE ONLY ONES WHO KNEW
ABOUT THAT KIND OF HURT.

BEFORE THEY SAID ANYMORE, MISTER JESUS SPOKE TO THEM: "I WAS HURT TOO. THE BAD MEN TOOK MY CLOTHES JUST LIKE YOUR DADDY TOOK YOURS."

"I LOVE YOU SO MUCH. I WAS HURT SO THAT I COULD KNOW HOW YOU FEEL. YOU ARE NOT ALONE."

"ARE YOU SURE ABOUT THAT, MISTER JESUS?" EMMA ASKED. "ARE YOU SURE YOU KNOW WHAT WE'RE TALKING ABOUT?"

MISTER JESUS PICKED UP EACH LITTLE GIRL AND HELD HER CLOSE FOR A LONG TIME.

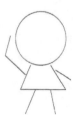

EMMA AND MANDY FINALLY SAW THAT MISTER JESUS REALLY DOES KNOW HOW THEY FEEL. BAD MEN TOOK HIS CLOTHES, JUST LIKE DADDY TOOK THEIRS.

YOU CAN TALK TO MISTER JESUS ABOUT HOW DADDY HURTS YOU, JUST LIKE MANDY AND EMMA DID. HE WANTS TO HEAR ALL ABOUT YOU—FOR YOU ARE HIS PRECIOUS LITTLE GIRL.

Mister Jesus Knows All about That

You can see how the woman who wrote this book is beginning to grasp that this Mister Jesus is the Man of Sorrows and acquainted with grief—with *her* grief. Mister Jesus says, "I was hurt too. The bad men took my clothes just like your daddy took yours." There is tremendous healing for survivors as they begin to study and truly grasp the suffering and death of Jesus. He *knows*—that is a phenomenal revelation. I recently had a woman come in to a session who is working through some of the Scripture on the crucifixion. She had barely sat down on the couch when she said, "They took his clothes. I never saw it before. They took his clothes." This is a woman who had many perpetrators and has countless memories of standing naked as an adolescent in a group of men. Something way down deep gets touched when such things are seen and understood. In the next book, you can see how the connection she established with Jesus began to extend to God as Father, as well.

MISTER JESUS'S ABBA

"GOD DOESN'T WANT YOU TO BE ALL
FILLED UP WITH FEAR; HE IS YOUR SAFE
ABBA AND HE WILL NEVER HURT YOU."

ROMANS 8:15 (PARAPHRASE)

THERE ONCE WAS A SPECIAL LITTLE GIRL NAMED EMMA. EMMA WAS A WONDERFUL LITTLE GIRL, AND MISTER JESUS LOVED HER VERY MUCH.

EMMA'S DADDY DIDN'T LOVE HER IN SAFE WAYS LIKE MISTER JESUS DID. HER DADDY HURT HER SOMETIMES AND MADE HER FEEL LIKE A BAD GIRL.

EMMA DIDN'T KNOW THAT NOT *ALL* DADDIES HURT THEIR LITTLE GIRLS.

MISTER JESUS KNEW THAT EMMA'S DADDY HURT HER AND THAT EMMA DIDN'T TRUST DADDIES ANYMORE. THAT MADE MISTER JESUS FEEL SAD.

SO MISTER JESUS DECIDED THAT IT WAS TIME FOR EMMA TO KNOW A SAFE DADDY, HIS ABBA.

ABBA MEANS "SAFE DADDY" WHO LOVES YOU WITHOUT HURTING, AND THAT'S WHAT MISTER JESUS'S ABBA IS.

MISTER JESUS KNEW THAT IT WAS IMPORTANT THAT EMMA MEET ABBA BECAUSE EMMA IS HIS CHILD TOO. MISTER JESUS'S ABBA IS GOD AND HE IS *EVERYONE'S* ABBA.

MISTER JESUS KNEW THAT ABBA IS SAFE, BUT EMMA DIDN'T. HE WOULD HAVE TO FIND A WAY TO MAKE HER SEE THAT ABBA IS A SAFE AND LOVING DADDY, NOT LIKE HER DADDY WHO HURTS HER.

SO MISTER JESUS SHOWED EMMA ALL ABOUT HIS ABBA.

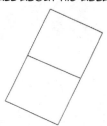

HE SHOWED HER A PART OF HIS BOOK THAT SAID, "GOD DOESN'T WANT YOU TO BE ALL FILLED UP WITH FEAR; HE IS YOUR SAFE ABBA AND HE WILL NEVER HURT YOU."

EMMA THOUGHT ABOUT THAT VERSE AND THEN TOLD MISTER JESUS ABOUT HOW SHE FELT.

"MISTER JESUS," SHE PRAYED, "I DON'T WANT TO KNOW YOUR ABBA. HE'S A DADDY AND THAT MEANS HE'S GOING TO HURT ME. I DON'T LIKE THAT."

MISTER JESUS WASN'T ANGRY AT EMMA FOR WHAT SHE SAID. HE KNEW THAT SHE WAS BEING HONEST WITH HIM AND TELLING HIM THE TRUTH.

SO MISTER JESUS ANSWERED HER.

"EMMA, I KNOW THAT YOU FEEL VERY SCARED OF MY ABBA. BUT ABBA IS SAFE. HE'S NOT LIKE DADDIES THAT YOU KNOW. HE WILL NEVER HURT YOU. I PROMISE."

EMMA THOUGHT ABOUT THAT. SHE DIDN'T THINK THAT DADDIES WERE SAFE, BUT MISTER JESUS *PROMISED* HER THAT ABBA WAS SAFE.

MISTER JESUS NEVER BROKE A
PROMISE AND EMMA KNEW THAT.
HE PROMISED THAT SHE COULD
ALWAYS TALK TO HIM AND HE KEPT
THAT PROMISE. HE PROMISED THAT
SHE'D NEVER BE ALONE AND HE
KEPT THAT PROMISE.

EMMA HAD NEVER KNOWN A DADDY
THAT KEPT HIS PROMISE BEFORE,
BUT MISTER JESUS *ALWAYS* DID.
SO EMMA DECIDED TO TRUST
MISTER JESUS.

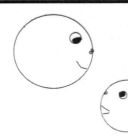

"MISTER JESUS, I'M STILL KIND OF
SCARED TO MEET YOUR ABBA, BUT
I'M GOING TO BELIEVE YOU WHEN
YOU SAY HE'S SAFE. BUT...WILL
YOU STAY RIGHT HERE WITH ME
WHEN I MEET HIM?"

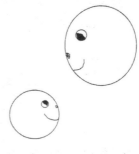

MISTER JESUS SMILED WITH A HAPPY
TEAR IN HIS EYE. "YES, EMMA, I'LL
BE RIGHT HERE WITH YOU. I LOVE YOU
AND I'LL NEVER LEAVE YOU—EVER."

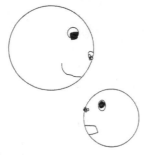

SO MISTER JESUS STAYED RIGHT
THERE WITH HER. EMMA BEGAN TO
TALK TO ABBA. "HI, ABBA, IT'S ME—
EMMA. I'M MISTER JESUS'S FRIEND."

ABBA WAS HAPPY TO HEAR FROM
EMMA. HE TALKED TO HER IN A SAFE
VOICE:

"MY PRECIOUS CHILD. HOW HAPPY
I AM TO HAVE YOU HERE AS MY
DAUGHTER. I LOVE YOU SO VERY
MUCH AND I'VE BEEN WAITING TO
HEAR FROM YOU!"

EMMA SAW LOTS OF LOVE IN ABBA'S EYES AND SHE FELT SAFE. SHE BEGAN TO TALK TO HER ABBA ABOUT EVERYTHING, JUST LIKE SHE DID WITH MISTER JESUS.

ABBA WAS VERY HAPPY TO FINALLY HAVE HIS LITTLE GIRL WITH HIM, AND EMMA WAS HAPPY TO FIND HER LOVING AND SAFE ABBA. SHE WAS GLAD THAT SHE BELIEVED MISTER JESUS'S PROMISE!

ABBA IS YOUR SAFE AND LOVING DADDY TOO. HE WILL NEVER HURT YOU LIKE YOUR DADDY DID, AND YOU CAN TELL HIM EVERYTHING— EVEN THAT YOU'RE SCARED TO TALK TO HIM! HE CAN HARDLY WAIT FOR YOU TO COME TO HIM AS HIS CHILD!

Mister Jesus's Abba

Keep in mind that the process involved here was long and arduous, and it was not completed with the writing of these books. However, they are signposts of God's work in her life and all the more potent for being *her own expression* of faith. This is not work I could have done for her. It is the wrestling of her own soul with the questions that loom large in the face of abuse.

APPENDIX B:

Lament

I have included a lament here that brings together various verses from the Bible and that expresses deep pain and sorrow to God. It is an exercise you can adjust to do with one person, but it is especially powerful to do with a group so that you hear and feel what a lament is really like. This lament has been spoken chorally by many groups around the world who are grieving many traumas and great losses. I am sure some of you reading now are grieving someone or something and so this will feel close to your heart.

Leader: Why, O LORD, do you stand far away?
    Why do you hide yourself in times of trouble?
All: My God, my God, why have you forsaken me?
    Why are you so far from saving me, from the words of my groaning? O my God, I cry by day, but you do not answer, and by night, but I find no rest.

Leader: How long, O LORD? Will you forget me forever?
    How long will you hide your face from me?
How long must I take counsel in my soul
    and have sorrow in my heart all the day?
All: Our eyes failed, ever watching
    vainly for help.
You have wrapped yourself with a cloud
    so that no prayer can pass through.

You have made us scum and garbage
   among the peoples.

Women: All our enemies
   open their mouths against us;
panic and pitfall have come upon us,
   devastation and destruction;
my eyes flow with rivers of tears
I have been hunted like a bird
   by those who were my enemies without cause;
they flung me alive into the pit
   and cast stones on me;
water closed over my head;
   I said, "I am lost."
All: Therefore I will not restrain my mouth;
   I will speak in the anguish of my spirit;
   I will complain in the bitterness of my soul.

Men: There is no faithfulness or steadfast love,
   and no knowledge of God in the land;
there is swearing, lying, murder, stealing, and committing
   adultery;
   they break all bounds, and bloodshed follows bloodshed.
Therefore the land mourns,
   and all who dwell in it languish
All: Therefore I will not restrain my mouth;
   I will speak in the anguish of my spirit;
   I will complain in the bitterness of my soul.

Women: So I am allotted months of emptiness,
   and nights of misery are apportioned to me.
When I lie down I say, "When shall I arise?"
   But the night is long,
   and I am full of tossing till the dawn.
My flesh is clothed with worms and dirt;
   my skin hardens, then breaks out afresh.
All: Therefore I will not restrain my mouth;

I will speak in the anguish of my spirit;
I will complain in the bitterness of my soul.

Leader: I loathe my life;
I will give free utterance to my complaint;
    I will speak in the bitterness of my soul.
I will say to God, Do not condemn me;
    let me know why you contend against me.
Does it seem good to you to oppress,
        to despise the work of your hands
        and favor the designs of the wicked?
Why did you bring me out from the womb?
    Would that I had died before any eye had seen me and
            were as though I had not been,
        carried from the womb to the grave.
Are not my days few?
    Then cease, and leave me alone,
        that I may find a little cheer before I go—
        and I shall not return—
        to the land of darkness and deep shadow,
        the land of gloom like thick darkness,
        like deep shadow without any order,
        where light is as thick darkness."
All: Therefore I will not restrain my mouth;
    I will speak in the anguish of my spirit;
    I will complain in the bitterness of my soul.

Women: My eyes will flow without ceasing,
    without respite,
until the LORD from heaven
    looks down and sees
All: Remember, O LORD, what has befallen us;
    look, and see our disgrace!

Men: My soul also is greatly troubled.
    But you, O LORD— how long?
Turn, O LORD, deliver my life;

save me for the sake of your steadfast love.
**All: Remember, O LORD, what has befallen us;
look, and see our disgrace!**

Leader: Why do you forget us forever,
why do you forsake us for so many days?
Restore us to yourself, O LORD, that we may be restored!
Renew our days as of old—
**All: Remember, O LORD, what has befallen us;
look, and see our disgrace! (L5:1)**

Leader: In my distress I called upon the
LORD; to my God I cried for help
Women: Hear my prayer, O LORD,
and give ear to my cry;
hold not your peace at my tears!
Hear my prayer, O LORD;
let my cry come to you!
Do not hide your face from me
in the day of my distress!
Incline your ear to me;
answer me speedily in the day when I call!
Men: Hear, O LORD, when I cry aloud;
be gracious to me and answer me!
You have said, "Seek my face."
My heart says to you,
"Your face, LORD, do I seek."
Hide not your face from me.
Turn not your servant away in anger,
O you who have been my help.
Cast me not off; forsake me not,
O God of my salvation!
**All: Hear my prayer, O LORD
Hear my prayer, O LORD
Hear my prayer, O LORD**

Endnotes

Chapter 2: Justice vs. Complicity

1. Matthew Henry, *Matthew*, Matthew Henry Commentary on the Whole Bible (Complete), N.p., 1706, http://www.biblestudytools.com/commentaries/matthew-henry-complete/mark/5.html. Commentary on Matthew 5:22.

2. Elie Weisel, Oslo, Nobel Acceptance Speech, December 10, 1986.

3. Frederic W. H. Meyers, "Saint Paul," archive.org/stream/saintpaul00myer/saintpaul00myer_djvu.txt.

4. Elie Weisel, *The Night Trilogy* (New York: Hill & Wang, 1972), 43.

5. Jeffrey Geller, *Women of the Asylum* (New York: Doubleday, 1994), 58.

6. *The Scottish Psalter of 1650*, http://www.cgmusic.org/workshop/smp_frame.htm.

Chapter 3: The Psychology of Evil and Sin

1. Oswald Chambers, *My Utmost for His Highest* (Westwood, NJ: Barbour Books, 1963), 298.

2. John Calvin, *Institutes of the Christian Religion*, 2.2.15 (John Knox Press: Westminster, 2001), 38.

3. Cornelius Plantinga, *Not the Way It's Supposed to Be: A Breviary of Sin* (Grand Rapids: Eerdmans, 1995), ix.

4. G. K. Chesterton, *The Complete Father Brown* (New York: Penguin Books, 1981), 218.

Chapter 5: The Fellowship of His Sufferings

1. Amy Carmichael, *Gold Cord* (London: S.P.C.K., 1982), 31.

Chapter 6: The Spiritual Impact of Abuse

1. Jeffrey Fleishman, "He Left Bosnia for Mount Airy. But His Heart Stayed Behind. Coming Home to the Ruins of War," October 14, 1997, http://articles.philly.com/1997-10-14/news/25539933_1_mostar-croats-neretva-river.

2. Ernest Becker, *The Denial of Death* (New York: MacMillan, 1973), 283–84.

3. C. H. Spurgeon, "The Minister's Fainting Fits," Lectures to My Students, Lecture XI, 1856.

4. Roy Baumeister, *Evil: Inside Human Violence and Cruelty* (New York: Henry Holt, 1999), 141.

5. Dorothy L. Sayers, *A Matter of Eternity* (Grand Rapids: Eerdmans, 1973), 56.

6. Klaas Schilder, *Christ Crucified* (St. Catherines, ON: Paideia Press, 1979).

7. George MacDonald, "The Truth in Jesus," *Unspoken Sermons* (Whitethorn, CA: Johannesen, 1997).

Chapter 7: Ministry to the Suffering

1. UN Women, "Facts and Figures: Ending Violence against Women," http://www.unwomen.org/en/what-we-do/ending-violence-against-women/facts-and-figures.

2. Bureau of Justice Statistics Special Report, *Intimate Partner Violence and Age of Victim*, 1993–9, October 2001.

3. Frye V. "Examining Homicide's Contribution to Pregnancy Associated Deaths," JAMA 285(11), (2001):1510–11.

4. National Crime Center and Crime Victims Research and Treatment Center. *Rape in America: A Report to the Nation.* Arlington, VA (1992):1–16.

5. U.S. Department of Justice, "Extent, Nature and Consequences of Rape Victimization" (1995–1996), https://www.ncjrs.gov/pdffiles1/nij/210346.pdf.

6. National Institute of Justice, *Victims and Perpetrators,* October 2010, http://www.nij.gov/topics/crime/rape-sexual-violence/Pages/victims-perpetrators.aspx#note5.

7. The Children's Assessment Center, "Child Sexual Abuse Facts," http://cachouston.org/child-sexual-abuse-facts/.

8. American Academy of Child and Adolescent Psychiatry, "Child Sexual Abuse," *Facts for Families Guide,* http://www.aacap.org/cs/root/facts_for_families/child_sexual_abuse.

9. Kimberly J. Mitchell, PhD; David Finkelhor, PhD; Janis Wolak, JD, *Risk Factors for and Impact of Online Sexual Solicitation of Youth. JAMA.* 2001;285(23):3011–14. doi:10.1001/jama.285.23.3011.

10. The Children's Assessment Center, "Child Sexual Abuse Facts," http://cachouston.org/child-sexual-abuse-facts/.

11. Shankar Vedantam, "Focus Urged on Sex Abuse of Boys Researchers Consider It a Hidden Epidemic. They Say It Can Be the Root of Addictions and Other Problems," *The Philadelphia Inquirer,* December 2, 1998, http://articles.philly.com/1998-12-02/news/25720606_1_sexual-abuse-david-finkelhor-sexual-offenses.

12. U.S. Department of Justice, "Runaway/Thrownaway Children: National Estimates and Characteristics," *National Incidence Studies of Missing, Abducted, Runaway, and Thrownaway Children,* October 2002, https://www.ncjrs.gov/pdffiles1/ojjdp/196469.pdf.

13. Redefining Refuge, "21st Century Slavery: Fact #4," http://www.redefiningrefuge.org/facts/.

14. Ibid., "Fact #6."

15. Ibid., "Fact #4."

16. World Report on Violence and Health, World Health Organization 2002, http://peacealliance.org/tools-education/statistics-on-violence/ - sthash.dDY5XcrG.dpuf.

17. L. Fox, G. Dunlap, M. L. Hemmeter, G. E. Joseph, & P. S. Strain, "The teaching pyramid: A model for supporting social competence and preventing challenging behavior in young children," *Young Children* 58 (4), (2003):48–53.

18. U.S. Census Bureau, Statistical Abstract of the United States: 2012 (131st Ed.), Transportation: Motor Vehicle Accidents and Fatalities Washington, DC, 2011; http://www.census.gov/compendia/statab/cats/transportation/motor_vehicle_accidents_and_fatalities.html.

19. Oswald Chambers, *Christian Disciplines*, vol. 1 (Grand Rapids: Discovery House, 2000), 276.

20. Handley C. G. Moule, *Messages from the Epistle to the Hebrews* (Glasgow: Pickering & Inglis, 1930).

Chapter 8: Shame and Trauma

1. Douglas Jehl, "Shame: A Special Report, Arab Honor's Price: A Woman's Blood," http://polyzine.com/arabwomen.html.

2. Sandra Cisneros, "The House on Mango Street," in *Growing up Poor: A Literary Anthology*, ed. Robert Coles, Randy Testa, Michael H. Coles (New York: New Press, 2002), 25.

3. Dorothy Allison, "A Question of Class," in *Growing up Poor*, ed. Coles, Testa, Coles, 76.

4. Sherman Alexie, "Indian Education,"*Growing Up Poor*, ed. Coles, Testa, Coles, 105.

5. Donald L. Nathanson, ed., *The Many Faces of Shame* (New York: The Guilford Press, 1987), 10.

6. Lawrence Langer, *Holocaust Testimonies: the Ruins of Memory* (New Haven: Yale University Press, 1991), 77.

7. C. S. Lewis, *Prince Caspian: The Return to Narnia* (New York: Macmillan, 1951), 233.

8. Dr. Donald Nathanson, *Shame and Pride: Affect, Sex, and the Birth of the Self* (New York: W. W. Norton, 1992).

9. Yotam Felder, "'Honor' Murders—Why Perps Get off Easy," Middle East Quarterly 7(4), (December 2000), http://www.meforum.org/50/honor-murders-why-the-perps-get-off-easy.

10. Jake Neuman, *Islam: Evil in the Name of God* (Felibri.com, 2009), 161.

11. Patricia Hurtado, "No Jail for Man Who Killed Wife," *Newsday*, April 1, 1989, www.stewartorden.com/dong_lu_chen%203.rtf.

12. Tamar Lewin, "What Penalty for a Killing in Passion?" *The New York Times*, October 21, 1994, http://www.nytimes.com/1994/10/21/us/what-penalty-for-a-killing-in-passion.html.

13. Elie Wiesel, *The Accident* from The Night Trilogy (New York: Hill and Wang, 1972), 239.

14. Elie Wiesel, Brown University, Providence, Rhode Island, April 5, 1990.

15. Primo Levi, *The Drowned and the Saved* (UK: Abacus, 1989), 150.

16. Ibid., 77–79.

17. *Equus*, Act II, Scene 34.

Chapter 9: Living with Trauma Memories

1. Langer, *Holocaust Testimonies*, 5.

2. Ibid.

3. Bruno Bettelheim, *Surviving and Other Essays* (New York: Alfred Knopf, 1979), 157–58.

4. Langer, *Holocaust Testimonies*, 6.

5. Ibid.

6. Ibid., 48.

7. Ibid., 49.

Chapter 10: Living with Ongoing Trauma

1. Fyodor Dostoevsky. BrainyQuote.com, Xplore Inc, 2015. http://www.brainyquote.com/quotes/quotes/f/fyodordost154352. html, accessed April 17, 2015. Read more at http://www. brainyquote.com/citation/quotes/quotes/f/fyodordost154352. html#ODzwfOAzWt5i4oQ5.99.

2. Mindy Belz, "The War of Northern Aggression," *World*, February 23, 2013, 56, http://www.worldmag.com/2013/02/war_ of_northern_aggression.

Chapter 11: The Many Faces of Grief

1. *Webster's Twentieth Century Dictionary*, s. v. "grief."
2. Walter Wangerin, *Mourning into Dancing* (Grand Rapids: Zondervan, 1992), 208–9.
3. Ibid., 215.

Chapter 12: Leadership, Power, and Deception in the Church and the Home

1. Timothy Keller, "The Disobedience of Saul," in *The Gospel According to David*, Sermon preached on January 4, 2004, http:// www.gospelinlife.com/the-disobedience-of-saul-5406.html.

2. George Adam Smith, *Four Psalms* (Hodder & Stoughton: London, 1896), 25.

3. Gavin De Becker, *The Gift of Fear* (New York: Little, Brown and Company, 1997), 67.

4. CNN.com, "Rader details how he killed 10 people," (June, 28, 2005), http://www.cnn.com/2005/LAW/06/27/btk/. This is just one example of many.

5. Child Advocacy Center, "Myths about Child Sexual Abuse," http://www.childadvocacycenter.org/about-child-abuse.php.

6. Anna Salter, *Predators: Pedophiles, Rapists and Other Sex Offenders* (New York: Basic Books, 2003), 29.

7. Ibid., 39–40.

Chapter 13: Sexual Abuse in Christian Organizations

1. The Lausanne Covenant, The Lausanne Congress, Section 5, 1974.

2. *Webster's Twentieth Century Dictionary*, s. v. "sexual," "abuse," "Christian," "organization."

3. Christa Brown, *This Little Light* (Cedarburg, WI: Foremost Press, 2009), 250.

4. Anna Salter, *Predators*, 29.

5. The Silent Majority: Adult Victims of Sexual Exploitation by Clergy, http://www.adultsabusedbyclergy.org/statelaws.html. Only thirteen states and the District of Columbia have laws against clergy sexual relations with a congregant.

Chapter 14: Complex Trauma

1. Judith Herman, *Trauma and Recovery: The Aftermath of Violence* (New York: Basic Books, 1992), 119.

2. Lenore Terr, *Childhood Trauma: An Outline and Overview*, American Journal of Psychiatry 148 (1991):1–20.

3. Luxenberg, Spinazzola and van der Kolk, *Directions in Psychiatry* (Long Island City, NY: The Hatherleigh Company LTD, 2001), 373–415.

4. Langer, *Holocaust Testimonies*, 6, 43, 56.

5. Diane Langberg, *Counseling Survivors of Sexual Abuse* (Maitland, FL: Xulon Press, 2003).

Chapter 15: Understanding Domestic Violence

1. Patricia Tjaden & Nancy Thoennes, U.S. Department of Justice, NCJ183781, *Full Report of the Prevalence, Incidence, and Consequences of Intimate Partner Violence Against Women: Findings from the National Violence Against Women Survey* (November 2000), http://www.ojp.usdoj.gov/nij/pubs-sum/183781.htm.

2. Bureau of Justice Crime Data Brief, "Intimate Partner Violence," 1993–2001, https://www.ncjrs.gov/app/publications/abstract.aspx?ID=197838.

3. Victoria Frye, "Examining Homicide's Contribution of Pregnancy Associated Deaths," *The Journal of the American Medical Association* 11 (March 21, 2001): 285.

Chapter 16: Understanding Sexual Abuse

1. U.S. Department of Justice, Bureau of Statistics. "Sex Offenses and Offenders: An Analysis of Data on Rape and Sexual Assault," February 1997, 10, http://www.bjs.gov/content/pub/pdf/SOO.PDF.

2. Dara Lind, "The FBI finally changed its narrow, outdated definition of rape," (November 14, 2014), http://www.vox.com/2014/11/14/7214149/the-fbis-finally-collecting-modern-rape-stats.

3. Rape, Abuse & Incest National Network (RAINN), "What the Sandusky Verdict Means for Survivors," (June 2012), http://rainn.org/images/news-room/News/06-2012/june-newsletter.html.

4. Vedantam, "Focus Urged," *Philadelphia Inquirer*.

5. Elizabeth K. Hopper, Ellen L. Bassuk, and Jeffrey Olivet, "Shelter from the Storm: Trauma Informed Care in Homelessness Service Settings," *The Open Health Services and Policy Journal* 3 (2010): 80–100.

6. Anna Salter, *Predators*, 11–12.

7. Diana Russell, "The Incidence and Prevalence of Intrafamilial and Extrafamilial Sexual Abuse of Female Children," *Child Abuse and Neglect: The International Journal* 7(2) (1983): 133–46.

8. Anna Salter, *Predators*, 36.

9. Ibid., 66.

10. Christine Bahls, "Sex Abuse: Youngsters Now Predators," *Philadelphia Inquirer*, September 1998.

11. Herman, *Trauma and Recovery*, 33.

Chapter 17: Narcissism and the System It Breeds

1. Frederick S. Stinson, et al. "Prevalence, Correlates, Disability, and Comorbidity of DSM-IV Narcissistic Personality Disorder: Results from the Wave 2 National Epidemiologic Survey on Alcohol and Related Conditions," *J Clin Psychiatry* 69(7) (July 2008): 1033–45, www.ncbi.nlm.nih.gov/pmc/articles/PMC2669224.

2. American Psychiatric Association, *Diagnostic and Statistical Manual IV*, 1994.

3. Joseph Braff, *The Unthinkable Thoughts of Jacob Green* (Chapel Hill: Algonquin Books, 2004), 173–74.

4. Lewis Carroll, *Through the Looking Glass* (New York: Macmillan Publishing, 1874), 364.

5. Adolf Hitler, *Mein Kampf* (London: Hurst and Blackett, 1925).

Chapter 19: Secondary Trauma

1. Herman, *Trauma and Recovery*, 140–44.

2. Philip Gourevitch, *We Wish to Inform You That Tomorrow We Will Be Killed with Our Families* (New York: Farar, Straus ad Giroux, 1998).

3. Karen Saakvitne and Laurie Pearlman, *Transforming the Pain* (New York: W. W. Norton, 1996).

Chapter 20: Beauty in Garbage City

1. Herman, *Trauma and Recovery*, 141.

2. John Bunyan, *Pilgrim's Progress* (New York: E.P. Dutton, Inc., 1907), 42.

3. Amy Carmichael, *Things As They Are* (London: R.W. Simpson & Co, 1903), 35.

Justice
Mercy
Compassion

The mission of GRACE is to empower the Christian community through education and training to recognize, prevent, and respond to child abuse. GRACE exists to equip and assist faith communities to mirror God's justice, mercy, and compassion for children and abuse survivors of all ages. GRACE is made up of highly trained and experienced multi-disciplined professionals and provides abuse prevention training, abuse response assistance, consultations, and independent investigations.

GRACE

**Godly Response to Abuse
in the Christian Environment**

netgrace.org